CHRISTIANOPHOBIA

CHRISTIANOPHOBIA
The Persecution of Christians under Islam

Raphael Israeli

WIPF & STOCK · Eugene, Oregon

CHRISTIANOPHOBIA
The Persecution of Christians under Islam

Copyright © 2016 Raphael Israeli. All rights reserved. Except for brief quotations in critical publications or reviews, no part of this book may be reproduced in any manner without prior written permission from the publisher. Write: Permissions, Wipf and Stock Publishers, 199 W. 8th Ave., Suite 3, Eugene, OR 97401.

Wipf & Stock
An Imprint of Wipf and Stock Publishers
199 W. 8th Ave., Suite 3
Eugene, OR 97401

www.wipfandstock.com

PAPERBACK ISBN: 978-1-4982-9200-9
HARDCOVER ISBN: 978-1-4982-9202-3
EBOOK ISBN: 978-1-4982-9201-6

Cataloguing-in-Publication data:

Names: Israeli, Raphael

Title: Christianophobia : the persecution of Christians under Islam / Raphael Israeli.

Description: Eugene, OR: Wipf & Stock, 2016 | Includes bibliographical references and index.

Identifiers: ISBN 978-1-4982-9200-9 (paperback) | ISBN 978-1-4982-9202-3 (hardcover) | ISBN 978-1-4982-9201-6 (ebook)

Subjects: LCSH: Islam—Relations—Christianity. | Christian martyrs—History—21st century. | Persecution—History—21st century. | Title.

Classification: BR1601.3 I87 2016 (print) | BR1601.3 (ebook)

Manufactured in the U.S.A.   06/14/16

To the memory of David Littman,
and in honor of Gisele Littman,
who spent much of their married life
rescuing and advocating for the rights
of Jewish and Christian minorities
trapped in the lands conquered by Islam

Contents

Preface | ix

Introduction: Islam and Christianity in Perspective | 1

Chapter One
Christian Minorities in the Arab World | 55

Chapter Two
Christian Minorities under African Islam | 117

Chapter Three
Christian Minorities under Asian Islam | 136

Chapter Four
Christian Minorities in the Holy Land | 165

Chapter Five
Muslim Minorities under Western Christianity | 199

Summary and Prospects | 228

Bibliography | 235
Analytical Index | 245

Preface

Bat Ye'or's seminal books[1] about the mistreatment, which at times ended in annihilation, of entire Christian communities in the territories occupied by the surging and conquering Islam of the Middle Ages—in the Near and Middle East, North Africa, Black Africa, Central Asia, and the Balkans—require a sequel today in view of the escalating clashes between Islam and the Christian minorities surviving under it, or between the host Christian majorities of the West and the Muslim guest cultures that have increasingly been challenging them. In the twentieth century alone, the Armenian genocide was perpetrated at the dusk of the Ottoman Empire during World War I, which was the last Muslim Empire thus far, and further attacks on Christian minorities have followed in Nigeria, Egypt, Iraq, Syria, Lebanon, and elsewhere. Today, it is the worldwide outrage that ISIS provokes, due to the oppression and extermination of Christian and other minorities in the territories it has taken over, and the rampage by other radical Islamic movements (Boko Haram in Nigeria, Al-Shabab in Somalia, the Muslim Brothers in Egypt and Gaza, Jabhat al-Nusra in Syria, Shi'tes in Iraq, Hizbullah in Lebanon, Hamas in Gaza and the West Bank, and ISIS in Iraq and Syria) against the Christian minorities they control, which is attracting the attention (and disgust) of the civilized world.

A dispatch from Beirut by *Al-sharq Al-Awsat* in August 2015[2] reported that the Islamic State of Iraq and Syria (ISIS) militants have abducted hundreds of civilians, including dozens of Christians, from a central Syrian town it captured earlier in the week, a development that has prompted hundreds of Christian families to flee to areas outside the control of the ultra-radical

---

1. See Bat Ye'or, *The Dhimmi': Jews and Christians under Islam*; and *The Decline of Eastern Christianity under Islam: From Jihad to Dhimmitude*, both published by Fairleigh Dickinson University Press, 1985 and 1996, respectively.

2. *Asharq Al-Awsat*, Saturday, 8 Aug 2015: http://www.aawsat.net/2015/08/article55344720/isis-kidnaps-dozens-of-christians-from-central-syrian-town-hundreds-of-families-flee

group. Syria-based activists who monitor the group's activity in the country said that in 2015 ISIS in effect kidnapped more than 220 residents from Qaryatain after overrunning the town, which is located in the central province of Homs, a few days earlier. Initial information indicates that ISIS took the abductees to the historic city of Palmyra, which it captured from Syrian government forces in May. At least sixty Christians are among the kidnapped. (The UK-based Syrian Observatory for Human Rights, which monitors the conflict in Syria through a network of activists, has confirmed the data.) ISIS accuses the 220 civilians of "collaborating with the [Syrian] regime, but the primary goal of the abduction is to use them as a bargaining chip," an activist, who goes by the *nom de guerre* Abu Muhammad, told *Asharq Al-Awsat*. There are around thirty Christian families living in Raqqa city, ISIS's main stronghold in Syria, Abu Muhammad said. "But they pay the *jizya* [a poll-tax levied on non-Muslims] in exchange for permission to stay," he said. Male and female members of the Christian families in Raqqa are forced to adhere to a strict dress code that ISIS deems in line with Islam. Meanwhile, the Christian Assyrian Network for Human Rights in Syria warned that ISIS might be preparing to launch a large-scale attack on the town of Sadad, 15 miles (25 kilometers) from Qaryatain. Sadad is home to around five thousand Christian families. Dozens of Christian families reportedly began to flee Sadad toward the government-held city of Homs and the capital, Damascus, and several Christian religious figures have appealed to the international community to stop the "potential aggression" by ISIS against their town. This is a tiny example of the plight that Syrian Christians must endure every day.

Unlike the Middle Ages, when it was the Christian powers of Europe who encroached upon the Islamic domain during the two centuries of the Crusades, in modern times, especially after the beginning of the demise of the Muslim Empires of the Ottomans and the Moghuls in the nineteenth century, it has been the strength of the Western Christian world that has been the moving force of modern history up until the end of World War II. Since then, the pendulum has been swinging again in the other direction, with the Muslim world upsurging again and counter-attacking. In effect, the two previous onslaughts of Islam on Christian Europe—the first in the Iberian Peninsula in the seventh century, which lasted almost eight hundred years (until 1492), and the second from the opposite direction in southeastern Europe, immediately thereafter, by the Ottoman Empire, which conquered the Balkans, and lasted until the end of the nineteenth century—have been followed by the third attempt after World War II, this time by peaceful means via immigration, both legal or forced. At the rate of hundreds of thousands annually, Muslim immigrants flow into Europe, first as *gastarbeiter*, and now more and more as asylum seekers, they have come to constitute sizeable minorities in Europe, amounting to about 6 percent of the total European population (30 million out of the 500 million population of the EU), with the major countries of Britain, France, and Germany counting them in the millions and the lesser countries in smaller but growing numbers.

We shall see a linkage between the conquest and territorial expansion at the hands of Muslim radical movements—like those in sub-Saharan Africa and the Middle East, who attack Christian populations with a view of diminishing them and scaring them away—and the international inundation of Western Christian countries, both in Europe and in Australia and the Americas, by the unrelenting flow of destitute immigrants from Muslim countries, for the most part, who simply abandon their miserable and oppressive turf, and head for the promise of a good life under Christianity. There is no doubt that many in the West's midst are latent agents, who exploit the almost free flow of "refugees" to the West, and the latter's generosity in welcoming them, to erect sleeper cells in the hosting countries, to be awakened when time comes.

The inbuilt paradox is there of Muslim radicals who despise Christianity and are pitted against it and committed to overrun it, but at the same time they line up at the door of Western embassies and consulates in an attempt to migrate there legally, and when not afforded that opportunity (which is the customary state of affairs), they venture at the risk of their own lives, putting in jeopardy their families, under the wild assumption that if they force themselves on the Westerners of the Christian world (or of Jewish Israel), theirs hosts, who exhibit far more clemency and compassion for them than the Muslim home regimes they flee, they would somehow be tolerated as "political refugees," at the same time that at home they left behind them persecuted Christian minorities which are being decimated.

Many valuable studies were published in recent years about similar or overlapping topics, such as Raymond Ibrahim's *Crucified Again: Exposing Islam's New War on Christians*; Tom Doyle and Tom Parks' *Killing Christians: Living Faith Where It Is Not Safe to Believe*; Michael Coren's *Hatred: Islam's War on Christianity*; George Marlin's *Christian Persecution in the Middle East*; Paul Rowe et al. (editors), *Christians in the Middle East Conflict*; Habib Malik's *Islamism and the Future of Christians in the Middle East*; and Betty Jane and Martin Baily's *Who the Christians in the Middle East?* However, as evident from merely reading the titles, not of these books treats the topic beyond the Arab world, the Middle East, or individual Arab countries. The innovation suggested by this volume is double: (a) it provides a comprehensive survey of the entire Islamic world, of which the Middle East is only a small part (the other parts are Africa and Asia), and (b) it makes links between the persecution of Christian minorities worldwide and the flocking of hundreds of thousands (soon millions) of Muslims from Islamdom to Christendom by trying to answer some major questions related to this world phenomenon, which is nourished, on the one hand, by the ejection from Islamdom of the persecuted Christian minorities and, on the other hand, by the attraction of the countries of Christendom as lands of asylum to the millions of Muslims who are driven from home by the corruption, turmoil, chaos, upheaval, and war of their homelands.

However, again paradoxically, as soon as sizeable Muslim minorities congregate in one location, grow in numbers, and acquire the requisite self-confidence of partners (no longer guests) or even proprietors by right, they can be found seeking to alter the tolerant system that had absorbed them, in order to shake it and force it to adopt their ways, rather than the other way around. And the more their radical elements at home are "successful" in oppressing and chasing Christians, the more self-confident and vocal they become in their demands, self-assured as they are that their "progress" at home guarantees their success in their host countries.

Apparently due to other diplomatic interests, or simply for fear of being accused of Islamophobia or of racism, the State Department, and other Western Christian diplomatic institutions, which used to stand at the forefront of human rights defense in the world, have recently abdicated their commitments on this score. Thus, at least as regards the persecution of Christian minorities under Islam, Muslim radicals feel free to persecute and cleanse their countries from the Christian populations who have inhabited those lands from long before the time they were conquered by Islam.

As always, I am indebted to the Harry Truman Research Institute for the Advancement of Peace for the funding, the office space, the secretarial facilities, and the collegial atmosphere that permitted me to carry out this investigation. I am particularly grateful to Enav Hecht and Edward Makhoul for their untiring efforts to sift through masses of materials to detect the relevant part of them. But I alone shoulder the responsibility for any misapprehension of fact or comment that may have befallen my text.

Jerusalem, Summer, 2015.

INTRODUCTION

Islam and Christianity in Perspective

Since its inception, Islam has positioned itself as the universal rival of Christianity, at whose boundaries it has been gnawing ever since, with varying degrees of success, depending on the fortunes of one faith or the other as the prevailing world engine of its era. When Islam sprung from Arabia after the death of its Prophet in 632 CE, in its frenzy of conquest and empire, motivated by the enthusiasm of a new world faith, it encountered either the Sassanian Iranians in the East, the Berbers of North Africa, or the Byzantine Christians in the North, and it battled until it subjugated them and ultimately converted their vast territories into Islam. On its way to empire it took over Syria and the Holy Land, Hellenistic Egypt and its Coptic Christians, Roman and Visigoth North Africa, rebellious Berbers and Kabyles in the Atlas mountains, and a myriad other minorities, many of them Christian, under the promise of ruling them with enough tolerance to allow them to keep to their scriptural faith if they were among the Scripturaries (*Ahl-al-Kitab*—Christians and Jews), or else the obligation to conform to Islam if they were pagans (*kuffar*), in accordance with the early Islamic definitions.

Today, the main and recurrent grievance of Islam focuses around the claim that it is being humiliated and discriminated against in and by the West, all subsumed under the complaint of "Islamophobia," at a time when it is Islam that launches terrorism against the West, enters its territory through legal and illegal penetration and immigration, claims the necessity to erect its mosques and cultural centers everywhere in the West, as of right, but forbids at the same time Western cultural and religious centers in its territory, persecutes Western-originating cultural and religious ideas in its lands, and explodes in violence and murder every time it senses that its honor, values, or religious tenets are hurt. It can expand in territory and in spirituality, it can propagandize its most radical views among its believers in their host countries in the West, and proselytize among unbelievers, and take over entire networks of education, viewing any check or question by the authorities as intrusion and discrimination, but woe to any people or authorities that question its freedom to do so, or resist its expansionist endeavors. Islamic civilization does use the same terminology that the West does, but it means different things when it says, for instance, democracy, freedom, pluralism, tolerance, co-existence; or conversely: terrorism, oppression, persecution, tyranny, and the like. Therefore, to be able to converse, or at least to understand each other, we must delve into some fundamental lexicography.

If we examine the most important terms that are tossed around by many Muslims in the present clash of worldviews and war of misunderstandings, we must analyze each term in its Muslim context so as to spare recriminations and aggravations and realize that our cherished democracy is not something Muslims aspire to; that justice for them means Muslim justice; tolerance to them is not unconditional acceptance of the other and the different; terrorism is what the others do; pluralism is altogether unheard of in their ideally monolithic societies; ending a conflict can only be done through victory, not compromise; sovereignty belongs to Allah, not to the people; legislation is not the prerogative of human citizens but of divine will; any retaliation against them is cowardice, genocide, and murder, and every wanton murder of innocent civilians of their foes is an act of heroism; Western values mean tyranny and corruption; reasoning must follow the Islamic way of thinking; they expect respect for Islam but dispense contempt for others; they regard their own shouting and rampaging as a show of force and indignation, but their foes' dignified quiet and restraint as evidence of weakness; everybody owes them everything, but they owe nothing to anyone; and they regard any attack on others as legitimate and necessary, while any act of self-defense by non-Muslims is nothing but aggression and arrogance.

Almost since its inception, Islam has recognized the division of humanity into three categories of people: the Muslims, the Scripturaries, who feared God and had a holy book, and the pagans who knew no one God. The lands of the globe were divided basically into two domains: the *Dar-al-Islam* (the Abode of Islam) and *Dar-al-Harb* (the Abode of War). While for practical purposes these categories are no longer operative because they would otherwise throw international relations into chaos, in the thinking and policies of radical Muslims, both those empowered and those in opposition to the rulers, this terminology has been revived and widely used to analyze internal and external affairs in accordance with the requisites of the Shari'a, that is the holy law of Islam. One has to realize that the religion of the radicals is the Islam of old, not an innovation (Allah Forbid!). Therefore, when the radicals or their deeds are condemned by other Muslims as "non-Islamic," this is merely a blanket statement calculated to skirt the embarrassment caused by the excesses of their coreligionists. Since the Shari'a submits only to eternal divine laws and cannot be amended, let alone abrogated at the whim of anyone, then it is either applied more or less strictly—as it is by the radicals when they hold power, as we see in ISIS territory nowadays—or it is partly or wholly ignored—as it is by the multitudes of Muslims, who have elected to succumb to the requirements of modernity, as has been the situation in most Muslim countries. The difference, then, is only in the degree of enforcement: the Muslims in general, while aware of, and caring about, the tenets of their creed, may be lax about the implementation of some of them, insistent as they may be on their Muslim identity and commitment; while the radicals impatiently display their burning passion for *full* implementation here and now, at almost any cost, including the use of violence.

The radical Muslims, today dubbed "Wahhabists," "Jihadists," or "Salafists," actually wish to emulate the times of the Prophet and his immediate successors (the *salafis*) and did not invent any new idea or add any new tenet to the pillars of the faith. In that regard, they wish to practice to the letter pristine Islam as it was understood in its beginnings, including Jihad to expand Islam and conquer territory, and the relations with non-Muslims under their rule. More moderate Muslims claim today that their Jihad is spiritual, mainly an improvement of the self, but when reading the platform of the Hamas or watching the deeds of ISIS, one has no doubt that their Jihad harks back to the Holy War that assured the spread of Islam by violence and force, and the rule over non-Muslims according to the eternal laws of the *dhimma* (protection). What is more, the Shari'a rules are not used only against Scripturaries but also against other Muslims who refuse to submit to their rule, as we see today in Syria, Iraq, Gaza under the Hamas, post-Qaddafi Libya, the civil war in Afghanistan, chaotic Yemen and any number of other Muslim territories infected by the devolution of power of the Islamic Spring.

When the Muslim conquerors overran much of the medieval world and imposed their rule, they eradicated the prevailing cultures, religions, and civilizations that they encountered, like the Sassanian/Iranian, the

Byzantine/Christian, the Berber/pagan, until little by little they were diminished and oppressed into annihilation, if not expulsion, population transfers, conversions (voluntary or forced), discrimination, and the heavy tax of the *jizya*, a poll tax that Muslims were exempt from paying and only Scriptuaries had to disburse as the price of their "protected" dhimmi status. This status was legal, social, economic, political, and religious and became part of the Shari'a, namely was enforceable and immutable like the other laws of Islamdom. But it was so oppressive that it generated the shrinking and then the quasi-disparition of some subjugated faiths, like Christianity in North Africa after the Muslim conquest of the seventh century. Essentially, it was made part of the obligations of any Muslim ruler to protect the life and property of the conquered Scriptuary people, provided they paid their *jizya* tax. The category of "protected" people comprised at first only Christians and Jews, but was later expanded to the conquered subjects of other faiths, like Zoroastrians and Hindus, as the borders of Islamdom continued to expand.

By the standards of those days, when religious fanaticism and intolerance were the norm, to be "protected" by a dhimmi status would have been a much more coveted position than, say, for a non-Christian to live in Christendom, where Muslims, and particularly Jews and thousands of sectarians, heretics, and apostates were pursued and put to the *auto-da-fé* mercilessly. At least under Islam, though the rules of dhimmitude[1] were often violated to the detriment of the dhimmis (i.e. even though the dhimmis respected the law they were often persecuted anyway), they were also sometimes broken in their favor (i.e., under a benevolent ruler, dhimmis could acquire high positions in government or in the royal court, in spite of the mistrust and contempt that they officially deserved). The main point was that Islamdom recognized a compartmentalization of society, whereby Muslims were at the center, full-fledged subjects of the Caliphate, while the Scriptuaries enjoyed a midway recognition and protection as long as they accepted the sovereignty of Islam and paid their poll tax. The pagans, if there were any left in the occupied Muslim territories, had either fled or converted to Islam, so the pagan world remained, by definition, confined to Dar al-Harb, against which perpetual war (Jihad) was to be waged until taken over and subjugated by Islam.

Thus, unlike Jews, who had nowhere else to go, since they were oppressed and persecuted in Christendom even worse than they were in Islamdom, Christians under Islam could retreat together with their defeated armies into the vast countries ruled by Christians, where they continued to

---

1. Bat Ye'or, *The Decline of Eastern Christianities*, chap. 3.

face belligerent Muslims and battle against them. This differential treatment of the Jews under Christianity and Islam is the origin of the mythical Golden Age of Jews under Islam, which mistook the relatively better Muslim treatment of Jews, compared to the hostile Christian attitude and practice against them, in absolute terms and mythologized them into a *Shangri-la* of happiness and bliss. At any rate, it is evident that while the Jewish communities in Islamdom kept expanding, because they had no other outlet available, Christian congregations kept shrinking throughout the years, while the international tensions on their shared borders kept intensifying.

After the abortive attempt of the Christian world to retrieve some of its lost territories through the Crusades, we come to the modern era when roles were reversed: the Muslim countries sank into backwardness, poverty, and under-development, while the Christian world made its eruption into the modern word as the hegemonic engine of humanity. Muslim lands were then colonized and humiliated, a process that escalated after the fall of the two great Muslim empires: the Moghuls in India by the British in the nineteenth century, and the Ottoman empire as a result of World War I, by the British, the French, and the Russians. When the Western colonial rule ended after World War II, signaling the termination of exploitation and cultural and political domination, the radical Islamic movements sought to restore Muslim pride to its origin. When carried to extremes in our days, those movements also produced chaos, devolution of power, ungovernability, tribalism, tyranny, hostility, war, and destruction.

Bat Ye'or has stunningly and accurately documented the saga of the fast-shrinking Christian minorities in the East under the sweep of Islamic conquest and dhimmitude in the Middle Ages[2]; more poignantly still, she has accounted for the reverse process of dhimmitude that has affected the Western countries when Muslim minorities began to migrate to the Christian world, and she has demonstrated that while Christians could be taken out of dhimmitude into the safety of Christendom, the dhimmitude state of mind could not be taken out of the Christian sovereign states in the contemporary world, which continue to behave as if they still were under Islamic dominion.[3]

We will have then to tackle and explain the current situation whereby it is Islam that flows westwards, to seek dominion over it by "peaceful" means, and seeking equal status as of right, at the same time that it not only does not maintain a similar atmosphere of coexistence with its Christian minorities at home, but it persecutes and oppresses them, as if signaling that

2. Ibid.
3. Bat Ye'or, *Eurabia: The Euro-Arab Axis.*

the entire world must be Islamized. In other words, Islam, being thought to be the faith of the future, is justified to demand that it be respected everywhere, but other faiths, notably Christianity, have no standing in the world and must yield to Islamic hegemonic ambitions.

Some naïve minds in the West have come to believe that dialogue and negotiations with Muslim leaders can and will alter those attitudes and lead to coexistence between Muslims and their rivals. The aftermath of the protracted "dialogue" between Iran and the six world powers in 2014–15, where, following the signed agreement in Vienna between the parties, Iran reverted to its virulent anti-American statements, should have been proof enough of that asymmetrical attitude to dialogue.

The problem is that dialogue has been treated in the West as if it were a real policy, whereas it is in fact a non-policy, designed only to fill an awkward vacuum and to make politicians, diplomats, and other dreamers feel virtuous for "doing something." But while world powers have regularly entered a "dialogue" with Muslims in good faith, fully intending to find common ground with their often-unruly Muslim interlocutors—for the Muslims, "dialogue" means something else entirely. For them, it signifies the submission of a lesser foreign culture and religion to their own superior one. Muslims hope to inspire in the Westerners (and Israelis) conversion to an Islamic view of the world. Anything short of that is regarded by them as an abject "failure of dialogue," and a signal to resort to threats of violence or acts of terrorism. They are well practiced at both, while the Westerners have literally become pushovers at this stage in their history. Except for the U.S., they hardly believe that anything is worth fighting over. Nor do they have a stomach for a fight of unlimited duration. They would rather capitulate than investigate in depth the meaning of tolerance, understanding, dialogue, and peace to Muslims.

The problem today lies in the juxtaposition of a resurgent Islam on the one hand, and a self-deprecating West on the other, unsure of itself, its values, or even what it stands for. Its people have made a virtue of instant self-gratification, and therefore they invest next to nothing in the future—hence they have stopped having children. Their preferred way of life amounts to a "credit card culture." They want everything, and they want it instantly. Never mind that their governments no longer raise sufficient funds from taxation to cover exorbitant welfare entitlements, or that a bleak financial future awaits tomorrow's pensioners. In short, the West has become a disgrace to its own heritage, in sharp reversal of its fortunes when at the turn of the twentieth century the Muslim Ottoman Empire was considered the "sick man of Europe," and was therefore no match for a confident West.

There is another drawback to this constant resort to "dialogue." It lulls the Western populations into believing that their governments are doing something constructive to avert violence or threats of violence in the future. In reality, nothing could be further from the truth, for this non-policy simply serves to embolden and concomitantly empower those Muslims whom Western governments have chosen to act as intermediaries with the wider Muslim community in their midst. Invariably, Western governments have elected these Muslims largely because they are the activists and therefore are prominent in the community, while the governments comfort themselves with the injudicious belief that these figures represent "moderate" Islam, or that dealing with Muslim governments can justify departure from the standard norms of justice, as the scandalous release by the Scottish authorities, in mid-2009, of the Lockerbie culprit has illustrated. However, these Muslims have known Europe and the West long enough to have learned to tailor their vocabulary precisely according to whom they are facing across the table. They speak the language of peace, reconciliation, and goodwill to Westerners, and reserve their true thoughts and beliefs for fellow Muslims. In other words, they have learned to "work the system," admirably so.

In effect, these "moderate" Muslim leaders gradually extract one concession after another from Western policymakers, rendering "dialogue" a one-way street. They enter each session with the full intention of testing the limits of the concessions they can extract, and it is a rare Western government minister who would risk disappointing them—or else the headlines in the papers the following day would be sure to inflame the Muslim community. Herein lies the value of the worldwide Muslim penchant for overreacting to every perceived slight, real or imagined, by demonstrating their "rage" loudly and violently. Temperament comes into play here too (watch the shifting moods of Qaddafi when he was courted by the West and the concessions he got from it, or the phenomenal concessions the West made to Iran when their leaders in Tehran poured their vitriol over their naïve and well-meaning interlocutors); for unlike other peoples who experience anger or humiliation, many Muslims are either unable or unwilling to contain those sentiments. One has only to recall the Arafat-orchestrated "days of rage" in the early stages of the *Intifadah* against Israel to understand that, in sharp contrast to Westerners, Muslims often make a fetish of celebrating their anger. Such an uncontrolled behavior is unthinkable in the West, but not because of lack of provocation against it, particularly since September 11. Funerals too are manipulated to vent wrath and fury, emotion, general mayhem, and impromptu rifle-shooting. The lack of dignity, even at what should be a somber occasion, is jarring to Western eyes. Bodies are held aloft and bounced along the route, in a manner that would be regarded as disrespectful to the deceased in other cultures. Bodies have been known to fall off the stretcher amid the *melee*, and processions have turned chaotic, as was recorded for posterity in the case of Iran's Ayatollah Khomeini's funeral. Iran's ambassador to Copenhagen, Ahmad Danialy, making his first public appearance in Denmark since being recalled by the Iranian Foreign Ministry in January 2006, following the Cartoon affair, addressed a public gathering and noted that the crisis had hurt the feelings of the Muslim world and caused a great deal of concern. He noted that:

> Now after the lapse of this period of unpleasant and bitter experience, I am very pleased to witness a beautiful and jovial gathering of the erudite and learned here in Copenhagen.... The conference is a step in the right direction for improving relations. The truth of the matter is that the world needs to direct new attention to one fundamental principle and that is: Respect for the sanctity of religions in all places and at all political, cultural and social levels....[4]

And this happened when the Ambassador was well aware that the damage, killing, and destruction had been caused by violent *Islamic* demonstrators worldwide during the Cartoon Affair, not by the cartoons, and of how his own President spoke about eliminating Jews and Israel, how his clerics deprecated Christianity and other faiths, and how the Iranian regime supported the burning down of Jewish synagogues in the West Bank and in European cities. (Matters have worsened since Iran's involvement in Syria, Lebanon, Iraq, and Yemen during the Arab Spring of 2010–15). But if the purpose of the Danish conference was not to elicit a mutual reconciliation but only "to introduce the Prophet (the Muslim one, not all the rest), the proper way," then why should we expect any care or concern, on the part of Muslims, for any faith except the Islamic one?

The conference that followed in the United Arab Emirates brought sixty young people from Denmark and the Arab world together, under the banner of "The Search for Mutual Understanding," namely that the Danes should learn to respect Islam, never mind their own beliefs and culture. The delegates discussed a range of issues that the Cartoon crisis revealed as sore points between religious Muslims, and secular Western culture, such as freedom of expression and the role the media can play in hindering or facilitating global understanding. The four-day conference, held in Abu Dhabi (May 2006), "exceeded the expectations of Jeppe Bruus Christensen," chairman of the Danish Youth Council, who naively and prematurely declared: "I don't think we should underestimate how important this is in the Arab

---

4. Cited in Israeli, *The Islamic Challenge in Europe*, 39.

world. It has gathered a great deal of attention." What he did not realize was that his statements were interpreted throughout the Arab world as a desperate attempt by Denmark to apologize for its "horrible" deed, and as a capitulation to Muslim demands. It did not earn Denmark any credit, but only scorn and contempt. Christensen felt that the two groups managed to "understand" each other and "accepted" mutual criticism, but he failed to comprehend that the Muslim goal was to assert its victory, not compromise, because its system cannot recognize that it can be at fault, unlike other (lesser) faiths. Thus, his feeling that the whole exercise "has been very constructive and positive," and that "we have been able to agree upon common values, such as having the right to criticize each other," would have been in vain had he read the Arab reports of the conference. Other participants from Denmark and the Middle East were more sober and realistic when they merely agreed that the conference "underscored the need for bridging the gaps that the conflict had revealed," and that "We have to accept that there are areas where we remain distant from each other." Moreover, to illustrate the depth of that gap, some Muslims continued to consider Denmark, which is one of the most open, tolerant, and hospitable countries of the world, to be "a racist and closed country."

Much closer to the reality was the evaluation by some Danish participants who heard their country being deprecated, albeit that it could be the model of tolerance for the entire Islamic world, when they said that "we have to acknowledge that that's the way it's going to be for some time." The conference also gave young Muslims the chance to meet their Danish counterparts and test the images presented by the media in their countries. "It's been very important for me to obtain the human aspect. To meet people and hear their opinion instead of seeing it in the media," said a nineteen-year-old Egyptian who admitted that preconceived notions, such as "the Danes hate us," were difficult to reject, but the conference's people-to-people approach helped. Another Arab youth, from Saudi Arabia, where Danish goods were initially boycotted, said that he was surprised in a positive way about the Danish young people, for "They were much more open and understanding about our culture than I had expected." But was he about theirs in the same way? He acknowledged that while dialogue and respect had been established at the conference, transferring the experience to his home country could prove difficult. He explained: "We'll be challenged when we come back to our countries, because some people have different attitudes. They use a different approach than dialogue, but we still need to work to spread the message that it is possible to live in this world together."[5] One wishes he were right.

The Cartoon Affair, which particularly targeted Scandinavia, especially Denmark and Norway, put those countries in disarray for they were the most forthcoming in terms of humanitarian aid to poor Muslim countries. Unlike Denmark, which apologized, saying that it did not intend to insult anyone, but still insisted on the principle of freedom of expression, the Norwegian government instructed its Embassies in the Middle East to apologize to Muslim countries, backed by Javier Solana's sycophant apology that he presented in his tour to the Middle East, expressing "solidarity" with Muslim nations, which implied his moral support for their outrageous rampages, for their boycott of member countries of the EU and for the vain killing of 200 people, Muslims and Christians, for that silly and unjustified outburst of violence that they spawned. Those *dhimmi*-like apologies, far from calming the moods, on the contrary increased the contempt that the Muslim world showed to those who came to admit their "guilt," and reinforced the belief that, unlike any other faith which can be trampled upon with impunity (like Christianity), supreme Islam was untouchable and unchallengeable; and that for saving the face of Islam in the eyes of those who should have been so certain of their faith that they should have brushed aside any insult to it, it was permissible to massacre many innocent people. The apologies were counterproductive for they caused more moral harm to the West than the initial "insults" to Islam. One example is that the Saudi media boasted at the price Denmark had to disburse for its "injury" of Islam: "

> Products of the Danish conglomerate Arla Foods will be back on the supermarket shelves in Saudi Arabia. The unofficial boycott has been lifted and this is only for Arla products. . . . This move comes following a recommendation made by five Islamic organizations which participated in an Islamic conference in Bahrain last month, to debate the issue surrounding the blasphemous cartoons. . . . Arla Foods has issued an apology to Muslims worldwide . . . and pledged to disseminate awareness about Islam and make donations to charity groups. Arla has a major dairy plant in Riyadh. . . . A new production facility planned for Saudi Arabia has been indefinitely put on hold. . . . [The Danish manager of the firm, Mr. Petersen, said:] we have deferred plans to set up the multi-million dollar production plant because of the boycott of Danish products and its adverse impact on our sales in the region. Arla had already invested $70

---

5. Ibid

million to build the new plant in cooperation with Danya Foods in Saudi Arabia.[6]

To exonerate themselves from any wrongdoing towards Christians, Muslims thinkers have tried to divert the debate to the eternal scapegoats—Jews. Sheikh al-Qaradawi, the senior spiritual leader of the Muslim Brothers throughout the Islamic world, aired an interview on Qatar TV[7] blaming the Jews for the evils of the world, in the context of the controversial movie *The Passion of the Christ*, which had just been released, while oppression against Christians in Islamdom kept escalating:

> This film exposes the Jews' crime of bringing Jesus to the Crucifixion. . . . Even though we Muslims believe that Jesus was not crucified, a crime was committed, and the people who paved the way for the crime, who helped to commit it, who brought Jesus to the crucifixion, and kept pursuing the issue, until the governor on behalf of the Romans in Jerusalem at that time sentenced him to death. . . . More than 30 years ago the Vatican issued a document exonerating the Jews from the blood of Jesus. Not all Christians accepted this document. The Pope in the Vatican and the Catholics are the ones who exonerated them. They exonerated them under political pressure. But the Protestants did not exonerate them, the Orthodox did not exonerate them, and Patriarch Shinouda in Egypt did not exonerate them, and kept saying that they bear the responsibility. . . .
>
> Do the Jews of yesterday bear the responsibility for the crimes committed by the Jews of the past? The principle is that they indeed bear the responsibility for these crimes, as long as they do not renounce them. If they glorify and take pride in what their forefathers did, . . . and consider it part of their religion and heritage, they bear the responsibility. As we can see, the Qur'an held the Jews of the Prophet's times responsible for what their forefathers did. It said: "We made Moses a promise extending over 40 nights, then you took the calf for worship, wrongfully. . . . They adopt the deeds of their forefathers, and so they bear responsibility for them, unless they renounce them. . . . Therefore, I say that the Jews of the 21st Century adopt the blame for what the Jews of the first century did. . . . This was a crime, and we ask Allah to absolve us of it . . . .

---

6. Ghazanfar Ali Khan, "Products of Danish Dairy Company Return to Supermarkets Shelves," in *Arab News* (Saudi Arabia) 4 April 2004.

7. Sheikh Yussuf Qaradawi, "Jews of Today are Responsible for Their Forefathers' Crime against Jesus," *Qatar TV*, 26 August 2006.

Much can be inferred from this expose, primarily that the punishment being meted out today to Christians in the Islamic world is due to the "crimes" that their forefathers, especially the Crusaders, had inflicted on Islam. Never mind the crimes of conquest, destitution, enslavement, and cultural imperialism that Islam had brought on entire Christian civilizations, and is continuing to threaten them with today.

The spirit of criticism against the deeds and attitudes of the Christian West against the world of Islam is indeed reflected even in remote and well-meaning Norway. Indeed, that country, which by hosting the abortive Oslo Accords in 1993 thought it was bringing peace and salvation to the world, and persists in allocating annually the Nobel *Peace* Prize, was jolted by the Cartoon Affair, not so much by the violence against some of its representatives and symbols in the Muslim world, but by what a prominent radical Muslim, who has been generously sheltered by her for years, had to say to and about his hosts. The Kurdish-Iraqi member and commander of *Ansar al-Islam* (The Supporters of Islam) Mullah Krekar, gave a press interview in the aftermath of the controversy over the Cartoons of the Prophet Muhammad to the Internet section of the daily *Dagbladet*. In it, he expounded his views on the relations between Islam and the West. Krekar, whose real name is Najm al-Din Faraj Ahmed, came to Norway as a refugee in 1991, where he established his *Ansar al-Islam* organization. While slated for deportation from Norway, he gave his interview to the press:

> On one side stands the Western way of thinking. This is the way of thinking that has taken its materialism, egotism and savagery from the ancient Greeks and Romans. This is the way that has altered true Christianity. An example of this is that Western Christianity today accepts men having sex with men. That was never accepted by Jesus. On the other side stands Islam, and now the West is trying to take over and change Islam in the same way Christianity was debased. There is only one civilization. But there are no different ways to think about it, and our way of thinking in Islam stands in opposition to the Western way of thinking. Today, it is our way of thinking which comes in and shows itself stronger than theirs. Islam has a stable foundation: one God, one Prophet, one Qur'an and one tradition. This generates hatred among those who think the Western way, and leads the losing party to use violence. And that is the violence and war against Islam. Democracy is just an excuse, it is Islam that they cannot stand. . . . The same with the hunt for Osama Bin Laden, it is just an excuse. It is Islam that the West cannot stand. The attack on Islam is like a hand: One finger is the

war in Iraq and Afghanistan, another is the imprisonment of Muslims at Guantanamo Bay. The third finger is the publishing of pictures of the Prophet Muhammad. We must see things as they are, and those pictures are one part of the military fight that the West is conducting against Islam.... By 2050, 30% of the European population will be Muslim....

We have no fear of the Western way of thinking. It can never win. In Iraq, the two sides stand against each other. On the side of Islam stand men who love death and who are willing to become martyrs for what they believe in. On the other side stand soldiers who fight for $1,000 a day. The number of dead American soldiers is proof of failure. The same is true in Afghanistan. From 2001 to 2004, there were five suicide attacks, in 2005 there were seventeen. While the front of the US and its allies is becoming smaller, Islam is widening its front. The reports from Guantanamo show the same. They are trying to rip belief from the heart of the Muslims, but it does not work. In Denmark they published cartoons, but the result was only to encourage people to rally behind Islam. I and all Muslims are proof of this. They have not managed to change us; it is we who will change them. Look at the development of population in Europe, where the number of Muslims increases like mosquitoes. Each Western woman in the EU produces, on average, 1.4 children, while each Muslim woman in the same countries produces 3.5 children. By 2050, 30% of the European population will be Muslim....

Muslims who go to Iraq and Afghanistan to fight—that is an honor. It is an honor in itself if it violates the rules here in Europe. Those who say that Osama Bin Laden is a terrorist are themselves killing our women, children and civilians. That is what we see and what we know. We are not influenced by the US words against Bin Laden, since they are talking about someone we know. We are fighting for the same goal, just under different circumstances. The goal is Islamic rule in an Islamic state. Shi'ite Muslims have achieved that goal in Iran and they are so strong that the West does not dare attack them. This is the only way we maintain a balance and achieve a lasting peace. Our Caliph is dead and we are orphans. Therefore we are fighting, like the Jews fought under David Ben Gurion, for our own state, a state ruled by a true Islamic ruler. Bin Laden is a good person to rule the Caliphate. Borders do not matter. Things are born, and then they grow bigger. The essential thing is Islamic rule. This was why the West destroyed the Taliban rule in Afghanistan. They feared the Islamic state. The ruler does not have to be a cleric, a good human being is enough, and Osama Bin Laden and Ayman al-Zawahiri are among several good people. Weren't Jewish leaders also terrorists before they had their own state?

Muslims in the West and in Norway do not want to understand that this is not their country. The Muslim state will be their home, no matter where it is located. Muslims in the West are like the Jews were. We are homeless and weak, and will remain so until we create our own country. Life here has no value for Muslims. Muslims can participate in elections and elect Karl Hagen or Kristin Halvorsen, but in themselves they have no value for society. When we get our own country, like the Shi'ites created in Iran, the Muslims will have full political and economic control. We have no role to play in Europe at this point. Our position is to maintain our numerical strength, but now you are putting us in the role of the accused. It is you and the West who should be telling us what the West can do for us. The West should protect Islam, and not the other way around. I am protected by the law in this country, but it is not a law that protects Muslims in particular. Neither could it protect Muslims against the attack that these cartoons constituted. It is not the West that is the victim in this case.[8]

It is extremely fascinating to get into the thinking of this cleric, especially in view of the hundreds of thousands of Muslims flocking to Europe following the summer of 2015 and their demand that it *must* absorb them. This account, made a decade earlier, should have been a warning of things to come, despite exaggerations and omissions of facts (like the claim that Muslims who dwell in fifty-seven Muslim-majority countries are "homeless" like the Jews, until they get their Caliphate, which has been under implementation by ISIS one decade later).

It is important to note that this statement does not reflect the odd thinking of an eccentric individual, dipped in megalomaniac delusions of bypassed ages. Elsewhere in the Islamic world, similar dreams are not only experienced but also articulated and blindly sermonized to vast ignorant masses who hold on to them in replacement of the grim realities amid which they live. Palestinian clerics, for example, who watch their dreams of a democratic/Islamic state being smashed by the hard politics that prevail, find it easy and comforting to take their revenge on the Christians and the Jews of the world, who are considered to be bound to sink and disappear while the fortunes of Islam are on the ascent. For, in their mind, the final stage of history will be the subjugation of all Christians under Islam and the extermination of every single Jew. For the Jews are so evil that they cannot

8. *Dagbladet* (Norway) 13 March 2006.

be subjugated like the Christians, and therefore the only way to deal with them is total genocide. As the preacher Ibrahim Mudayris put it: "The day will come and we shall rule America, Britain, we shall rule the entire world, except the Jews." This means that no peace, reconciliation, or coexistence are to be sought from the non-Muslims, since only total victory, subjugation, and enslavement of those who will have been spared from genocide, are the modes of survival of Infidels under world Islamic rule. On a Friday sermon of Ibrahim Mudayris on Palestinian TV,[9] which was mostly devoted to the extermination of the evil Jews, several anti-Christian references are worth mentioning too:

> The Jews are a virus similar to AIDS, from which the entire world is suffering. This has been proven in history.... You will find that the Jews were behind every conflict on earth.... Do not ask Germany what it did to the Jews, since the Jews are the ones who provoked the Nazis so the world would go to war against them.... The Palestinians are the strongest nation on earth. Look at all civilizations and empires. Where did Great Britain disappear? Where did the Czar of Russia disappear? Where did Nazi Germany disappear, which massacred millions and ruled the world? If Allah will, He will get rid of the US like he got rid of them.... He is the one who can remove the US and bring it down, and so He shall do.... We [Muslims] had ruled the world, and the day will come, by Allah, and we shall rule the world again. The day will come and we shall rule America, Britain, and the entire world, except the Jews. The day will come when all shall rest from the Jews, even the trees and the stones, which have suffered from them. Listen to your beloved [Muhammad] who tells you about the most dire end awaiting the Jews. The tree and the stone want the Muslim to bring every Jew to his end. You all know the *hadith*....[10]

The purpose of this volume is to survey the situation throughout the Islamic world in order to test the extent to which the rise of radical Islam has not only polarized the attitudes of Islam towards their Christian minorities in the countries they rule, but also, concomitantly, how the aggravation of the mistreatment of Christians in Islamdom has affected the mounting self-confidence of Muslim minorities in the West in their vocal and often-violent

---

9. Ibrahim Mudayris, Friday Sermon, *Palestinian TV,* 13 May 2005.

10. Ibid. The infamous hadith, which is frequently repeated by clerics and other Muslim leaders relates that "The hour of Resurrection will not come until the Muslims make war against the Jews and kill them, and until a Jew hiding behind a rock and a tree will say: 'Muslim, Servant of Allalh, there is a Jew behind me, come and kill him.'"

demands for parity of recognition; a confidence based on the self-assurance that they will inherit those lands too.

This examination of the various areas of the globe will be regional, taking into account the major concentrations of Islam and the extant vestiges of Christian minorities in their midst. That database will allow us to follow the major foci of anti-Christian persecution under the various Islamic regimes in the contemporary world, region by region. At the outset, the conquering power of Islam was in the minority while the process of Islamization took many decades, sometimes centuries, but in view of the doctrine of *Dar-al-Islam*, which made the definition of the *Pax Islamica* contingent upon its Muslim ruler, not on the composition of the population, it was the overwhelming military power of the occupiers and their zeal to Islamize their new conquests that determined the political and social fate of the new subjects of Islamdom.

In China, for example, Islam came during the Tang Dynasty (seventh to tenth centuries) and for a long period thereafter there was no question of the Muslims Sinicizing or the Chinese Islamizing. For Islam was brought to the Middle Kingdom by Persian and Arab traders who remained in constant contact, until the end of the Mongol rule in China (fourteenth century), with their countries of origin. Although they settled in China, they remained out of it, so to speak, because of the virtual extraterritorial rights accorded to them, together with the freedom to conduct their lives as they wished. Neither did the Muslims in China attempt to spread their faith overtly, because they must have been aware, from the very outset, of the vitality of the Chinese system and of the strength of the Unitarian Chinese state attached to that system, which would make any mass Islamization unlikely, if not impossible. So "Muslims in China," rather than "Chinese Muslims," would be the right way of defining the Muslim settlement during the Ming reign (1368–1644). Under this dynasty, however, Chinese Islam, responding to vigorous local pressures, underwent a process of material acculturation into its Chinese environment. Arabic names, which were theretofore exclusive among the Muslims in China, gave way to Chinese names, or at best continued to survive alongside the newly adopted Chinese names. Arabic and Persian speech, which had been the *lingua franca* of all Muslims in China, yielded before the irresistible sweep of the Chinese tongue, although some interspersed words of the previous languages remained in use. Mosques, whose dominant architectural feature—the Minaret—had been transplanted into China, also changed their shape under the Ming; not only did they adopt the Chinese pagoda shape, which made them outwardly indistinguishable from Buddhist or Daoist temples, but they were scattered between regular dwelling houses so as not to attract attention.[11] It will become thereafter the main pattern of Muslim expansion, that conquest by force of arms would often occasion the elimination of the previous cultures, while propagation through trade (like in Southeast Asia) or Sufi mystics (like in Central Asia) would strike compromises with the existing local cultures and permit either their co-existence with Islam or their merger into new syncretic realities like in black Sub-Saharan Africa or in East Asia.

The current and false stereotype is that the Middle East, or the Arab world, equals Islam. The truth is that the demographic center of gravity of Islam long ago shifted eastwards to Asia. If we divide roughly the 1.5 billion Islamic population into three unequal parts, we find that:

1. The first part of over half a billion is located in the Arab world (320 million), Iran, Turkey (75 million each), and Black Africa (at least 150 million). Altogether over 600 million souls;
2. The second part dwells in the Indian Sub-continent and around it: India and Pakistan (180 million each), Bangladesh (100 million), Afganistan, the republics of Central Asia, East Asia (ca. 50 million). Altogether over half a billion.
3. The third part in southeast Asia, first in Indonesia, the largest Islamic country with 220 million Muslims, and then Malaysia and Muslim minorities in Thailand, Nepal, Mianmar, the Philippines, amounting to at least 50 million Muslims. In total, something around 350 million Muslims.

In addition to these figures, which are distributed between fifty-seven Muslim-majority states, we ought to add the Muslim diasporas in Europe, amounting to more than 30 million, and others in the Americas, counting at least 10 to 15 million Muslims.

The Islamic world, like a living organism, senses from one end to the other any tremor that shakes any part of it, and responds in unison to any challenge to it. Thus, worldwide crises like the Cartoon Affair, the Rushdie Affair, the Iranian Revolution, the American interference in Afghanistan or Iraq, or the Israeli incursion into Lebanon or Gaza, immediately provoke reactions and outbursts of sentiments everywhere in the Islamic world. Matters concerning the Middle East and Israel are immediately reflected in the Muslims minorities in Europe and the West in general, usually with violent demonstrations, both against Israel and America, whose national banners and effigies of their leaders are burned in tandem, and against the policies of

---

11. Israeli, "Established Islam and Marginal Islam in China."

the host countries where they sought asylum, and where they are given the freedom to express themselves. The fact that their original homes persecute their Christian minorities and do not permit them the freedom to express themselves the way Muslims do in the West is of little concern to them. Accordingly, the major chapters of this book will center on the following areas:

THE CORE AREAS OF THE MIDDLE EAST

The Middle East is the core area where Christianity was predominant when Islam sprung out from Arabia in the seventh century and launched its conquests. It took over greater Syria with its myriad Christian denominations and made Damascus the capital of the first Arab Dynasty, the Umayyads (660–750), which was followed by the legendary Abbasids based in Baghdad (750–1250). Then, the gradual conquest and elimination of the Byzantine Empire on the Anatolian Plateau was also started by the Islamized Turks, who came from Central Asia, and were to advance thence to the Balkans in the heart of Europe. In Egypt, they subjugated the Copts in their own country and advanced towards the rest of North Africa, up to the Atlantic Ocean, annihilating the bases of Christianity that had evolved there for a couple of centuries under the Visigoths. Thus, while other faiths and ethnic groups, like Jews, Berbers, Kabyles, pagans, animists, and all sorts of other denominations and groupings, were able to preserve themselves after the Muslim conquest in North Africa, Christianity was almost totally extirpated from the land. This is because Christianity was a rival that breathed down the necks of the nascent Muslims, while the others were not.

After it secured its hold on the entire landmass of North Africa, and having attained the frontier of the ocean which signaled its finality, the conquerors of Islam turned northwards to the Iberian Peninsula where they maintained their rule for some eight hundred years, and using it as their catapult, they launched their onslaughts on the south of France until they were arrested in Poitiers by Charles Martel in 732. Until today, Poitiers is remembered in Islamic circles as a travesty of history, and the loss of Andalusia (1492) is recalled as a traumatic event that still demands reversal, as do the loss of Palestine (to Israel) and parts of Kashmir (to India and China).

Yet Muslims still like to preserve their self-image as a tolerant culture, which allowed the "Golden Age" for Christians and Jews to flourish under their aegis in Spain. However, Fernandez-Morera Dario, in *The Myth of the Andalusian Paradise: Muslims, Christians and Jews under Islamic Rule in Medieval Spain*, thoroughly debunks that myth; indeed, he tears it into pieces.

A thoughtful summary by Jonathan Adelman, University of Denver, in August 2015,[12] is worth noticing. He says that "in the nightmarish maelstrom that defines the Middle East today, there are few places of refuge for Christians, except for Israel," for Jesus of Nazareth was born in Bethlehem, lived in the Galilee, and was crucified in Jerusalem. Many Christian holy places from the Via Dolorosa to the Church of the Annunciation[13] are in Jerusalem, and others are in Israel or the West Bank. He stresses that while Iraq, Syria, Yemen, Sudan, and Libya are disintegrating, and Egypt is embattled, the Christians are in dire trouble in a region that is increasingly growing Islamic and radical. Worse, he reminds us, in Iraq and Syria Christians face enslavement, torture, massacres, and crucifixion at the hands of ISIS. ISIS sees them as the dreaded Crusaders, who need to be destroyed or repressed, even though these Christian communities have lived in Syria for the past two thousand years and had nothing to do with the Crusades. ISIS marks Christian houses with an N for Nazarene to single out their victims. Only Lebanon could be a place of refuge, but the Christian population has plunged in one hundred years from 78 percent to 34 percent of the country, and Hezbollah calls the rules of the political game. In the twelve years since Saddam Hussein was overthrown by American military intervention (2003) almost a million Iraqi Christians have fled Iraq or been killed. Barely 500,000 Christians remain behind. In Iraq Christians are less than 4 percent of the population, but 40 percent of the refugees. In Syria, 30 percent of its 1.5 million Christians have fled the country. Adelman rightly emphasizes that the Arab Christians are further divided between Eastern and Western churches in over a dozen denominations. In Lebanon some Christians support Hezbollah while others oppose the radical pro-Iranian Shi'ite group. The Christians, through low birth rate and massive emigration, have dropped from 20 percent of the Middle East in 1900 to 4 percent today and will drop to 3 percent by 2050. The stateless Christians, unlike the Jews before 1948, lack a military, secret police, or government. The Christians have found that without a strong state or patron, they are often hopeless in the face of repressive states or movements.

Discussing the international stance of the Middle East Christians, Adelman laments the fact that he United States and Europe, though heavily Christian, have provided little military protection or financial aid to the

---

12. Adelman, "The Christians of Israel: A Remarkable Group."

13. The Basilica of Annunciation is in fact in Nazareth, the author probably meant the Church of Nativity in Bethlehem.

embattled Christians. President Obama won't even label ISIS as Islamic fundamentalists. By contrast, the 160,000 Israeli Christians live as citizens in a democratic First World country with freedom of religion, rule of law, and open elections. Christians can move anywhere, even building a number of churches recently in Tel Aviv. The government safeguards the Christian holy places and is lenient on the right of return of Christian refugees. Since 1967 Christian, Islamic, and Jewish holy sites are open to pilgrims of all religions. The Christian churches own a significant part of Jerusalem, including the land on which the Knesset sits.

The greatest problem for Christians in Israel often comes from the Muslims. Most Arab Muslims count their blessings for living in a free, open, and prosperous country, but a growing minority, especially in the north, is virulently anti-Christian, using physical attacks, provocative speech, and seditious billboards. These radicals call the Christians, "the descendants of apes and pigs." (They apply this genealogical libel mainly to Jews, following the Qur'an.) While Bethlehem was once 90 percent Christian, today it is 65 percent Muslim. Adelman mentions that after 2007 the Hamas takeover of Gaza led to the remainder of the Christians fleeing to the West Bank. While the Christian element in Israel dropped from 8 percent in 1910 to a projected 1.8 percent in 2025, mainly due to the ten-fold increase of the Jewish population since 1948, the Christians plummeted from 11.6 percent of the West Bank and Gaza in 1910 to a projected 1 percent in 2025, mainly due to emigration of the Christians.

Today 60 percent more Christians live in Israel than in the Palestinian territories. A small, new Christian party, *B'nai Brith*, calls on its youth to serve in the Israeli army and hundreds each year do so. Its leader, Reverend Nadaff, declares, "We love this country," but Israeli Christians have several problems. One is lacking the benefits given to Israelis who serve in the army.[14] Another is the provocative and occasional defacing and vandalizing of Christian monuments and cemeteries by a group of radical Jews. Christians also complain of the high cost of land and housing. Their small size and internal divisions make them a peripheral political force.

Outside of the Gulf States, with over a million (mainly Asian) Christian laborers, Israel is the only place in the Middle East where the Christians are growing in number. They are excelling in education, doing well in

---

14. Christians in Israel have long preferred their Arab nationalist links with their Muslim Arab compatriots, to their citizenship in the Jewish State of Israel. However, the Druze, for example, who are serving in the Israeli military and are recognized as a corporate minority that enjoys the privileges of the Jewish population, have decided, due to their break with Muslim Arabs who are persecuting them, to throw their lot with Israel and its Jewish-majority population.

business and the professions, and feeling relatively safe from their radical tormentors. In today's troubled Middle East, that is a remarkable feat of which Israel can be proud, concludes Adelman.[15]

CHIRISTIANOPHOBIA IN TURKEY

A special, and alarming case of a Christian minority under Islam is Turkey. It is special because it neither belongs to the Arab hardcore of the Middle East, which is tackled here separately, nor to Asian Islam, due to its affiliation to NATO and its European pretensions, which have been blunted by the EU refusal to let it join the Union. And yet, it is listed with the score of 52/100 in the World Watch,[16] that is to say it occupies a middle ground after Mali and before Kazakhstan in its persecution of Christianity. It is also special in the sense that its founders, who originated in Central Asia, had occupied and eliminated the thriving Christian Byzantine Empire, turning its prevalent creed into a persecuted minority in the Anatolian plateau and even in the European part of present day Turkey, Thracia. Not only did the Turks occupy and destroy the Christian culture of Byzantine Anatolia, but they made sure that almost all the vestiges of Christianity were eliminated over the years, and they have titled their Sultan Mehmet II, who subjugated the glorious Christian Capital of Constantinople, as "the Conqueror," forever glorifying his name. But no other feat of the Muslim conquerors has shaken the Christian world as much as the re-baptizing of Constantinople as Istanbul, and the transformation of the greatest structure of Christianity, the immense Hagia Sophia Church (the Greek for Holy Wisdom), into a mosque. That shock, which modern Turkey had been trying to assuage since the end of the Ottoman Caliphate after World War I by converting the structure into a museum, has emerged once again since Tayyip Erdogan came to power in 2003, and Muslim pressure has been building up to revert the structure to its Islamic glamour by returning it to its usage as a mosque.

Before that outrageous conversion by force—a practice that has long been embraced in the entire Islamic world, where conquered Christian churches or Jewish synagogues have been converted into mosques, thus demonstrating who was the sovereign in place—the Hagia Sophia had been for almost a millennium Eastern Christianity's greatest cathedral. Built in 537 CE in the heart of the Christian Empire, in Constantinople, the largest

15. Ibid.

16. The World Watch is an NGO that advocates for Christian minority rights, and publishes an annual list of Christian minorities, where the countries are graded on a scale of percentage points for their tolerance of their minorities.

and most glamorous city of the Middle Ages, it had been also a stalwart symbol of Christian strength and defiance to the advancing Islamic troops which advanced up at its periphery until it succumbed in 1453. Finally, when it fell to the Ottomans, the city was ransacked, churches and crosses were desecrated, and icons were defaced. Minarets were added to the majestic structure of the Cathedral. In the 2000s, according to the *Hurriyet Daily News*, a parliamentary commission was considering an application of Turkish citizens to reconvert Hagia Sophia into a mosque once again, and reopen it to Muslim worship. Other great historical cathedrals have known the same fate. For example, in the northern city of Trabzon, a thirteenth-century church, also called Hagia Sophia, was converted into a mosque, turned into a museum under the secular government of post-Ottoman Turkey, and now the local authorities have decreed that its original frescoes, which had been restored under the civil governments, would gain be covered and the structure turn again into a mosque.[17]

Studios Monastery, a fifth-century Christian structure dedicated to John the Baptist, as well as the fifth-century Mor Gabriel Monastery, are also at risk of turning into mosques, although the latter is a functioning institution, with a few dozen monks dedicated to worship and scholarship. But it was sued for pursuing "anti-Turkish" activities, such as occupying lands that belong to Muslim villagers. Unsurprisingly, the Supreme Court in Ankara ruled in favor of the Muslims, saying that the Monastery's possession of those lands for fifteen hundred years was no proof of ownership, and that the structure had been built on the ruins of a mosque—even though it was built when there was no Islam and no Muhammad, and certainly no mosque, in existence! The Orthodox Patriarch, whose dwindling power and authority are much in painful evidence for the vestiges of the Christian minority, is naturally protesting these blatant land grabs, but apparently in vain, as the de-Christianization and increasing Islamization of Turkey continue at full pace, while the Christian West is looking on indifferently and showering favors and benefits on Erdogan, in spite of his annihilationist intolerance.

A report by *Reuters* in 2012 reflects on this state of affairs in NATO-affiliate and American-ally Turkey that nobody seems able or willing to stop:

> Thousands of devout Muslims prayed outside Turkey's historic Hagia Sophia Museum on Saturday, May 23, 2012, to protest a 1934 law that bars religious services at the former church and mosque. Worshippers shouted: "Break the chains! Let Hagia Sophia Mosque open again! Allahu Akbar!," before kneeling in prayer as tourists looked on. Turkey's secular laws prevent

17. Raymond Ibrahim, *PJ Media*, 18 June 2013

Muslims and Christians from formal worship within the 6th Century monument, the world's greatest cathedral for almost a millennium before invading Ottomans converted it into a mosque in the 15th Century.[18]

It is evident that, with its three thousand active mosques, Istanbul is hardly in want of places to pray! But the whole of Turkey has been swept by the Islamic zeal that Erdogan and his government have enforced since 2002. The ambience they have created, which glorifies Jihad and Islamic conquests, also produced the massive staged prayers marking the 559th anniversary of the Ottoman Mehmet the Conqueror, who decimated the Byzantine Empire and generated the Islamization of Istanbul and the entire Anatolian heights. His followers, who still adore him and are proud of his heritage, believe it is their legitimate right to rededicate Hagia Sophia as a mosque. Not only do they not repent or apologize for their outrageous confiscation of that glorious cathedral and conversion into a mosque, but they consider that it is an insult to the seventy-five million Islamic majority that "unjustified" Western pressures are keeping that mosque closed to Muslim worship. This is also an oblique warning to the growing Muslim of communities of Europe that, wherever and whenever they achieve local majorities in their diasporas, they will be apt to advance "legitimate" demands of this sort. Erdogan himself expressed this skewed view of history by declaring in May 2012, on the anniversary of the fall of Constantinople to the Turks, when countless Christians were slaughtered, raped, and enslaved that, "that was the true time of enlightenment."[19]

In June 2010, sixty-two-year-old Bishop Luigi Padovese, the Head of Turkey's Catholic Church, was brutally murdered, depriving the 30,000 member Catholic community (a third of the total Christian population) of its leadership and further terrorizing the minute vestiges of the Christian communities into either lowering their public profile or emigrating. Ironically, the bishop was known for his relentless efforts to improve Christian-Muslim relations in Turkey, when he was repeatedly stabbed near his home in Iskanderun (Alexandretta, hinting to his Syrian affiliation), by his Turkish driver and bodyguard, Murat Altun, who also decapitated his victim while shouting: "Allah Akbar! I have killed the Great Satan!," as "ordered by God," as he later admitted to the police. The tragedy of that Jihadi murder is that while the Western leniency toward the Muslim world was intended to win the hearts of Muslims, both domestically and internationally, it has backfired and reinforced the Jihadists into more terrorism and denigration

---

18. Ibid.
19. Ibid.

of what they regard as the sinking Christianity, both in the international arena and within the Christian minorities that they oppress all the more in the Islamic lands. The murder was further aggravated by the denials and obfuscation of the embarrassed authorities, backed by the shameful pretext-manufacturing of the Vatican and the Western governments, who since September 11 have attempted to divorce Islam from acts of violence and international terrorism. Obama continues to wrongly praise the "strong, vibrant and secular democracy of Turkey," just as he is denying, against all the evidence, any link between Islam and Jihadi terrorism.[20] Who else in the world champions Jihad but Muslims?

The slain bishop's mission had been to save Christianity from extinction and to foster conditions for its rebirth, and he therefore rejected the hallowed notion of dhimmitude, under which Christianity was a "protected" minority faith, given to the whims of unpredictable Muslim rulers, and probably viewed Ankara's attempts to gain access to the EU as a golden opportunity to win concessions from the Turks on this score, but he must have been frustrated in his efforts, as he was witnessing the frenzy of the crowds who demanded more Islamization of their society, apparently with the encouragement of their government.

Nonetheless, to preempt the world protest for the murder and the police investigation, the Turkish provincial governor announced that it was not a politically-inspired murder, but the deed of one lunatic person, and there was even a claim in the media that he was not a Muslim but a convert to Catholicism; police sources leaked word that the assassin had been forced to suffer abuse in a homosexual relationship with the bishop, evidently capitalizing on the sexual scandals that were rife in the Catholic world in those days, and therefore the murder was an "act of legitimate self-defense." Though some high officials have expressed their regrets and condolences for that senseless murder, neither President Gul nor Prime Minister Erdogan found it necessary to apologize publicly for it. In effect, the spirit of Islamic Jihad emerged victorious from this clash, and even the Regensburg papal speech in September 2006, in which he broached the question of violent Jihad, and which was insultingly dismissed and called names by the Turkish hierarchy, had to be toned down in advance of the Pope's official visit to Istanbul in November, 2006.[21]

Unlike the arrogant reaction of the Turkish leadership to the murder, and the dhimmi-like submissiveness of the Vatican and the West, which elected to harmonize their speeches to the tune of Erdogan, the beleaguered

---

20. EIbner, "Turkey's Christians under Siege."
21. Ibid.

Turkish Christians, who must deal with the day-to-day struggle for survival, accepted neither the denials nor the obfuscations of their failed protectors. The Archbishop of Smyrna (now Izmir), Ruggero Franceschini, the slain bishop's successor, angrily rejected the explanations of his predecessor's assassination, and dared to declare publicly that the Pope had received bad counsel prior to his denial of the religious and political motives of the murder. After visiting Iskanderun, where he knew the family of the murderer, he dismissed as "pious lies" the official explanations, and confirmed the political and religious motives behind that senseless killing. He saw it as the deed of anarchic groups who wish to destabilize the government and to manipulate public opinion. He suspected that the crime was stage-managed by Turkey's "deep state," an underworld where powerful state elements, including the military and security services, acted in conjunction with violent extremist groups, such as the ultra-nationalists "Grey Wolves" and the radical Islamic Hizbullah. That deep state, known as "Ergenekon," was a source of anti-church activity, which included an Islamic-style ritual murder of three evangelical Christian book publishers in Malatya in April 2006, and the murder of another Catholic priest, Andrea Santoro, in the Trabzon Church in February 2006. The convicted killer, then a sixteen-year-old boy, who shouted the familiar "Allah Akbar" before pressing the trigger, was apparently provoked by the passions aroused during the Danish Cartoon Affair of 2006. Prosecutors in Turkey also ascribed to Ergenekon the January-2007 manslaughter, by another seventeen-year-old boy, of the Armenian Christian journalist Hrant Dink, who was a vigorous campaigner against the denial of the Armenian massacre by the Turks. Expectedly, he had been indicted for "insults to Turkishness," another secularized version of "blasphemy" in other Islamic lands, which resulted in his Turkish lawyer's body being found hanging, the day after the bishop's murder.[22]

This attribution of Christianophobia to Ergenekon has been a way for the state elites to escape the blame for the plight of the diminishing statute of Christianity in the Turkish Muslim state. However, the older generation among Christians reminisces over the state-sponsored mass deportations and massacres that had culminated in the Armenian genocide in World War I. It was indeed during the twentieth century that the Christian population was reduced drastically, almost to extinction. The most memorable in recent memory in this litany of anti-Christian attacks was the 1955 anti-Greek pogrom in Istanbul, in which many Jews and Armenians also perished.

The younger generation remembers the attack against a Slovenian priest by a group of Muslim teenagers in a Christian compound of Smyrna

---

22. Ibid.

(Izmir now) in February 2006, and six months later the slaying of another seventy-four-year-old priest in Trabzon, about which later murdered Bishop Padovese told the media: "The climate has changed. It is the Catholic priests that are being attacked." In December 2007, another priest was stabbed by another teenager as he was leaving Sunday Mass.

A leader of the Protestant community, Rev. Behnan Konutgan, also complained about many cases of violence against his church property and physical harassment of his congregation. In 2009, the normally subservient Patriarch of the Ecumenical Church of Constantinople, Bartholomew I, appeared on CBS's "Sixty Minutes" and shocked the Turkish establishment by his forceful, frank, and daring confession that Turkey's Christians were second-class citizens, and that he personally felt "crucified" by the state, which wanted to see his church extinct. He also complained that Erdogan had never responded to any of his frequent petitions about the situation. Instead of addressing the Patriarch's substantive grievances, the authorities reacted with fury, charging that the metaphor of "crucifixion" was inappropriate' since no crucifixions were ever practiced in Turkey! In effect, one of the ruling AKP's leaders retorted that if anyone felt he was being crucified, it is the politicians, security officials, and others, while the Patriarch, who is a spiritual leader, should be much more cautious when making such a statement, for anyone who loved his country ought to be more responsible than that. The charge of irresponsibility and disloyalty to the state sounded ominously threatening.[23]

In spite of the government's attempts to show a smiling face to Europe and the US regarding Christianity, as if they could care less, domestically Erdogan held a tight hold on the development of Christian institutions, for example, by refusing to reopen the Haki Theological Seminary, the only Christian Orthodox institution where clergy could be trained, under the pretext that Greece and Bulgaria ought to improve the conditions of their Muslim minorities first. Thus, instead of ensuring the liberty of the church to train its own clergy, Turkey holds its Christian minority hostage to the improvement of the fate of Muslim minorities in Christendom, as if the West should make the erecting and financing of new mosques in its territories conditional on the opening of churches in Saudi Arabia.

In the meantime, churches in Turkey have been constrained by the General Directorate of Foundations, and choked in their inability to retrieve through legal suits their confiscated properties. The four-year (2006–10) state prosecution of two Protestant evangelical converts from Islam, on the charge of "insulting Turkishness" (a variant of "blasphemy" or "heresy," in

---

23. Ibid.

view of the unity of religion and nationality in Turkish perception), though it ended in October 2010 for "lack of evidence," the converts were forced to pay fines, otherwise they would have been convicted and imprisoned for "collecting information on citizens" (i.e., information of their fellow Christians).

Bishop Padovese had seen before his death his plea rejected to reopen the Church of St. Paul of Tarsus and change its status from museum to a place of active worship. But in spite of the involvement of the Pope and the Bishop of Cologne, and their pledge to support the erection of a major mosque in Germany in return, Ankara turned down those pleas. In this atmosphere, where Christians are considered subversive to the state, and the hostile media is constantly cultivating suspicions against them, the national intelligence report, exposed by the *Cumhuriyet* paper in June 2005, revealed similar Christianophobic sentiments when it put Christian missionaries on a par with Islamic terrorist groups, who "cover Turkey like a spider web and promote divisions in sensitive areas." Other officials accused the Christians of "breaking up the historical, religious, national, and cultural unity of the people of Turkey," for "Turk" and "Christian" are viewed as mutually exclusive terms. They further said that "Christian missionaries exploited religious and ethnic differences and natural disasters to win the hearts of poor people," although that effort has resulted, in seven years of evangelization, in only 338 converts to Christianity (and six converts to Judaism), out of the 75 million Muslim Turks.[24]

The sweeping victory of Erdogan and his party in the October 2015 elections, which were a corrective to the previous election of June 2015 in which he had lost his absolute majority in Parliament, may render things still worse for Christians in the country. For, though Erdogan has failed for now to obtain a yet larger majority to enable him to change the constitution and turn his regime from republican-parliamentary to a presidential and Sulnatate-like authoritarian rule where he would reign supreme and no constraints would check his power, he still emerged all- powerful and poised to pursue his campaign of Islamization (vis-à-vis) the Christians, and Turkification (vis-à-vis the Kurds) that won him his latest victory. So, from his imposing new 1,100-room palace in Ankara, from which he can inspire awe, he will pursue his terrorism towards a docile media, intimidation of political and ethnic rivals domestically, and a high-handed policy towards the Kurds, which his international critics in America and Europe would not dare to contradict.

---

24. Ibid.

CHRISTIAN MINORITIES UNDER AFRICAN ISLAM

After it completed the conquest of North Africa, from Egypt, Sudan, and Somalia, to Mauritania, and was stopped in its endeavor to turn north into Europe, expanding Islam, which had encountered the vast barrier of the Sahara, a no less formidable obstacle than the Atlantic, used trade routes of the vast desert, the Jihad movements, and the various Islamic sultanates that rose in Dar Fur (Sudan) and West Africa (Mali and the Volta Basin), to spread their faith in the continent.[25] Today's points of Muslim upheaval, which carry with them vast and inhumane persecutions of Christians, are the Horn of Africa—notably Somalia, where the fanatic Al-Shabaab Movement radiates out from into adjoining east African countries—and Nigeria, the most populous country of Africa, half Muslim and half Christian, where the outrageous *Boko Haram* practices daily rampages against the Christians that no rule seems able to stop. Lately, we hear that this movement not only targets innocent Christians simply because of their Christianity, kidnapping, murdering, raping, and terrorizing them in the thousands, but that it also entertains ambitions of rule and empire, which might hark back to the revival of the old Muslim sultanates.

CHRISTIAN MINORITIES UNDER ASIAN ISLAM

Islam did not encounter much Christianity to battle against in the process of its Asian expansion, though it did learn to accommodate other faiths like Hinduism, Buddhism and animism, except for the only Christian country in Asia—the Philippines—where the southern islands of Mindanao and the Sulu had been Islamized by Malay Islam, which predominates southeast Asia. Its largest impact is noticeable in the Indonesian islands where local Hinduism and Buddhism, which began adopting the Muslim traders in the fourteenth century in an eclectic way, led ultimately to a syncretic Islam of a very special brand. On the one hand, it is said to be more inclusive and tolerant than the Islamic streams of the Middle East and West Africa, which have been causing the upheavals of the past decades, but on the other hand, there are there also periodic explosions of terrorism, like in Bali (2002), the cruel oppressions of the Chinese minority in the 1960s, and a rather harsh, heavy hand on the dissident sect of the Ahmadiyyah within this multifarious archipelago of cultures, religions, and ethnic groups. In nearby Malaysia, where the Muslim majority is flimsy, the Chinese community, which is the most successful and thriving economically, is being

---

25. Levtzion (ed.), *Conversion to Islam*.

discriminated against. Under the general atmosphere of favoritism to the Muslim faith, it is easy to grow xenophobic and intolerant, and so manifestations of Christianophobia are quite current there and have become *cause célèbre* from time to time, though it is the Islamophobic phenomena in the Buddhist cultures of Mianmar and Thailand which gain the most attention in the West and in Islamdom.

CHRISTIAN MINORITIES IN THE HOLY LAND

The Holy Land is the place where it all began, with the birth place of Jesus Christ. However, the fate that Palestinian Muslims are scheming for their Christian minority is exemplified best and most concretely by adoption of Jesus by Yasser Arafat as his "Palestinian" hero, whom he sanctified by his union with Suha, a Christian, who gave birth to their daughter, born (of course) a Muslim, as Muslim law prescribes. The Palestinian Christian minority, which has survived since the Crusader times, especially in the Christian holy cities of Jerusalem, Nazareth, and Bethlehem, has been dwindling ever since the Palestinian Authority took over the rule in part of those cities. Nazareth and Jerusalem, which have been under Israeli rule, and Haifa which is no holy city, have become asylum locations for the Christians of the Holy Land, who are fleeing either the Palestinian rule, or the mixed towns in Israel, where they share their villages with Muslims who demonstrate no tolerance for them, much less for their growing accommodation of late with the Israeli state in which they wish to integrate.

MUSLIM MINORITIES UNDER WESTERN CHRISTIANITY

To lend a comparative dimension to this volume, it would be instructive to learn the mirror image of the persecuted Christian minorities in the Islamic world, as it is reflected in the existence of the Muslim minorities in the West. As against the ever-increasing—in both numbers and influence—Muslim communities in the West, which even entertain ambitions to increasingly change the countries of their asylum to march to an Islamic tune, Christian minorities in Islamdom have been shrinking and threatened to the verge of extinction. While Christians under Islam continue to seek to move to Christian countries, as millions of Lebanese and Syrians had done to South America, and more recently Palestinians, Afghanis, Kurds, and Syrians, to Europe and North America, Muslims in Christendom show no propensity to return to their original homes; quite the contrary, they keep absorbing a relentless stream of illegal new immigrants, coming from the countries of Islam. That tendency stems not only from the preference that Muslims accord to the West, compared to the miseries of their own countries, but very often, after they settle down and realize what a good move they made by changing their place and style of life, they begin talking about adapting the host countries to their culture, rather than plying themselves to the cultures that had generously absorbed them in their midst.

Open Door USA, which publishes the World Watch List, ranks all countries where Christian minorities are persecuted—thirty-two out of fifty of which are Muslim-majority—and lists them in percentage points out of one hundred, relatively to the degree of persecution and oppression they practice towards their Christian minorities. Interestingly enough, North Korea, which is probably the most oppressive regime there is, is the worst (92/100), but most of the following countries are Islamic, with Somalia (90/100), Iraq, Syria, and Afghanistan leading (81–86/100), and then all the rest.

Of course, when it comes to Muslim minorities in Christendom, it is the choices of the targets that the Muslim guest culture elects to attack in their host countries that is of concern to us here. In one of the pieces highlighted by eminent specialist Raymond Ibrahim,[26] for example, he expands on why Muslim rapists prefer Western blond women.[27] He says that the Muslim penchant to target "white" women for sexual exploitation—an epidemic currently plaguing Europe, especially Britain and Scandinavia—is as old as Islam itself, and even can be traced back to Muhammad. Much literary evidence attests to this in the context of Islam's early predations on Byzantium (for centuries, Christendom's easternmost bulwark against the Jihad). According to Ahmad M. H. Shboul (author of *Byzantium and*

26. Raymond Ibrahim is a Middle East and Islam specialist and author of *Crucified Again: Exposing Islam's New War on Christians* (2013) and *The Al Qaeda Reader* (2007). His writings have appeared in a variety of media, including the *Los Angeles Times, Washington Times, Jane's Islamic Affairs Analyst, Middle East Quarterly, World Almanac of Islamism*, and *Chronicle of Higher Education*; he has appeared on MSNBC, Fox News, C-SPAN, PBS, Reuters, Al-Jazeera, NPR, Blaze TV, and CBN. Ibrahim regularly speaks publicly, briefs governmental agencies, provides expert testimony for Islam-related lawsuits, and testifies before Congress. He is a Shillman Fellow, David Horowitz Freedom Center; a CBN News contributor; a Media Fellow, Hoover Institution (2013); and a Judith Friedman Rosen Writing Fellow, Middle East Forum. Ibrahim's dual-background—born and raised in the U.S. by Coptic Egyptian parents born and raised in the Middle East—has provided him with unique advantages, from equal fluency in English and Arabic, to an equal understanding of the Western and Middle Eastern mindsets, positioning him to explain the latter to the former.

27. Raymond Ibrahim, *FrontPage Magazine*, 30 July 2015.

the Arabs: *The Image of the Byzantines as Mirrored in Arabic Literature*) Christian Byzantium was the "classic example of the House of War," or *Dar al-Harb*—that is, the quintessential realm that needed to be conquered by Jihad. Moreover, Byzantium was seen "as a symbol of military and political power and as a society of great abundance." Author Shboul continues:

> The similarities between pre-modern Islamic views of Byzantium and modern Islamic views of the West—powerful, affluent, desirable, and the greatest of all infidels—should be evident. But they do not end here. To the medieval Muslim mind, Byzantium was further representative of "white people"—fair haired/eyed Christians, or, as they were known in Arabic, *Banu al-Asfar*, "children of yellow" (reference to blond hair). The Byzantines as a people were considered as fine examples of physical beauty, and youthful slaves and slave-girls of Byzantine origin were highly valued.... The Arab's appreciation of the Byzantine female has a long history indeed. For the Islamic (saying of the Prophet), Muhammad is said to have addressed a newly converted [to Islam] Arab: "Would you like the girls of *Banu al-Asfar*?" Not only were Byzantine slave girls sought after for caliphal and other palaces (where some became mothers of future caliphs), but they also became the epitome of physical beauty, home economy, and refined accomplishments. The typical Byzantine maiden who captures the imagination of *litterateurs* and poets, had blond hair, blue or green eyes, a pure and healthy visage, lovely breasts, a delicate waist, and a body that is like camphor or a flood of dazzling light.[28]

Ibrahim warns us nonetheless, that while the essence of the above excerpt is true, the reader should not be duped by its overly "romantic" tone. Written for a Western academic publication by an academic of Muslim background, the essay is naturally euphemistic to the point of implying that being a sex slave was desirable—as if her Arab owners were enamored devotees who merely doted over and admired her beauty from afar. Indeed, Muhammad had asked a new convert "Would you like the girls of *Banu al-Asfar*?" as a way to entice him to join the Jihad and reap its rewards—which, in this case, included the possibility of enslaving and raping blonde Byzantine women—not as some idealistic discussion on beauty.

This enticement seems to have backfired with another Muslim who refused Muhammad's call to invade Byzantine territory (the Tabuk campaign). "O Abu Wahb," cajoled Muhammad, "would you not like to have

---

28. Shboul's essay is found in Michael Bonner (ed.), *Arab-Byzantine Relations in Early Islamic Times*, 240, 248.

scores of Byzantine women and men as concubines and servants?" Wahb responded: "O Messenger of Allah, my people know that I am very fond of women and, if I see the women of the Byzantines, I fear I will not be able to hold back. So do not tempt me by them, and allow me not to join and, instead, I will assist you with my wealth." The Prophet agreed, but was apparently unimpressed—after all, Wahb could have all the Byzantine women he desired if the Jihad succeeded—and a new Sura of the Qur'ran (9:49) was promptly delivered condemning the man to hell for his reported hypocrisy and failure to join the Jihad.

Thus, a more critical reading of Shboul's aforementioned excerpt finds that European slave girls were not "highly valued" or "appreciated" as precious statues, but they were held out as *sexual trophies to entice Muslims to the Jihad*. Moreover, adds Ibrahim, the idea that some sex slaves became mothers to future caliphs is meaningless since in Islam's patriarchal culture counted, while mothers—Muslim or non-Muslim—were irrelevant in lineage and had no political status. And talk of "*litterateurs* and poets" and "a body that is like camphor or a flood of dazzling light" is furthermore anachronistic and does a great disservice to reality: these women were—as they still are—sex slaves, treated no differently than the many slaves of the Islamic State today. Ibrahim suggests another relevant parallel between medieval and modern Islamic views: white women were and continue to be seen as sexually promiscuous by nature—essentially "provoking" Muslim men into lusting after them.

Some of these themes are discussed in *Byzantium Viewed by the Arabs* by Nadia Maria El Cheikh.[29] She writes: "*Fitna*, [an Islamic term] meaning disorder and chaos, refers also to the beautiful *femme fatale* who makes men lose their self-control. *Fitna* is a key concept in defining the dangers that women, more particularly their bodies, were capable of provoking in the mental universe of the Arab Muslims." After explaining how the fair haired/eyed Byzantine woman exemplified Islam's *femme fatale* of *fitna*, Cheikh writes:

> In our [Muslim] texts, Byzantine women are strongly associated with sexual immorality. . . . Our sources show not Byzantine women but [Muslim] writers' images of these women, who served as symbols of the eternal female—constantly a potential threat, particularly due to blatant exaggerations of their sexual promiscuity . . . .

29. Cheikh, *Byzantium Viewed by the Arabs*, 123–29. Cited by Ibrahim, *Crucified Again*, 123–29.

Cheikh documents how Muslims claimed that Byzantine (or "white Christian") females were the "most shameless women in the whole world"; that, "because they find sex more enjoyable, they are prone to adultery"; that "adultery is commonplace in the cities and markets of Byzantium"—so much so that "the nuns from the convents went out to the fortresses to offer themselves to monks." And she concludes:

> While the one quality that our [Muslim] sources never deny is the beauty of Byzantine women, the image that they create in describing these women is anything but beautiful. Their depictions are, occasionally, excessive, virtually caricatures, overwhelmingly negative.... Such anecdotes [of sexual promiscuity] are clearly far from Byzantine reality and must be recognized for what they are: attempts to denigrate and defame a rival culture through their exaggeration of the laxity with which Byzantine culture dealt with its women.... In fact, in Byzantium, women were expected to be retiring, shy, modest, and devoted to their families and religious observances.... [T]he behavior of most women in Byzantium was a far cry from the depictions that appear in Arabic sources."[30]

Based on all the above, Raymond draws authoritatively some historic facts: Byzantium was long viewed by early Muslims as the most powerful, advanced, and wealthy "infidel" empire, one highly desired—not unlike modern Islamic views of the West today. And Byzantine women, or "white women," were long viewed as the *"femme fatale"* of Islam—from a carnal perspective, the most desired, though from a pious perspective, the most despised of women. Today, we find all these same patterns at work—including the idea that "white women" are naturally promiscuous and provoke pious Muslim men into raping them. In December 2014 in the UK, while a Muslim man raped a British woman, he told her that "you white women are good at it"—thereby echoing that ancient Islamic motif concerning the alleged promiscuity of white women. Turning to today's problems in the UK, Ibrahim claims that it is also home to one of the most notorious Muslim-led sex ring scandals: in Rotherham and elsewhere, thousands of young native British girls have been systematically groomed, trafficked, beaten, and sexually abused by Muslims—even as the "multiculturalist" authorities and police stood by and watched. In fact, he says, and it is well known[31] all throughout Europe—particularly in the Nordic nations—thousands of "Byzantine-type" women have been violently raped and egregiously beaten

---

30. Ibid.
31. See Israeli, *Islamic Challenge in Europe*.

by Muslims. In Norway, Denmark, and Sweden—where fair hair and eyes predominate—the number of rapes has astronomically risen since those nations embraced the doctrine of multiculturalism and opened their doors to tens of thousands of Muslim immigrants.

Ibrahim cites the Gatestone Institute:[32]

> Forty years after the Swedish parliament unanimously decided to change the formerly homogenous Sweden into a multicultural country, violent crime has increased by 300% and rapes by 1,472%. The overwhelming majority of rapists are Muslim immigrants. The epidemic is so bad that some blonde haired Scandinavian women are dying their hair black in the hopes of warding off potential Muslim predators. Nor is this phenomenon a product of chance; some modern-day Muslims actually advocate for it. Back in 2011, a female politician and activist trying to combat sexual immorality in Kuwait suggested that Muslims import white sex slaves. After explaining how she once asked Islamic clerics living in the city of Mecca, concerning the legality of sex slavery, and how they all confirmed it to be perfectly legitimate, she explained
>
>> A Muslim state must [first] attack a Christian state—sorry, I mean any non-Muslim state—and they [the women, the future sex slaves] must be captives of the raid. Is this forbidden? Not at all; according to Islam, sex slaves are not at all forbidden. [As for what sort of "infidel" women are ideal, the Kuwaiti activist suggested] Russian women (most of whom are fair haired and eyed; ironically, Russia is often seen as Byzantium's successor): In the Chechnya war, surely there are female Russian captives. So go and buy those and sell them here in Kuwait; better that than have our men engage in forbidden sexual relations. I don't see any problem in this, no problem at all.

In sum, concludes Ibrahim, the ongoing epidemic in the UK, Scandinavia, Australia,[33] and elsewhere—whereby Muslim men sexually target white women—is as old as Islam, has precedents with the Prophet and his companions, and, till this day, is being recommended as a legitimate

---

32. The Gatestone Institute, formerly Stonegate Institute and Hudson New York, is a think tank based in New York City that specializes in strategy and defense issues. Gatestone was founded in 2012 by Nina Rosenwald, who serves as its president. Former U.S. Ambassador to the United Nations John R. Bolton is its chairman. Gatestone publicizes the writings of authors as diverse as Alan Dershowitz, Robert Spencer, and Israeli-Arab journalist Khaled Abu Toameh.

33. Israeli, *Muslim Minorities in Modern States: The Challenge of Assimilation*

practice by some in the Muslim world. Thus, the frictions between Islam and non-Muslims, including in the sexual area, is not likely to recede either when non-Muslim women are taken prisoners under Islamic rule or are assaulted in their own countries by immigrant men.

Julius Werner, who has covered other problems of human rights among the Palestinians,[34] has shed some light on the wider perspectives of this dire issue. Unlike the situation in other countries, Palestinian Christians as such have no history, since Palestine itself had never existed as an independent entity, and therefore it could never devise any policy towards its Christian minorities; and when it did, under the Palestinian Authority Territories since the 1993 Oslo Accords, its record has been quite pitiful (Number 26 in the World Watch of fifty countries, with the ranking of 58/100). Here too, the Palestinian Christian minority has stood in the forefront of local nationalism, and has often gained favor with the Muslim populace by championing the Palestinian cause. Their alternative was much less pleasant: when they realized that they could not contend with the mounting wave of Muslim radicalism in the past decades, many of them have elected to emigrate to the West, particularly to Christian South America. Thus, typically Christian cities, like Bethlehem and Ramallah (and Nazareth in Israel), have grown Muslim with the crushing new Muslim majority, signaling to the local Christians that they are no longer the masters of the towns of their roots, birth, growth, and identity. This renders in turn the remaining Christians more extremely nationalistic (see, for example, the cases of Hanan Ashrawi, a member of the executive board of the PLO, or the Latin Patriarch, Michel Sabbah in Jerusalem, or Azmi Bishara, an Israeli Arab from Nazareth, who served as a member of the Knesset, and then defected to Hizbullah and run away from justice in Israel, to live in exile in Qatar and other Arab lands).

Logically, one would think that as the number of Christians living in Muslim countries decreases, the less acute should be their problem in society. But in reality it is not necessarily so, because the more the radical movements like Hamas, Hizbullah, or the Boko Haram experience "success" in "cleansing" their societies from a Christian presence, the closer they feel to realizing the end of "Crusaders" in the Muslim lands, an end earmarked to constitute the revived Caliphate. Being so close to the ultimate goal only boosts their eagerness to squeeze the Christians even more (and also the Jews if that were possible) out from the Domain of Islam.

While Weiner set out to discuss the issue of human rights for Christians under the Palestinians, the entire notion becomes laughable, because there is no recognition of human rights in any Muslim country. Even the

---

34. Weiner, *Human Rights of Christians in Palestinian Society*.

border cases of Turkey and Indonesia in the two ends of the Muslim world, which pride themselves for being democratic, because they indeed run free elections, as a matter of fact put journalists in jail or oppress minority groups like Christians, Chinese, Kurds, Muhammadis, and Ahmadis, which their Muslim states cannot tolerate. For human rights, one needs the structure of a state of law, while those countries are ruled by tribal, religious, clan, and family ties and obligations, where the concept of "honor," personal and collective, or religious imperatives, dominates the scene and conditions societal behavior. Human rights as recognized and stated by the UN are not accepted by Muslim nations, who have made it abundantly clear that this issue, like many others in international affairs, is culture-bound, and therefore they reject lock, stock, and barrel this whole concept. It is then absurd to even raise the issue of human rights in a Muslim context.

Certainly, Ashrawi and her like would often attack the West and Israel for depriving Palestinians and others from human rights, but within their own societies that issue is seldom, if ever, invoked. For it would be like describing to viewers the violent game of American football using the gentle language of basketball, which is replete with warnings, caution, penalties for foul play, and strict rules of conduct deriving from commitment to fair play. Human rights standards are impossible to detect in Palestinian or other Islamic societies, for what is considered violation for the West is standard conduct in Islamic and other authoritarian regimes. Exactly as one cannot point out to any particular spot on a totally filthy cloth, or try to detect gentlemanly conduct in a brutal mafia gang, so it is vain to search for human rights violations in a society that does not even understand what they are, and in any case openly rejects the Western notions thereof.

Islamic countries have already come up with their "Islamic Human Rights" version, as if such were not a contradiction in terms. Prerequisites for human rights are Western-style democracy, tolerance, and freedom, which do not exist in the Western sense in *any* Muslim society. Seeking for them in an Islamic context would be equivalent to sending a blind person into a dark room to look for a black cat that is not there.

An American analyst of Serbian descent, Srdja Trifkovic, who knows something about minority rights, wrote that the fourteen centuries of Islam have fatally undermined Christianity in the land of its birth, and accompanied by the indifference of the post-Christian West in the recent decades, has brought Christianity in Islamdom to its impending demise.[35] He claims that in Syria, the Obama administration is openly supporting the rebels, who are Muslim radicals, and who ultimately act to hamper and subjugate

---

35. Trifkovic, "The Disappearing Middle Eastern Christians."

the 2.5 million remaining Christians (after the exit from Syria of an equal number of refugees since the start of the civil war in 2011) who are the allies of the regime. The West, including the Americans, however, with their rebel allies and the Turks, have sworn to remove Assad from power, in spite of the ominous warning that his fall will cause the murder of his Christian allies. The suspicion exists among some American analysts, that the Obama policy in the Middle East has been impacted by a network of Muslim Brother agents who are working in cohorts with his administration, to bring about the removal of Assad and the victory of Muslim radicals, which will by necessity be fatal to Syrian Christianity. That was illustrated in the fact that in October 2010, Dalia Moghahed, Obama's adviser on Muslim affairs, blocked a delegation of Middle Eastern Christians, led by Lebanon's Maronite Patriarch, from meeting Obama and members of the national security team at the White House, at the request of the Muslim Brothers in her native Egypt.

The Muslim Brothers and their Sister Organizations: The Engine behind the Persecution

The Muslim Brothers and their affiliates in the Arab world, which must be accounted for as the major Islamic element in the persecution of Christians in their territory, was founded in Egypt in 1928 by Hassan al-Banna, but grew by leaps and bounds during the 1930s and 1940s during their association with the Nazis. After the War, while they concentrated their struggle against the British, who occupied the Suez Canal, and against the Zionists in Palestine, they began to implant their cells in Europe and America, to the point that today there is almost no Muslim population in the West where the Brothers did not take root. So much so, that far from the initial practice of the Brothers to maintain some secrecy in the general public until entrenched in the populace, both domestically and in foreign lands, today the Brothers aspire for rule in their countries, and have even succeeded briefly in Tunisia and Egypt during the Islamic Spring; and many Muslim groups in the West boast their affiliation with what has become the worldwide Muslim Brothers Organization, which is openly committed to the practice of Shari'a law domestically in their countries of origin, and to a world Caliphate, including in their host countries of asylum.

Hassan al-Banna in Egypt and his deputy Haj Amin in Jerusalem forged a partnership with the Nazis, in the Arab world, Berlin, and Bosnia, during the years that led up to World War II, where they found common cause against the West and the Allies, and siding with Hitler and his Axis.

That hostility against the West has persisted after the war, especially after the defeat of the Axis countries by the West, and the Arabs by Israel in the Middle East. The perennial attempt by Muslims to take revenge on the Christian West, which is too mighty to beat, has led them to take the easier option of attacking the weaker Christian minorities in their midst, and the Jewish State in the Middle East, in what psychologists would call a "displaced aggression." At the same time, they never desisted ever since from attempting to undermine Christianity on its own turf by seeking to immigrate into its territory, and engaging in illegal infiltration there when their legal immigration is inhibited. After the war, the banner of virulent anti-Semitism and Christianophobia would definitely pass from areas of defeated Nazi domination to the Islamic world led by the Arabs, and by Muslim radicals like the Muslim Brothers, al-Qa'ida, and Iran, and now ISIS.

The writer, who detected and researched the ideological link between Islamic radicalism and the Nazis is the German Matthias Kuntzel, a political scientist, in his book *Jihad and Jew Hatred*, published in German, English and Hebrew.[36] The only drawback in this seminal volume is that the author follows today's vogue among Western scholars for differentiating between Islam and "Islamism," as if they were two different religions or systems of belief, attributing the built-in hatred toward Christians (and Jews) only to the latter, while the former seems to be generally exonerated, under the recurrent platitude embraced by Western politicians, that "Islam is a religion of peace." The problem is that it is becoming more and more difficult to differentiate between these two putative brands of Islam, if there ever were any difference, since the Muslim Brothers have moved to the international Muslim consensus, and have been embraced by the West as a brand of "moderate and reasonable" Islam, while ISIS, al-Qa'ida, and similar movements are viewed as the "bad guys." Kuntzel's focus on the Muslim Brothers in Egypt not only interpreted that movement as the beginning of modern radicalism in Islam, but he found extraordinary organizational similarities between it and Nazism and fascism in general; for example, the subordination of the individual to the collective will, the worship of iconic leadership, hostility towards liberal and democratic principles, vitriolic rejection of Communism, extreme opposition to capitalism, and a strong ambition among Muslims to establish a universal Muslim state (Caliphate), ruled by the Shari'a, similar to the Germanic 1000-year Reich that Hitler had in mind.

In this kind of similar ambience of continual fighting under strict rules of conduct and their relentless enforcement, the predominance of men was

---

36. Kuntzel, *Jihad and Jew-hatred: Islamism, Nazism and the Roots of 9/11*. Much of the following discussion is based on the first chapter of this book.

paramount, the submission of women obvious, as was martyrdom for the sake of the collective. These similarities and affinities between the two ideas and nationalities emerged during the 1930s and contributed to the forging of the alliance between the two by the time the war broke out. It was the Muslim Brothers (MB) who translated Hitler's *Mein Kampf* into Arabic and distributed it throughout the Arab world, and helped channel to Haj Amin in Palestine—who was facing similar challenges—arms and funds from Germany, which sustained him in his major revolt against the British (and Zionism) in Palestine during the lead-up to the war (1936–39).

Of course, the centre of gravity of Kuntzel's interest in the Muslim Brothers was not only their inspiration by Nazi doctrine, but their extended influence on Haj Amin and Palestinian Arabs, which facilitated the Palestinian Mufti's close collaboration with Hitler. That caused him to move to Berlin during the war, and after the war to invite some Muslim Brothers troops to participate with the Palestinians in their war against the Jews in 1948–49.

Kuntzel also laments the fact that the victorious allies, instead of punishing the Muslim Brotherhood and their supporters, including Haj Amin, after the war, for their collaboration with the Nazis and for concocting with them the ruin of Britain, on the contrary came to view their restored good relations with the Arab world as outweighing any doctrinal "deviation" by the Mufti and his Muslim Brothers allies.

This historic myopic policy is what required David Cameron's government in Britain to launch in 2014 an official investigation into the dangers that the Muslim Brothers pose today to British security and worldwide interests. For, to this day, the Muslim Brothers continue to declare their abhorrence of the West, and to hardly hide their ongoing admiration for Hitler and the Nazis. In the current unrest in the Arab world, which has been wrongly dubbed the "Arab Spring," some of those themes are re-emerging and reflecting on Christian persecution in the Muslim world. Britain and the West, who were prepared to sacrifice their long-term interests for a temporary rehabilitation of their positions in the Middle East, may be now paying dearly for that momentary lapse in their thinking. Indeed, with British and American silent consent, France had permitted the Mufti, back then, to run away from her territory and so avoid his trial as a war criminal, and seek refuge in Egypt, which had become, just like Syria, Argentina, and Paraguay, a shelter for Nazi criminals after the war. The consequences of this short-lived policy are now being reaped in both the Islamic subversion in Europe and the massive expulsion of Christians from the countries of Islam, which had been Christian lands before the Islamic conquest.

In spite of the many differences between Nazism and fascism on the one hand, and the authoritarian regimes in the Arab and Islamic worlds on the other, there is a lasting red (now green) thread that continues to connect between the two, long after the former has waned away in Europe and the latter has begun to shake off the unbearable regimes that have oppressed Arab peoples for so long. These connections persist, in spite of the doctrinal reversals that have gripped the Arab world since the end of the War, and caused them to attribute Nazism to Israel. Devout Muslim radical practitioners—like the Muslim Brothers, Hamas, Hizbullah, and similar movements—indeed often attempt to wash themselves clean of Nazism by projecting it on Israel and accusing her of having adopted it. What truly unites these movements with bygone European fascism are indeed their common enchantment with modern technology (today it is internet, satellites, social networks, and up-to-date television and radio broadcasting, and the most modern weaponry, including weapons of mass destruction); their fascination with violence and war, and the cultivation of supreme sacrifice, to the point of encouraging self-immolation, like the *Islamikaze* (wrongly viewed in the West as "suicide bombers"); and the rejection of democracy and liberal values. And perhaps above all, the never-ending obsession with eliminating Christians and Jews wherever they can be found.[37] No wonder that spectacular acts of international terrorism, like 9/11, the London and Madrid mass killings in civilian subways, hijacking airplanes and killing their passengers, or the Bali and other senseless bombings, have all an element of fanatic madness in them, reminiscent of the abuses of the Nazis. Even the Twin Towers' attack is strikingly identical to Hitler's similar fantasy to see Manhattan burning.[38]

The Party of Muslim Brothers platform proposed a new political organization in modern Egypt, modeled on the medieval universal Caliphate, based on *Shari'a* law and obeying the global Caliph, which also prohibited any other competing all-encompassing theory, like Communism or any other party. The Muslim Brothers, again like its Nazi model, also professed a social and moral puritanism which sought to control individual desires and ambitions, by strictly adhering to conservative modes of conduct, avoiding material temptations, and aspiring to spirituality, a controlled asceticism that lent priority to satisfying the needs of the collective before turning to address personal necessities. In this light, or rather obscurity, one has to reconsider *kristallnacht* (1938) and other abuses by Nazi thugs towards their Jewish victims that they wished to subdue by terror and violence, as well

---

37. See Israeli, *Muslim Anti-Semitism in Christian Europe*, especially chapter 1.
38. See Jeffrey Herf's splendid Introduction to Kuntzel's *Jihan and Jew-Hatred*.

as the violent outbursts of the Muslim Brothers then against Christians in Egypt, Lebanon, and Nigeria, which burned down night clubs and movie theatres, inherited from the hated imported Western culture.

Since the Muslim Brothers, particularly their prominent leader, Sayyid Qut'b, who inherited the clout of Banna after his assassination, saw Jews as the evil of the world and the cause of its misfortunes, as agents of Western-style decline and corruption, then, of course, all acts and institutions of immorality, like theatres, movies, prostitution, drugs, and the deterioration of manners and values in all societies were due to the Jewish management of world affairs. Those ideas have become so rooted in general Islamic and Arab culture, and so closely associated with Christian depravity, that one can still detect them, without much effort, more than half-a century after Nazism was routed and eradicated. In this mindset Jews and Christians together form a continuum of Western depravity threatening the Islamic world.

However, nothing illustrates the great doctrinal breakthrough of the Muslim Brothers better than the operationalization of the idea of *Jihad*, from a dormant ideal whose time was past, to an active tool to combat present-day enemies, binding on every individual Muslim, not only the Muslim *Umma* as a whole. The rationale was that when the house is burning, it was incumbent on each individual Muslim to carry a bucket of water and contribute to the extinction of the fire the best he can, regardless of what the state, the public, or the community do or refrain from doing. The idea was that the Qur'anic tenet of *Jihad*—which had been the driving force of Islam at its inception, and the engine of its expansion, but had become over the years mostly viewed as merely an endeavor for self-striving and improvement, for example, by spreading and propagating Islam—ought to be revived and converted to the use of force in order to propagate Islamic activity. In other words, *Jihad* should be developed into an active tool, as of old, to spread the word of Allah worldwide.

Al-Banna gave this idea a very active twist, as in the times of the Prophet, essentialized in the popular slogan that is still central to Muslim Brothers and its affiliates: *"Allah is our aim, the Prophet our model, the Qur'an our constitution, Jihad our path, and death for Allah the sublimest of our ambitions."* By promising eternal martyrdom to the casualties in battle, he turned death for the cause not only into something that does not inspire fear and abhorrence, but into *a desirable ideal* that every young Muslim can and should embrace, thus avoiding the torment of this-worldly life and taking the shortcut to the eternal hereafter under the blissful protection of Allah.

The revival of Muslim Brothers and *Salafi* Islam in the Arab and Islamic world following the so-called "Spring" of 2011–12, attests to the tenacity of this thinking, and the incessant flow of young Muslim volunteers to the killing fields of Bosnia and Afghanistan in the 1990s, and then of Syria and Iraq in the 2000s, is the best proof of its vitality. Thus, that enthusiasm is not only deployed to fight against the Western alliances on Islamic turfs, but also to rampage pitilessly against Christians in the Muslim world and to subvert the Christian countries where they sought asylum, and continue to assault relentlessly with their waves of illegal migrants.

At first, the Egyptian civilian constitution of 1923, in that first manifestation of democracy in the Islamic and Arab worlds, which did not last, had proclaimed full equality to all citizens, and no religious loyalty was referred to as a matter of state concern, for faith remained the private domain of each individual, and the reigning monarchy was declared "constitutional." During that period, under the political domination of the Wafd Party, Christians and Jews were part and parcel of the social, economic, and political system, and they were welcome in all walks of life. The Christians were then a mere domestic issue, as one of the three important denominational communities in the country, and no attention was yet paid to the international issues of Christianity or to Egypt's relations to major Christian countries. But with the advent of the Nazis, and the growing mimicking of what had been unfolding in Nazi Germany, young Egyptians were urged by the Muslim Brothers to buy only Muslim goods, to prepare themselves for *Jihad* to "defend the Al-Aqsa Mosque," and ultimately they were urged to apply their Jihad against the British and in favour of the Nazis, particularly in Bosnia[39] and Palestine, and to regard with suspicion their large Christian and Jewish minorities whose hearts were with the Allies, not with the Axis powers.

Thus, Germany identified its interest as lying with the Arab world. In consequence, many Arab students were invited to study in Germany, German companies took in Arab interns, Arab political leaders were invited to attend the annual marches and processions of the Nazi Party, and senior Arab military officers were invited to attend maneuvers of the *Wehrmacht*. In Berlin an "Arab Club" was founded, which became a center of propaganda for Palestine and against the Jews, and later a center for the Arab and Muslim broadcasts, under the Nazi regime, during the entire extent of the war. The Nazi Ministry of Propaganda, via its representative in Jerusalem, Dr. Franz Reichart, maintained close relationship with the Mufti, and channeled monies to Arab media and agents. In 1937, an SS delegation, where Adolf Eichmann was a member, went to the Middle East for a study tour, followed by many other high-level delegations. In Damascus, they set up in 1939 an "Arab Club," which served as a clandestine base to train

---

39. See Israeli, *The Death Camps of Croatia*.

"volunteers" to the Arab Revolt that was raging in Palestine against the British Mandate, and to undo the project of a Jewish National Home in the land. The Germans responded positively to the urgings of the Mufti and supplied weapons and funds, which maintained the momentum of the Revolt during its last two years (1937–39).[40]

As the British were striving to put an end to the Arab Revolt in Palestine, the Nazi press was enraged about the "cruelty with which the British were quelling Arab freedom fighters." So much so, that the active support lent by the Nazis to the Mufti, against the British and the Jews, was taken by some as a general rehearsal preceding the real war.[41] The British, who were eager to preserve their good relations with the Arabs in view of the approaching war, looked with horror at the rise of radical Islam in Egypt, Iraq, and Palestine, and at the extraordinary convergence of this movement with European fascism, especially the effort deployed by Nazism to aid the Arab cause and thus jeopardize British positions in the Middle East. So, as the Arab street was boiling hot with anti-British sentiment and pro-Nazi demonstrations, and as Jewish synagogues were being torched on *Kristallnacht* (9 November 1938) throughout Germany, Britain was caught in panic under its spineless government, which sold off Czechoslovakia to Hitler in Munich, and it resolved to abolish the recommendations of the Peel Commission, cancel the first Partition Plan for Palestine, and put a sweeping ban on Jewish immigration under the infamous White Paper.

The greatest drama of the Brothers' success since their inception eighty-five years earlier was their masterful rise to power in Egypt under President Mohamed Mursi in the year 2012–13, until they were toppled, outlawed, and prosecuted in Summer 2013 by the very Minister of Defense, Abd al-Fattah al-Sisi, that Mursi had appointed when he took up the presidency. As a matter of fact, of all Islamic countries affected by the "Spring," Egypt was the most important and most significant, due to both its size and might, and to its centrality in the Arab world, without which no war and no peace in the Middle East could be decided. In the Egypt of the "Spring" era (2011–13), the Muslim radicals (Brothers and Salafis) offered the most viable alternative to Mubarak's rule and also a likely example that other "Spring"-stricken countries could try to follow.[42] The new Muslim Brother President, Muhammad Mursi, pledged that his presidency would maintain a civil and democratic rule, together with equality between the genders and civil freedoms, and promised that he would honor all the Egyptian interna-

40. Kuntzel, *Jihad and Jew-hatred*, 40–48.
41. Ibid., 50.
42. See Israeli, *From Arab Spring to Islamic Winter*.

tional obligations, including the peace with Israel, in complete reversal of the traditional Muslim Brother opposition to any peace or settlement with Israel. He was buttressed in government by the 75 percent fundamentalists in the Egyptian Parliament who supported him (45 percent from the Brothers and 30 percent from other Salafists) and by the new constitution that he had had adopted by popular referendum, against the deep division of public opinion, but with vast demonstrations by his supporters, opposed by the bourgeois-liberal and Westernized urban opposition, who were also more tolerant of other faiths and of the Coptic minority.

In view of the Muslim Brothers' ideological commitments, anyone could follow the first practical steps of the Mursi government in the real world, and observe to what extent was he able to harmonize policy-making with his Muslim Brother doctrine. One was stunned not so much by the reaction of the people, who'd had enough of Mubarak's corruption and were waiting for a change, which they got finally, but by the hypocrisy of the West, which never raised a voice against the previous regime's corruption, the rigging of elections, the arrest of dissidents, and the perpetuation of illiteracy, poverty, and disease in Egyptian society.

One is also dismayed to see the runaway demographic growth, which has brought the country from a 30 million population sixty years ago, when it exported food and others goods, to a poor, import-dependent society of 85 million souls today. When President Obama decided to appeal from Cairo to the Islamic world, in 2009, he did not say one word of criticism against that destructive state of affairs, nor did he pay attention to the crying of the political prisoners who were rotting in prisons, hoping thereby not to damage the famous stability that was the top-priority in his calculations. All Mubarak could assume then, was that America stood firmly at his side without qualification and "had his back." So what incentive would he have had to improve?

The Americans were loath to take any measure against the Mubarak regime, which turned the American-supported peace treaty with Israel into a bad farce, as Egyptian tourism to Israel was completely discontinued, anti-Semitic attacks on Israel and the Jews, with *Sho'ah*-denial a major theme, inundating the Egyptian press, including the state controlled one, Sinai being invaded by terror, smuggling, and illegal migrants, and Mubarak—unwilling or unable to do much about it—was hiding behind American support without any incentive to mend his ways, until he was abandoned by his allies and thrown to the dogs.

What these groups hold in common is the view that they must eradicate infidels, in other words non-Muslims. This is further evidenced by the horrendous "suicide bombings" carried out by the Jihad group, also believed to be situated in Sinai, against the Israeli and US embassies in the capital city of Uzbekistan. The attacks killed at least nine people, while wounding many more.

However, some have been questioning the credibility of the danger posed by that medley of incoherent groups, which was directed "only" against non-Muslims, domestically and internationally. As far as individuals belonging to towns predominantly inhabited by the desert-dwelling Bedouins, these fears were underestimated because, it was said, they were "merely based on rumors." They claimed that while they had heard of the presence of militant groups in the deserts of Sinai, they hadn't come across them. While they could confirm the militants' existence in the area, it appeared that the Egyptian security forces were dependent on the Bedouins to attempt restraining the radical groups' activities. This appears to be their preferred method, as opposed to direct armed intervention, so as to avoid straining the tension between the Bedouins and the government's forces. Furthermore, the security forces considered armed intervention to result in large losses that simply could not be afforded amidst the country's general turmoil.

Israelis had all along heeded Mubarak's warnings that the alternative to him were the Brothers, because they understood that those waiting in the aisles to inherit his position were not some enthusiastic democrats, as it was naively believed in the West, which took at face value the sloganeering of the demonstrators who screamed "democracy!" from the top of their lungs, but multi-generational adepts of the Brotherhood who had been dreaming of this day, and who looked more like the Taliban than the members of the American Congress, or MPs of the British Parliament. In fact, if we take for guidance the declarations of Ahmed Badi', the chief spiritual guide of the Brotherhood, to wit that "the foundation of Israel was the most grievous international disaster that ever happened," and called the Arab armies to challenge her, there is not much room for optimism. Nonetheless, Mursi kept repeating that he was obligated to respect all the international obligations of his country, including the peace with Israel, though he usually added: "but also Egypt's interests." Many thought then that they were watching a sophisticated deception campaign of the Brotherhood to mislead the entire world, until its rule took root together with its self-confidence to do what it wished and finally realize its dream of Islamizing Egyptian society, in line with its step-by-step long-haul strategy.

In an article published in July 2012, where Mursi, in his inauguration speech, was cited as committing himself to international treaties and agreements, and declaring himself as carrying a message of peace to the world, the authors estimate that it accords neatly with the Brotherhood's sophisticated strategy for dealing with outsiders. They cite Mustafa Mashhur, the guide of the Brothers from 1996 to 2006, who had explained in his *Jihad Is the Way* his movement's beliefs and aspirations, especially the role of violent *Jihad* in bringing about a world under a unified Islamic Caliphate. These references, which are true to what al-Banna himself had written in the 1930s in the beginning of the movement, gave reason to doubt Mursi's reassurances. For one thing, *Jihad Is the Way* defined Israel and Israelis as "the criminal, thieving gangs of Zion," and Mashhur stressed that the claim that Israel is foundation on stolen land is not an opening position for negotiations, but a *non-negotiable* article of "faith and religion." Further, he claimed that the land was stolen not only from Palestinian Arabs, but from Islam; in his words: "Know that the problems of the Islamic world, such as Palestine . . . are not issues of territories and nations, but of faith and religion. They are problems of Islam and the Muslims, and they cannot be resolved by negotiation . . ."—words that are echoed by the Charter of Hamas, which is also an adept of the Brotherhood.

Mashhur explained that: "*Jihad* and preparation for *Jihad* are not only for the purpose of fending-off assaults and attacks against Muslims by Allah's enemies, but are also for the purpose of realizing the great task of establishing an Islamic state, strengthening the religion, and spreading it around the world." Like Banna who had exalted Jihad and martyrdom, and like Hamas, which glorifies them in its Charter, Mashhur writes that "Martyrdom for Allah, is our most exalted wish," and Mursi never rejected this ideology. So how are these contradictions to be understood? Why did Mursi talk peace when he also adhered to an ideology of Jihadist war?

The answer lies in the fundamental principles of the Muslim Brotherhood—principles largely overlooked in the West. As opposed to the ideology of al-Qa'ida, which preaches continuous confrontation and attacks on infidels regardless of the immediate political costs, the Brotherhood, contend the authors of *Jihad Is the Way*, places the highest priority on careful preparation and the strategic timing of political and military activity. *Jihad Is the Way* stresses the necessity of timing the eventual *Jihad* prudently; as evidence, they cite a Qur'anic passage in which Muhammad does not rush to fight until the timing is right. When the Muslims were a persecuted minority, the Prophet Muhammad did not instruct the Muslims to retaliate. Instead, he taught them *Sabr*, patience and resilience, and when the conditions were right, permission was given to fight. *Timing*, therefore, is an integral part of the Brotherhood's political and military decision-making. Indeed, as the Brotherhood sends their youth to *Jihad* at the appropriate time, they are not pushing them towards self-destruction. Rather, they contend that abstaining from *Jihad* at its appropriate time is destruction.

Similarly, it is not necessary for the Muslims to repel every attack or damage caused by the enemies of Allah immediately, rather only when their ability and the appropriate circumstances allow for it.

According to noted scholar Mordechai Kedar,[43] the history of the Brothers at some key points is worth mentioning. It was when the British ruled Egypt after World War I and tried to influence it to Westernize that local reactions to those endeavors found expression in the public square. One of them viewed the Pharaonic heritage as reflecting the national character of Egypt; others saw the Arab nation (of Muslims, Christians, Jews, and others, all of whom spoke Arabic) as the province of affiliation; and there were also those who saw the Greek (Alexander the Great, Ptolemy) and the Roman past as the source of European identity of the Egyptian people. All of these trends were anti-Islamic, and the Brotherhood, headed by the founder of the movement, Hassan Al-Banna, saw the occupation by the Christian, wine-drinking, and pork-eating British, as the source of all the cultural problems of the Land of the Nile, so they placed the struggle against the foreign occupation at the top of their priorities, and as a secondary task the purification of Egyptian society from the influence of Western culture, which in their opinion was rotten, corrupt, permissive, and not suitable to Islamic society. The struggle over the course that culture ought to follow placed the Brotherhood in conflict with the new socio-political theories that debated the sources of collective inspiration and identity of the Egyptian people. In answer to all of these trends, the Brotherhood claimed that "Islam is the Solution"; for it was forbidden for a Muslim society, whose Divine Guide is on high, to search among other cultures for solutions and arrangements that are the mere works of man.

The third task that the Brotherhood took upon itself was to prove that indeed "Islam is the solution," by imposing Islamic *Shari'a* in all spheres of life: private, family, political, economic, and diplomatic. This task, which aspires to impose the rules of Islam on politics and the state, has created the concept of "political Islam" (in contrast to other religions, which separate between religion and state). The symbol of the organization expresses this ideology well: the color of green represents Paradise and the favorite color of the Prophet, two swords in the center express the two basic avowals of Islam—there is no God but Allah, and Muhammad is his Messenger—and one word, which appears in the Qur'an just once, written above: *Wa-aidu* ("and prepare"). This word is the beginning of a passage from the Qur'an:[44] "and prepare whatever you can of your strength and your harnessed horses

---

43. Kedar, "The Brothers and the Muslims."
44. Sura 8:59

in order to impose fear (*irhab*, i.e., terror) in the hearts of Allah's enemy and your enemies."

When the Muslim Brotherhood was founded in Egypt, King Fuad the First ruled, and in 1936 his son Farouk succeeded him, and ruled until the Officers' Revolution in July 1952 overturned him. During the monarchy, the Brotherhood acted very freely, because the regime was incredibly ineffective. In December 1948, an activist from the movement assassinated the prime minister, Nukrashi, and two months afterward the movement's founder and leader—Hassan al-Banna—was murdered, apparently by agents of the regime.

The regime of the Officers was much more determined and decisive, and in general conducted a stubborn battle against the Brotherhood because it saw them and their activities as an attempt to undermine its own legitimacy and stability. In 1966, President Gamal Abd al-Nasser hung the ideologue of the movement, Sayyid Qut'b, because in his writings, he claimed that any regime that does not implement *Shari'a* is like the age of ignorance (*jahiliyya*) that preceded Islam, which was idol worship, and therefore justifies a Jihad against it.

Because the Brotherhood was marginalized politically during the years of the Officers' Regime, they found their fertile field of activity among economically and politically marginalized people, and turned their energies to charitable activities within the society of the tens of millions of Egyptians living in the poor, chaotic neighborhoods at the margins of the cities, without running water, without sewage, without electricity, without telephone lines, without medical services or educational services, without work, and without hope. It was the Brotherhood who supported these miserable people for years, out of a feeling of commitment, responsibility, and mutual trust rooted in Islamic values, which did not differentiate between religion, society, politics, economics, and culture. The regime allowed them to operate among the weak neighborhoods, since it did not see acts of charity and kindness as a danger to the stability of the regime, and because the burden on the state of caring for the poor population was eased thanks to the Brotherhood's activities.

The people held the Brotherhood in high regard, because for many years, it supported the poor among the people wholeheartedly; and because the Brotherhood did not appear as corrupt and greedy as the "fat cats" who ruled the state. Moreover, the Brothers related to the people with respect, unlike the officials of the system, who humiliated them and oppressed them cruelly.

Those who initiated the street riots that broke out in Egypt on the 25th January 2011, which some call the "Arab Spring," were throngs of Egyptian secular youth, some of whom were educated, who were sick of the corrupt and cruel regime, which was slated to be passed down to the son of the ruler. The Muslim Brotherhood did not take a meaningful part in the demonstrations at first, but rather sat on the sidelines watching to see which side would win. After the military forced Mubarak to resign on the 11th February, the Brotherhood went out to al-Tahrir Square in order to take advantage of the opportunities for which it had waited patiently for many years. The Qur'an states that "Allah is with the patient,"[45] and indeed Allah is with them: in the period that preceded the November 2011 elections to parliament, the Brotherhood activated Operation Da'wah' (Islamic outreach), in order to translate their investment of years of community efforts into political support by the public.

Spokesmen of political Islam, headed by Yussuf al-Qaradawi, mobilized themselves in support of the Brotherhood, and the result was that almost half of the seats of parliament were won by the "Party of Freedom and Justice," the representative of the Brotherhood, and a quarter more of the seats were won by the "Party of Light" (*al-Noor*), the representative of the more conservative *Salafi* groups. This is how the decisive majority of the Egyptian parliament was suffused with the color green, the color of the Islamic Paradise, in a truly democratic way.

It is important to note here that one of the most eloquent spokesmen of the Brotherhood, Sheikh Safwat Higazi, appeared on the 1st May 2012, and gave a speech that was broadcast live for thousands of people to see and to hear, as part of the Brotherhood's preparations for the presidential elections. In his fiery discourse, Higazi announced that the goal of the Brotherhood was the unity of all the Arab states into one giant Islamic Caliphate, under Mursi's flag, whose capital will be "not Mecca and not Medina but al-Quds [Jerusalem]." His words reflect very well the goal of the movement—to erase the heritage of colonialism (and Christianity), principally the borders marked by colonialist interests, which damaged both the Arab world and Islam; the elimination of Israel; and imposition of Islam on Judaism (and Christianity). It might be that this refers to a far-off hope and not to immediate plans, but the cheers of support from the throats of the masses who crowded into the streets, expressed the collective energy behind the idea, just waiting for the suitable moment to turn it into reality. Besides this, Israel must take very seriously the hopes of others, because the State of Israel itself is exactly the realization of such hopes, and its enemies learn from it how to realize hopes as well.

45. Sura 2:152

A new turn in the relations between the Islamic world and the West, was marked on the eleventh anniversary of September 11, when a large coordinated attack on the American Consulate in Benghazi by forces of al-Qa'ida and their affiliates, burned down the embassy, killed the Ambassador, who happened to visit, and decimated in arson the entire consulate and its attached property. The official trigger of that heinous attack was an idiotic film made by a private individual, a Copt in exile in America, which grossly mistreated the figure of the Prophet Muhammad, who is deeply venerated in Islam. Although it is clear that the attack must have been prepared months before that film was made and distributed, it was very easy to incite the ready-to-explode Muslim crowds, from Casablanca to Jakarta, with anything that smacks of Islamophobia, on the one-hand, and anti-Americanism and Christianophobia, on the other. Indeed, American (and also British and German) embassies were attacked in several Arab and Muslim countries, from Africa to the Far East, and fierce and violent demonstrations erupteded in many Muslim cities, accompanied by the chanting of anti-Western slogans and the burning of foreign flags, notably American and Israeli. It is noteworthy, that precisely Cairo—which had been chosen by Obama to "engage" the Muslims and "open a new page" with them at the beginning of his term, when his ally Mubarak still ruled the place—had been taken over by the Muslim Brothers, who proved unable (and perhaps also unwilling) to prevent the attacks on the American Embassy.

Although many Muslims who commented on this new outburst of maddened fury attributed this string of violent acts to that film, it is worth mentioning that prior to September 11, there was no such film to provoke this new manifestation of the 2005-6 drama of the cartoons in Denmark. And since the lessons were not learned there, the same scenario was bound to be repeated, and will be replayed more and more in the future. This is due to the basic religious, legal, and cultural differences between Islam and the West regarding freedom of expression and creation, tolerance of others and their ideas and religions, the separation between church and state, the relative self confidence of the culture and its readiness to compete with others in the open market, and the extent to which any democratic country can interfere with, and be held responsible for the non-criminal acts of its nationals.

Muslim countries have been trying to impose universally, via the UN and other international bodies, their own norms of morality and respect for religions, that they themselves do not respect. For example, enormous demonstrations and protests are raised by Muslims in the West when they are not afforded enough facilities for their prayers, while in Saudi Arabia, which finances most Muslim installations in the West, does not permit *any* non-Muslim house of prayer on its land. If, for example, the West had made the building of new mosques conditional on opening Saudi Arabia to the same freedoms of worship of all religions, the situation might be amended.

In Summer 2013, when Defense Minister Sisi, Mursi's appointee, realized both where his President was taking Egypt, on the one hand, much to the delight of the supporters of the Brothers among the rural and less educated population, and the growing discontent among the liberal and Westernized urban population, on the other, he decided to move, arrested the elected President, removed him from power, and ultimately put him on trial, and initiated a new referendum to change the constitution once again, and have himself elected as the new President one year later (Summer 2014).

Mursi's supporters domestically, and radical Muslim countries like Turkey, condemned his removal as a "coup," a thesis that the US also subscribed to, with all the attending strain in the relationships with Egypt, while Sisi's partisans hailed his counter-revolution as a salutary demarche which was necessary to return sanity and pragmatism to Egypt. The one-year eventful experiment of the Muslim Brothers rule came to a close, but the question remained nagging: how was it possible that within the space of one year the same Egyptian public first voted overwhelmingly for Mursi and then for his constitution in 2012, but then, on the opposing pole, voted for Sisi and his constitution in 2013? Something was definitely wrong, or strange in the workings of that "democracy."

Since World War II the Brothers, who have strengthened their positions in Europe through political and cultural activities—by such personalities as Tariq Ramadan, the grand-son of Hasan al-Banna, who is based in Geneva and has been recognized as one of the prominent Muslim intellectuals of Europe; and by such organizations as CAIR in the US, which has gained access to many avenues of power in Washington—have also been struggling in the Muslim world to reinforce their positions, mostly as opposition to the existing regimes, and more rarely as partners in the government. In Egypt, their birthplace, they came to power by free elections for one year (2012–13) after the toppling of Mubarak in the Arab "Spring," but they were reversed by the military. In Jordan they were part of the government coalition for a few years under King Hussein, before election reforms restricted their constituencies. The Nahda party in Tunisia, and its parallels in Algeria and Morocco, acted also as branches of the Brothers, though under different names. In Syria, they had been oppressed and almost wiped out by Assad's father in the 1980s, but their successors of various brands have been rebelling since 2011 against the Assad government. Among the Palestinian population, the Muslim Associations, which grew out of the early cells of the Muslim Brothers, were renamed Hamas during the First Intifada (1987–92) and gained currency among their people by brandishing the double banner of Islam and Palestinian nationalism, as if there were no built-in contradiction between the two. In Israel, the Muslim Movement, especially its Northern Branch under Sheikh Ra'id Salah, generally toed the line of the Jordanian Brothers. Saudi Arabia, Kuwait, and other Gulf donors also maintained for decades their financial and spiritual support to the Brothers, with Qatar in particular, which gave shelter to Sheikh Qaradawi, and allowed him its *al-Jazeera* network as a channel for his worldwide Islamic *da'wa*. Thus, he actively endorses the Muslim Brothers' organization and its bids to take over power in some Arab countries, provided Qatar Emir remained outside the scope of the Islamic propaganda worldwide. So much so, that the other Gulf states, fearing that Qatar's protection and support for the Brothers undermined their own monarchic regimes, have resented Doha and finally cut diplomatic relations with it in 2014.[46]

Nonetheless, in November 2014, fearing its growing isolation in the Gulf area, Qatar agreed to conform to the regional consensus, at least outwardly, and its ambassadors returned to UAE, Saudi Arabia, and Bahrain. That was allowed following an unannounced meeting between the Gulf Cooperation Council (GCC) leaders that ended on 17th November after resolving a long-standing schism with fellow member-state Qatar, as *Al Arabiya News* channel's correspondent reported. The assembly reached an agreement that "promises the opening of a new page that will present a strong base, especially in light of the sensitive circumstances the region is undergoing," the GCC said in a joint statement. Additionally, the annual GCC summit was also confirmed to take place on December 9th to 10th in Doha, the correspondent reported. The leaders, who travelled with their foreign ministers and other cabinet members or senior officials, were greeted by Crown Prince Mugran bin Abdulaziz al-Saud, and GCC Secretary-General Abdullatif al-Zayani, according to the Saudi Press Agency (SPA). Kuwait's Sheikh Sabah al-Ahmed al-Sabah has been leading efforts to bridge the gap between Qatar and Saudi Arabia, the United Arab Emirates, and Bahrain. The spat had been instigated by Qatar's support of certain movements and groups that stirred unrest in some states, said Khaled al-Matrafi, regional manager of *Al Arabiya News* channel in Riyadh. These groups, which adopted "orientations and policies that opposed those of the GCC, posed the most major points of conflict and led to the withdrawal of the ambassadors,"

46. For this passage, see Hatina and Kupferschmidt (eds.), *The Muslim Brothers*.

he said. Most important of all, Doha asked Brotherhood leaders to leave Qatar following diplomatic pressure from Saudi Arabia.[47]

The international politics of the Muslim Brothers of course did not deflect attention from its domestic oppression and persecution of the Copts in Egypt or in nearby Libya, where Copts had gone to look for job opportunities. Raymond Ibrahim reported a string of acts of terror directed against Copts in the Summer of 2015, two years after the takeover by the Sisi government, which has been trying hard to quell the Brothers and their rampages:[48]

1. On 30 July 2015, according to sources in Libya, there were reports, including from the *Libyan Herald*, that on 23rd July, the Islamic State [an affiliate of ISIS], executed another Egyptian Christian they seized over a week previously at a roadblock near Nufaliya, an Islamic State stronghold southeast of the city of Sirte. He was identified as Bekhit Nageh Efrank Ebeid, a twenty-five-year-old migrant worker from Egypt.

2. On 22nd July 2015, soon after the end of the month of Ramadan and Eid al-Fitr, another Christian church in Egypt came under attack. The Father's Church on Gamal Abdel Nasser Street in eastern Alexandria was attacked on 21st July by unknown assailants—three men—using Molotov cocktails and other homemade bombs, which were hurled at the church.

3. During the height of one of the most brutal months of Muslim persecution of Christians, the U.S. State Department exposed its double standards against persecuted Christian minorities. Sister Diana, an influential Iraqi Christian leader, who was scheduled to visit the U.S. to advocate for persecuted Christians in the Mideast, was denied a visa by the U.S.

So, we see that the involvement of Muslim hatred and mistreatment towards Christians is not a novel development, emanating from Western colonization of Western support for Israel. It has been deeply incrusted into the Arab and Muslim psyche as the rival religion with which it fought since its inception. Even the special status accorded to Christians and especially to the Christ in the Qur'an (*'Issa*), which is usually presented as a sign of Muslim tolerance, turns into horror when one realizes that Jesus is part of an Islamic

---

47. Saudi, UAE, and Bahraini Envoys to Return to Qatar," *Al Arabiya News* 17 November 2014.

48. Online: http://www.raymondibrahim.com/islam/why-muslim-rapists-prefer-blondes-a-history/%20-%20disqus_thread.

eschatology that places him in the position of fighting the anti-Christ before he converts himself into the Islamic faith. In the meantime, Christians in the Islamic world—which is, from another perspective, an occupied Christian territory for the most part—are doomed to live as submissive dhimmis and accept their fate as dictated by Muslim rule.

CHAPTER ONE

Christian Minorities in the Arab World

Almost everywhere the Arab world has taken root, in the entire expanse of the Middle East and North Africa, from Morocco in the West to Iraq in the east, except for the Arabian Peninsula, had been wholly or partly the domain of ancient and medieval Christianity, until Islam invaded its territory, supplanted its culture, erased its faith and tradition, and committed millions of occupied people into slavery, death, destitution, and Islamization, for the most part forced, less frequently voluntary. While one has to recognize that this was the norm of those days in any occupied land, due to the lack of awareness of human rights for individuals and right of self-determination for nations, it is also necessary to point out the contradiction between what the Qur'an proclaims, and Muslims boast about, that *"there no compulsion in religion,"* and the *reality* of entire communities coerced to embrace Islam, or else to stay under their *dhimmi* status once they recognize, accept, and submit to Islamic superiority, sovereignty, and rule. That reality, which had compelled entire Jewish communities to convert to Islam under the Almoravid and Almohads in North Africa in the tenth to twelfth centuries, and elsewhere under Islam before and after, had been practiced more extensively vis-à-vis the Christian communities even before they became minorities, and has been pursued to our days in the domains of ISIS, in the Sudan, against the Copts by the Muslim Brothers, and in other remote areas in Africa and Asia, where mass communications do not quite reach, nor do the great champions of human rights who plead on behalf of the helpless.

Throughout the Arab world, concurrent with the revival of Islam in the past few decades, an expression of discontent with the non-Muslim communities in general, and Christians in particular, has been in evidence, for the revival of the Islamic vocabulary by Muslim radicals also means that tools for diminishing the "others" (from the perspective of Islam) and for mistreating Christians and other non-believers have been forged and drilled into the common people's minds, so as to win the hearts of their constituencies. All too often, when those revivalist tendencies were not openly supported by the governments in place, the latter latently encouraged them, especially on Islamic festivals such as Ramadan, or the Night of the Hijra, so as to make the lives of the Christian minorities more and more unbearable, and compel them to emigrate from their lands which had been invaded and taken over by the conquering Muslims more than a millennium earlier.

In August 2005, for example, when the Christian leader John Garang died, an incited violent Muslim crowd attacked Christian neighborhoods in Khartum, killing thirty-six of them, and robbed their properties. The authorities did not demonstrate much eagerness to restore order, and even forbade UN personnel from being interviewed by the media on those events.

It was British reporter Edward Melnick who defined that state of affairs as "Christianophobia,"[1] typical of oppressive regimes, who fear their Christian minorities might encourage the rise of Western ideas that might threaten their regimes. To his mind, in twelve Muslim countries that he surveyed, there was a real danger that Christians would become a "threatened species," on the verge of being extirpated from its "biblical roots" and becoming extinct. If ISIS and other Muslim radicals, like *Ansar Beit-al-Maqdas* in the Sinai and others in Libya, Afghanistan, Pakistan, Syria, Sudan, Yemen, Somalia, Nigeria, and Mali, have their way, they may achieve that goal as they expand their conquests. Even when there is a government to stand against those destructive and murderous elements, like in Egypt and Nigeria or Afghanistan, it looks more and more helpless as its coercive ability diminishes and the radical Muslims' terrorizing effect surges.

Now that Christians in these countries are suspected of their alliance with America, which has itself become unpopular due to its deal with Iran, the persecution of Christians and the xenophobic attitudes towards them, are bound to sore. In the World Watch List of countries published by Open Door USA, indicating where Christian persecution is worst, seventeen Arab countries are counted out of a total of fifty countries across the world. The worst are: Iraq (86/100), Syria (83/100), Sudan (80/100), Saudi Arabia (77/100), Libya (76/100), Yemen (76/100), Qatar (64/100),

---

1. Edward Melnick, *Daily Telegraph*, 25 December 2012.

and the Palestinian territories (56/100). Egypt, which comes only in 23rd place in the general count (61/100), after Qatar and India, is nonetheless prominent in the Middle Eastern statistics due to its large population of Copts, amounting to around 10 percent of the population or something like nine million people. Conversely, Lebanon, whose Christian population is largely threatened, does not figure in the list because nominally Lebanon is a Christian-dominated country,[2] though for all intents and purposes it is Shi'ite Hizbullah that calls the shots.

Long ago, Muslim radicals had released their popular slogan that "after the people of Saturday [the Jews] will come the people of Sunday [the Christians] of the Middle East." But having encountered some difficulties in realizing that scheme, mainly because of Israel's refusal to disappear, they have reversed the order, which they find slightly more feasible. Thus, they started with the Christians of Lebanon, with the civil war of the 1970s, followed by cruel and relentless rampages against the Christian minorities in the rest of the Arab world, and are now busying themselves with either domestic tribal civil wars (as in Syria, Iraq, Yemen, and Libya); or aligning with either of the two major rival camps that are struggling for the soul of revolutionary Islam: the Sunna, which comprises close to 90 percent of all Muslims and the Shi'ia, which predominates in Iran, Iraq, and Lebanon.

The tensions, much less the violence against Christians in the Middle East, are rarely reported in the Arab media, due to the self-indicting nature of the Muslim oppression against their minorities. The Arab Christians, as a minority, fear that an open confrontation with the majority can only worsen their situation. On their part, the Muslims, save for the most radical among them, who do not usually shoulder state responsibility and care little for questions of public relations and reputation, wish to avoid open hostility with world Christianity for intimidating their minorities. For example, during the Nazareth crisis over the Basilica (see below), when the Catholic Patriarch of Jerusalem and the Vatican Custodian in Jerusalem threatened to close all the churches in the Holy Land in protest of the Muslim seizure of Christian land, the Arab media could not avoid jumping into the fray and candidly, if reluctantly, reporting about the controversy. For example, when Sheikh Yussef Salameh, the under-secretary of *Awqaf* (holy endowments) of the Palestinian Authority participated in the Inter-cultural Conference in Tehran in May 1999, he praised the seventh-century system of dhimmitude under which monotheistic non-Muslims were inferior to Muslims, as the proper paradigm for relations between Muslims and Christians today. He also said in the same breath that "Islam [always] respected people of other

---

2. See Nissan, *Politics and War in Lebanon*, 63.

religions and did not hurt them.³ One wishes he knew better the history of his faith.

CHRISTIANOPHOBIA IN MOROCCO

Even at the edge of the Islamic world, Morocco, where French colonization and the close relationship the Kingdom maintains with the West have had an attenuating effect, anti-Christian attitudes linger, though they do not get much publicity. Thus, although Morocco has been ruled for a millennium and a half by the Malekite School of Law, the second most radical and puritanical School after the strict Hanbalites of Arabia, which had extirpated Christianity from the land where it had been implanted since Roman times, the Kingdom has preserved an image of tolerance and openness. A report from March 2010, however, recounted the story of Christian aid workers who were deported by the authorities from the five major cities of the realm,[4] raising the question whether or not this was an act of modern Christianophobia (since it was in this case directed to foreign visitors, not to indigenous Christians, as is the case in other Muslim lands), or a lingering vestige of the ancient radical Islam vis-à-vis Infidels, as in Saudi Arabia. Jack Wald, who had spent ten years as a pastor in Rabat's International Church, a Protestant congregation in the capital, viewed the deportation as a change in the government policy, which had previously been a party to an unspoken truce with Christian missionaries, that was going to affect the entire ambience for Christians in the country.[5]

That incident was triggered in an orphanage for thirty-three abandoned children in the Middle Atlas, when Moroccan police showed up in the village Ain Leuh, 50 miles south of Fez, and separated orphans form their adoptive parents, and accusing the volunteers of spreading Christianity, a major crime in the world of Islam. In any event, anguished Dutch, British, Kiwi, and American volunteers were evacuating their households and hugging for the last time their weeping adopted Moroccan children, whose loud wailing shook up all present. That scene, which is known to have repeated itself in many Muslim countries, dramatized the tension between the role Christian aid groups played in needy Muslim lands, and the local anxieties that the generous aid efforts were nothing but a façade for covert missionary work.

3. *Al-Hayat al Jadida*, 12 May 1999.
4. German, "Morocco Orders Dozens of Christian Aid Workers in Five Cities to be Deported."
5. Ibid.

Moroccan officials claimed they were merely targeting isolated cases of law-breaking, and their act had nothing to do with Christianophobia, though for the victims, it was the sudden eruption of a coordinated campaign that reversed an unwritten understanding, for indeed the orphanage manager confirmed that his personnel was not proselytizing. But in fact, many evangelical workers have been quietly doing their job for years in this puritanically Muslim country, where identity has been focused for its 98 percent Muslim inhabitants on the triangle: Allah, the Motherland, the King. Jean-Luc Blanc, the Head of the Casablanca Evangelical Church, said that while previously Morocco would deport annually one or two token missionaries, who had crossed the red line of proselytizing, the mass expulsion of 2010, interestingly just prior to the eruption of the Arab "Spring" upheaval in all North Africa (Christmas of that year, first in Tunisia and then in Egypt and Libya), was quite startling, compared with the liberal policy of King Mohammed VI.[6]

In this instance, Christians were expelled from Fez, Tangiers, Essaouira (Mogador), Rabat, and Marrakesh, while several dozen more were "marked for expulsion," according to pastors in the various cities, and according to the American Embassy officials who confirmed that Americans were included in the "marked for expulsion." Moroccan officials reiterated, however, the freedom all foreign creeds enjoyed in the country, "as long as they did not undermine Moroccan Islam," noting that they had moved against extremist Muslim groups as well, to signal that not only were Christians not singled out for harsh measures, but that they took action against *any* group that "manipulated the religion of the people." However, the victims of the Village of Hope Orphanage, who were sacked, insisted that they acted within the contours of law. New Zealander Chris Broadbent, who had managed the orphanage office, explained that the interned children spoke Moroccan Arabic, studied the Qur'an, and learned Muslim prayers, as stipulated in Moroccan law, though outside the classrooms Christians were raising the children in their households, because no one else looked after them, a fact that was well known to Moroccan officials.

In a similar case, the Children's Haven Orphanage in the city of Azrou was targeted, though the authorities were aware of the charitable service done there. At that fifty-year-old institution, directed by an American, Jim Pitt, there were ten foreign personnel caring for thirty Moroccan children. However, during the March 2010 crisis, Moroccan investigators visited the place, but police had found nothing that contradicted the charitable purpose of the facility, where no proselytizing was done.

6. Ibid.

Logically, the People of the Book (Christians and Jews) under Islamic rule should have joined efforts to fight Christianophobia and anti-Semitism, which are both rife in the Arab world. But as it often happens, victims of the same malaise, rather that collaborating to resist their oppressors jointly, turn against each other, either to find favor with the oppressor in the hope to escape the Muslim heavy hand, or out of their own phobia against their fellow mistreated people. This is the case of many Christians who, under oppression and persecution by Islam, have become more anti-Semitic towards Jews and haters Israel than even their Muslim masters, in order to seek favor with them, or when their own Judeophobia was even more difficult to contain than their own suffering at the hands of their Muslim oppressors. It happened with Christians who were involved in the creation and leadership of nationalist Arabism, who had to demonstrate their loyalty to Arab nationalism by adopting a more extreme anti-Israel and anti-Zionist positions than their Muslim partners, and by making those positions part of their ideology. For example, Michel Aflaq, the founder of the Ba'ath Party, or the Marxist founders of the Palestinian extremist factions, Wadi' Hadad and George Habash.

George Saliba, The Syriac's Orthodox Church Bishop in Lebanon, gave an interview to *al-Dunya TV*, in the context of the Arab "Spring" disturbances in the entire Arab space:[7] "The source behind all these movements, all these civil wars, and all these evils in the world is nothing other than Zionism, deeply rooted in Judaism. The Jews are responsible for financing and inciting the turmoil, in accordance with the *Protocols of the Elders of Zion*."

These remarks, comments al-Tamimi, are not an isolated case among Middle Eastern Christians, especially after the assault in October 2010 of the Iraqis on the Syriac Catholic Church in Baghdad, leaving fifty-eight dead and sixty-seven wounded, in the worst attack against Christians in Iraq since 2003. Two months later the Melikite Greek Patriarch, Gregory III Laham characterized terrorist attacks on Iraq's Christians as "part of the Zionist conspiracy against Islam." He further affirmed that "all this behavior has nothing to do with Islam, but it is actually planned by Zionism, aiming at undermining and giving a bad image of Islam." He also absurdly said that the massacre was a conspiracy against the Arabs and the predominantly Muslim Arab world, which aims at depicting Arabs and Muslims in Arab countries as terrorist and fundamentalist murderers in order to deny them their rights, and especially those of the Palestinians![8]

7. Tamimi, Aymen Jawad al, "Middle East Christians and Anti-Semitism," Dunya TV, 24 July 2011, cited by *Jerusalem Post*, 2 August 2011.

8. Tamimi, "Middle East Christians and Anti-Semitism"; Tamimi, "Krudish-Christian Rivalries."

In fact, that trend of blaming all the problems of the world on Israel had been embraced before by other Christians in the Middle East. In an article published in the establishment *Al-Ahram* in Cairo, an enlightened Coptic scholar, Dr. Babawi, lambasted the American Congress for not stopping the "Israeli artillery attacks on the Nativity Church and al-Aqsa Mosque" (see below for the context of those incidents in the chapter about Christianophobia in the Holy Land), and he urged American Copts and Muslims to demonstrate against "mad [Ariel] Sharon." This personal broadside against Prime Minister Sharon sought to twist the Nativity event, where Palestinians invaded the Holy Church at gun point, by imputing the moral wrong to Israel, who tried to dislodge them from there. But no one could have missed the point: a prominent Copt in Egypt, a member of a persecuted and dispossessed minority (see below for details) in an Islamic country, must be more Arab than his compatriots to evince his loyalty, and there were evidently no better grounds for that exercise than an anti-Jewish attack.[9]

The bishop of the Assyrian Church in Lebanon followed suit by asserting that though the heads of the church today are not Jewish, they are "led by Jews, whose faith is inimical to God, to the people and to Christianity." He cites Jesus as having said to the Jews: "you are the sons of Satan, and you practice the will of Satan, your father," to which they supposedly answered: "No, we are not the sons of Satan we are the sons of Abraham." But he insisted: "Had you been the sons of Abraham, you would be acting according to the precepts of Abraham. . . . You are the sons of Satan." This wholesale discredit of the Jews, to gain favor with the thugs of Hizbullah, defies logic insofar as the dwindling Christian minorities in the Islamic world should have made common cause with the Jews, but it is evident that Muslims exploit the intimidated and persecuted Christians to prove the universal disgust that they sense towards Jews.

Many of the anti-Jewish stereotypes among Muslims are imported from Western Christianity, while others are Muslim-made, but both parties liberally borrow from each other, through the intermediary of the Eastern Christians in the Muslim world, who master both cultures and traditions, including as regards anti-Semitism, and who have not been reformed by the far-reaching concessions made to Judaism by the Catholic Church.

Furthermore, during the Palestinian Intifada, which had pushed the Islamic martyrs to the forefront of Palestinian experience, some Christians found the "martyrs" comparable to Christ's martyrdom, even as they violated the holiness of the Nativity at the height of their exhibitions of violence:

---

9. *Al-Manar TV* (Lebanon-Hizbullah), 24 April 2002.

We kneel before the Palestinian people in the Nativity. They starve and thirst, but they are steadfast. . . . The one who said: "I am hungry," when he was on the Cross was our lord Jesus himself. . . . Our Palestinian people in Bethlehem die like a crucified martyr on the rock guarded by Israeli soldiers, armed from head to foot, who have no compassion, love, life or tolerance. . . . The Jew has a principle from which we suffer, and which he tries to impose on people, and that is the principle of Gentiles. To him, the Gentile is a slave. They give the Palestinians working in Israel only a piece of bread and tell them: "this piece of bread that you eat is taken from our children, and we give it to you so you will live as free men in your land, but as a proletariat and a slave in Israel, to serve us . . . ." The *Protocols of the Elders of Zion* are based on this principle, and anyone who reads the *Protocols* feels that we are in this period with Jews.[10]

Patriarch Laham, cited above, apart from blaming the attacks on Christians on a Zionist conspiracy, rather than on Muslims, also warned of the dangers of Christian emigration, which would mean demographic extinction. This too, he said, was "solely attributable to the Israeli-Palestinian conflict."

Another Iraqi priest, Father Suheil Qasha, claimed in an interview[11] that Jews considered Gentiles to be beasts, and asserted that the real danger to Middle East Christians emanated from Zionism. He went on to state that those who [perpetrated the attack on the church in Baghdad] were certainly not Muslims, but "probably those trained and supervised by global Zionism." One wonders what he would have said today when he watches the thousands of Christians and Yazidis slaughtered by ISIS in Iraq.

The Copts of Egypt too are not exempt from these calumnies. The Coptic Orthodox Church is the largest in the Middle East and North Africa. As a certain Father, Marcos Aziz Khalil, wrote in the newspaper *Nahdat Misr* (the Egyptian Revival): "the Jews saw in the Church their Number One enemy, and without its priesthood the Church loses its most important component. Thus the Masonic Movement was the secret tool the Zionists had to create, to inspire revolution against the clergy."[12] Many explain away this anti-Semitism by the fact that Christians living in the Arab environment have absorbed much of the anti-Jewish sentiment among the populations of the Middle East, or that they have been too cautious not to contradict in the open the prevalent anti-Semitic mood. However, Tamimi, the author of this

10. Ibid.
11. NBN TV, 9 November 2010. Cited Ibid.
12. Ibid.

information, believes that the anti-Jewish hostility among Middle Eastern Christians goes much deeper than that.

The test cases are, of course, the other non-Jewish minorities that have been oppressed and decimated over the centuries in Islamdom, being subjected to discrimination and violence, including the Bahais, the Yazidis, or the Mandeans, who have never blamed the Jews for their misery, nor have they developed anti-Semitism as part of their doctrine. The Bahais, for example, whose thriving world center is in Haifa, Israel, certainly cannot blame Jews for any wrong doing, although their persecutors can blame them for "collaborating with Israel." Rather, they have always identified their problem in Iran and the wider Muslim world (i.e., the problematic enforcement of the *Shari'a* law, and the mistreatment of non-Muslims or ex-Muslims who are accused of heresy) on the supremacist attitudes promoted by Muslim radicals. The author also believes that ultimately the anti-Semitic attitudes of Christians are anchored in the old accusation of deicide attributed to Jews, an accusation no longer valid in Western Christianity since the Pope exonerated the Jews from that charge. But a priest like Saliba cited above, continues to claim that Christian anti-Semitism was a natural response because "Jews repaid Christ for his miracles by crucifying him." Pope Shenouda III of the Coptic Church in particular, lambasted the Western churches for exonerating Jews for Christ's death, in a televised interview on 8th April 2007. He argued that Jews were Christ-killers because, he claimed, the New Testament says they were.

It is clear that the Eastern churches, which did not embrace the *Nostra Aetate* declaration of 1965, which was issued in the Second Vatican Council, have perpetuated, and even aggravated the sentiment of anti-Semitism in their midst. Thus, the burden of alleviating those blames of deicide, rests on Middle Eastern Islam and then on the dwindling Christian churches that have adopted the Judeophobic attitudes of their Muslim societies.

A curious theological contradiction remains nonetheless: if the entire concept of the passion of Christ, which engaged him to carry on his shoulders all of humanity's sins, should be eliminated, then the notion of the absolution of the sins that are committed by all human beings, would be found faulty. Therefore, even if Christians wrongly insist on holding the Jews responsible for Jesus' death, far from blaming them for causing the suffering of the passion by crucifying him, Christians should, on the contrary, *thank* the Jews for having allowed that process of suffering, from the *via dolorosa* to the cross. Of course, it was the Romans, not the Jews, who executed Jesus—since the authority and rule was in their hands and they used to crucify any rebel against their government.

In the panel organized in London by Lapido Media, its Chief Executive, Jenny Taylor, complained that the media did not cover the current wave of anti-Christian rampages throughout the Arab and Muslim world due to their "secular blinders." She charged that the Western media reported on Middle Eastern religious affairs as if they were left-wing underdogs versus right-wing overdogs, with the Christians being lumped together with the overdogs. Another participant in the briefing, historian Tom Holland, emphasized that Egypt, where the rampages against the Copts under the rule of the Muslim Brothers (2012–13) drew most attention, was not a developing nation that needed help to emerge as a Western democracy, but was an ancient culture, on par with China or Iran. The audience in Whitehall, which was packed, heard also a long litany of atrocities reported by Arabic-speaking correspondents who were present on the ground during the vicissitudes of the Arab/Islamic "Spring" that erupted in late 2010 and does not seem to have come to rest. Bishop Angaelos, a former Secretary to the Coptic Pope and now the Head of the Coptic Church in the UK, also spoke about the distortions in the Western media, producing as an example the biased report about a field hospital in a mosque in the most affluent part of Cairo, as if it reflected a civil war where each denomination looked after its own patients, and assured the audience that there would never be a civil war in Egypt, because its demography "did not fit that scenario," alluding to the hopelessness of any organized rebellion against the established authority in view of the minority status of Christians in the Middle East (10 percent in Egypt and down to 4 percent or less elsewhere).[13]

Nina Shea, from the Hudson Institute in Washington also mentioned the Christians in Syria, who were being attacked by al-Qa'ida, Jihadists, and other rebels, and she illustrated the terror imposed on the beleaguered Christians by stressing that "when the rebels conquer a town, they set up *Shari'a* courts and mini-*Shari'a* states. The Christians, given the choice to be killed of leave, are fleeing. If they stay, the humiliating and costly *jizya* tax is levied on them, but if they cannot pay they are killed." She also said that refugees did not dare to seek refuge in refugee camps run by the rebels, for they could be recruited to fight in their ranks. An additional threat looms on their horizon for according to the Damascus Plan drafted by the Free Syrian Army for the aftermath of the civil war, retribution killings would be enforced against any who did not oppose the Assad regime, which they are intent to remove from power.[14] A similarly atrocious assessment is given by

---

13. Lapido Media, 20 September 2013.
14. Ibid.

Paul Merkeley,[15] who wrote, under a photograph of Muslim demonstrators carrying the signs "Islam will Conquer Rome" and "Jesus is the Slave of Allah" that:

> As the Middle East comes under the rule of Salafists, Christians are in jeopardy. In Afghanistan, Christians are put to death under blasphemy and apostasy laws enforced by a government installed, maintained, and subsidized by the West. Elsewhere, as in the Coptic community, churches and businesses are burned, Christians are forced to convert to Islam, and whole communities flee brutal persecution. Yet, the secular Western press and politicos, all the way up to the Obama White House, ignore the plight of the Copts and pretend that the Islamists, such as the Muslim Brothers, are moderate and tolerant.[16]

Raymond Ibrahim, the noted champion of human rights in the Arab world, where they do not exist, also reflected on the puzzle of our time in which while politicians, media, and academics insist on the abuses that the "poor Palestinians are suffering from Israel," the Muslim persecution of Christians is almost ignored. He says that some hundred million Christians are persecuted every year, and every five minutes a Christian is martyred somewhere, and 85 percent of this persecution occurs in Muslim lands, with the result that while in 1900 20 percent of the Middle East was Christian, today it is merely 2 percent. He stresses that within one week in his native Egypt alone, the Muslim Brothers have attacked, destroyed, and torched some eighty-two churches, some of them dating back to the fifth century when Egypt was Christian-majority, before the Islamic onslaught and conquest. Al-Qa'ida flags have been hoisted atop churches, and Christian priests, women, and children have been beheaded. This pandemic of Christianophobia extended from Morocco in the West to Central Asia and Indonesia in the East and south to sub-Saharan Africa, throughout an enormous variety of cultures, races, languages, and socio-economic conditions, all in the name of Islamic dominion. Throughout those vast swaths of territory, Christianity and Christian evangelists are attacked, imprisoned, and sometimes killed, churches are torched, banned, or destroyed, Christian women are being abducted, enslaved, raped, and/or forced to renege on their faith.[17]

---

15. Merkeley, "Effects of the Arab Spring so Far on Christians in the Middle East," 160.

16. Ibid.

17. Ibrahim, "Why the Media Do Not Cover Jihadist Attacks on Middle East Christians." See also Kashan, "Arab Christians as Symbols."

Ibrahim also explains why the West, especially America, far from helping these persecuted Christians, on the contrary exacerbates their sufferings. In Tunisia, Libya, Egypt, and Syria, it was the Arab "Spring," which the US supported, that provoked the deterioration of the Christians' position in the context of the chaos that those aborted local revolutions had produced. In Iraq and Syria, whence a mass emigration of Christians has proceeded, the bewildered victims are asking: "Why is the US at war with us?" One reason is that media in the West ignore the atrocities meted out to the Christians, therefore public opinion is simply ignorant of what is happening. Instead, the media are lamenting how Israel harshly treats the Palestinians, claiming that it justifies in their eyes the counter-violence of Muslims. Little did the public know that since the media describes Israel as the predominant force in the region, thus placing the Muslims as the underdogs, the latter cannot suddenly be depicted as the overdogs who oppress Christians.

An opinion is also often voiced that since Christian countries had colonized the Muslim world, indigenous Christians are always suspected of continuing to represent and reflect the old colonizers, as a sort of "fifth column." Ibrahim advisedly wrote:

> No matter how many rockets are shot into Tel-Aviv, by Hamas and Hizbullah, and no matter how anti-Israeli bloodlust is articulated in radical Islamic terms, the media will present such hostility as ironclad proof that Palestinians under Israel are so oppressed that they have no choice but to resort to terrorism.... However, if radical Muslims get a free pass when their violence is directed against those stronger than them, how does one rationalize away their violence when it is directed against those weaker than them—in this case millions of indigenous Christians?[18]

George Catan, a liberal expatriate Palestinian writer, who lived in Syria (when that could be called living, prior to 2011), had the unusual courage to shake the Arab world by his castigation of it over the fate of Christians. Of course, he could do that because in Syria the secular Assad regime, usually considered as the "regime of minorities coalition," had a vested interest in protecting the Christians more and better than any other Muslim country. He drew the attention of his compatriots to the statistical facts of the constant decline in the numbers of Christians in Islamdom, and in consequence in their influence in their countries, compared to their more prominent role in past centuries. He also warned his nation from achieving a Christian-free territory in the Arab world, for the emigrating Christians would elect to

18. Ibid.

move to Western countries rather than stay under the backwardness and tyranny of the Arab world. Rather, he counseled the Christians to stay put where they were, and struggle for human rights and democracy in their lands. He admits that Christians had occupied leading positions under the Umayyads, the Abbasids, and the Fatimids (the Muslim dynasties that ruled much of the Arab world from the eighth century to the twelfth), and had been instrumental in transmitting ancient philosophy and sciences to the Arabs. They had also introduced to the Arab world many European ideas during the Renaissance, contributed to the development of the Arabic language, and championed the uniqueness of Arab culture against the background of the Ottoman tyranny and backwardness. Their contribution was invaluable to the rise of modern Arab states, based on nationalism, not on religion, and took an active part in politics during the "liberal age" in the first part of the twentieth century.[19]

If Catan were to judge the success of the Christians in achieving their goals of democracy and progress in the Islamic world by today's yardsticks, he would have to admit their failure and his own despair from the lofty hopes they and he had entertained in seeing their and his goals accomplished, as their massive emigration to the West massively attests. He himself admits that with the rise of the semi-secular military regimes in Egypt, Syria, and Iraq in the 1950s, the Christians who had starred before in the conduct of secular politics, like the establishment of the Ba'ath Party and the Communist Party, withdrew from politics, although at that point they were not yet particularly oppressed, a deterioration that would dawn much later, at the end of the twentieth century and the turn of the twenty-first, when Muslim radicals emerged and took hold of the new political trends in their respective countries. Those radicals, now at the helm, launched a policy of hatred, oppression, and discrimination against non-Muslims, primarily Christians, and under ISIS also of Yazidis, Shi'ites, Assyrian and Chaldean Christians, and others. Copts, for example, who had been active in the Egyptian Parliament, government office, local councils, municipalities, and the military, were "cleansed" from their public service and their institutions became easy prey for attacks and destruction. He stresses that the Saddam regime of terror had also given free hand to the Salafis, so that after his fall, six Christian churches were blown up in one Sunday, which caused the Christians to emigrate in great numbers.[20]

---

19. George Catan. 17 January 2006. Online: www.metransparent.com/texts/george_catan_eclipse_of_christianism_in_orient.htm

20.. Ibid.

Although Palestinian himself, Catan does not exonerate his compatriots from Christianophobia. He explains that the armed Muslim militias (Hamas and Islamic Jihad) in the West Bank and Gaza, which regard Palestine as a *waqf* (religious endowment), mind the protection of the Muslim holy places, but not those of the Christians (and certainly not those of the Jews), and reports that the few Christian women who remained in Gaza wear the veil so as to escape the scrutiny of the Islamic groups. He also mentions that the last place where alcohol could be bought was bombarded, though it belonged to international institutions. He reminds us that Christianity had been totally uprooted in Saudi Arabia, and that the hundreds of thousands of Christians who enter the country from neighboring or far away countries seeking work, cannot build churches and could be exposed to whipping and imprisonment of expulsion even if they practiced their worship in the privacy of their homes, at a time when the Saudi regime spends millions of its oil profits to erect glamorous mosques across "infidel Europe." Similarly, in Lebanon, the rate of Christians has diminished from 50 percent prior to the civil war (1976) to 35 percent now (2006), while 3.5 million Christians are counted out of a total of 5 million expatriate Lebanese. Thus, while oppression and discrimination had caused Christians to convert to Islam, nowadays it precipitates a vast emigration, which threatens the very survival of Christianity in its original locations. Catan fears that far from auguring the rise of democratic and multi-cultural societies in the Arab world, this situation, which encourages purely Islamic societies, does not even invite the revival of Pan-Arabism, for all those movements have taken the path of Islamization, for the most part identifying Arabism with Islamism, thus totally excluding Christians, who have already been banned in a few countries from teaching Arabic, the language of the Holy Qur'an. Thus, the only remaining option for them is to cling to their land and act for the growth of democratic and tolerant societies in the Arab world where human rights prevail, and where nationality is equal for all without discrimination. That is possible through the establishment of Christian political parties that would not mix between religion and politics, in coalition with women's rights, human rights groups and others who hoist the banner of liberty and fight discrimination.[21] However, apart from Israel, which lends itself to such trends, it is feared that no Muslim country of this sort can encourage the thriving of Christian minorities in its midst.

---

21. Ibid

THE COPTS OF EGYPT

Surprisingly perhaps for some, the main Arab country militarily and culturally, Egypt, which is also credited with moderation, has been the most *in*tolerant towards its Coptic Christians, the ethnic and cultural element of the country that maintains the link to its ancient Pharaonic and Hellenistic roots, and that watches before its eyes its land being subtracted from underneath its feet, and itself either forced to Islamize, to be perennially humiliated in its *dhimmi* status, or to be ultimately obliged to emigrate to the safety of the West.

The persecution of the Copts had already come to a flash point under Sadat, when in 1981 the violent events of Zawiya al-Hamra had caused much killing and destruction to the Copts, and major embarrassment to the authorities who were desperately attempting their *rapprochement* with the West. In those years, *Le Monde* correspondent in Cairo, Jean-Pierre Peroncel-Hugoz, who undertook to divulge the story to the West, at a time when Sadat was its darling, compelled the Egyptian President to expel him due to his poignant and scathing reports on the helplessness, if not the complicity, of the Egyptian authorities in the face of the mounting virulence of the Muslim Brothers, especially in Upper Egypt.[22] Sadat himself was caught up in those days between his overt manifestations of Islamic piety and his overtures towards the Brothers, whom he legalized, and the virulent outbursts of Muslim radicals who ran their rampages of murder and arson against the Copts and their institutions almost unchecked.

The condition of the Copts in Egypt has worsened since the American administration of Obama—who appointed Dalia Mogahed (ominously meaning a Jihad fighter), a woman of Egyptian origin, as presidential adviser on Islamic affairs—has been edging towards adopting the Muslim Brothers as its "moderate" allies in the Middle East. That had brought the Americans to abandon President Mubarak, their ally of thirty years at the outbreak of the Arab Spring in 2011, and to press for the free elections that crowned the Muslims Brothers as the legal rulers of Egypt in 2012. For that reason, they also condemned General Sisi's counter-revolution in 2013, which removed President Mursi from power, and they insisted on dubbing it, with some justification, as a "military coup."

The Copts, already facing discrimination and harassment from Mubarak's regime, saw that things got much worse after Mubarak's removal and even before Mursi's short tenure (2012–13) began. Indeed, on New Year's Day in 2011, a powerful car bomb targeted a Coptic church in

---

22. Peroncel-Hugoz, *Le Radeau de Mahomet*.

Alexandria, killing twenty-five parishioners and wounding nearly a hundred, just as they were finishing midnight liturgy. The next event was the Maspero Massacre, when on 9th October 2011, twenty-seven unarmed Christian protesters were killed and hundreds more injured, by the military. But an official commission of inquiry surprisingly absolved the Army of all responsibility for the killings.[23]

Trifkovic further relates that on 1st August 2012, Sherif Gadallah, a prominent lawyer from Alexandria, submitted a report to the Public Prosecutor demanding the exclusion of Copts from the committee that was in charge and a suggested new draft for the Constitution, that the new regime of President Mursi was planning. At that same time, in the village of Dahshur south of Cairo, a Muslim crowd torched and looted Coptic homes and businesses, after 120 Coptic residents had already fled the village. While the security forces were present when the rampages took place, they did not interfere to put an end to them. The Coptic Church understandably criticized the authorities for their idleness, and demanded that the culprits be arrested, that a better security be afforded to the Copts, and compensations be disbursed to the victims of that attack, accompanied by the return of the fleeing refugees to their homes. The victims thought that those violent events were a continuation of the indifference of the Mubarak regime to their plight. Noted Egyptian novelist, Alaa al-Aswani came to their defense by suggesting that the US would not have agreed to the expulsion of its Muslim nationals, just because of Bin Laden's terrorism. They feared that Mursi's appointees from the Muslim Brothers to the security and justice apparatuses, would not shield them from their persecutors, hence the support they showed for Sisi's counter-revolution of 2013, which seemed to them much more promising for their safety.

The spiritual leader of the Muslim Brothers authorities, Sheikh Ali Gomaa, the Grand Mufti of the country, who had dubbed Christians as infidels in a earlier video, had in fact been called a "champion of moderate Islam" in an article in the *US News*, which explains the considerable *rapprochement* between the Obama Administration and the Muslim Brothers in Egypt that had caused the eager recognition by America of the Mursi government and their abandonment of long-term ally Mubarak. The result was, as the daily *Al-Fajr* reported,[24] that Jihadi organizations were openly distributing leaflets inciting for the killing of the Copts and warning them of their tragic end if they did not return to the truth of Islam. The leaflet also urged the

---

23. See Trifkovic, "The Disappearing Middle Eastern Christians."
24. *Al-fajr* (dawn) 14 August 2012.

supporters of such goals to assemble in the Sheikh Ahmed Mosque in Kasfrit after the Friday prayer in order to join forces.

In official Egypt, which since President Sadat (1971–81) had striven to maintain in a good relationship with the West, a correct attitude towards the Copts was hailed, if not always respected. It was Sadat himself who had declared that Egypt was an "Islamic land" and urged the Copts to reconcile to that idea, and he later exiled Pope Shinouda III to the Libyan desert when he protested the rampages against his community during the Zawiya al-Hamra events of 1981.[25] During the short tenure of Muslim Brother President Mursi in Egypt (2012–13) things got openly worse. Egyptian cleric Safwat Higazi, for example, made the following statement:[26]

> This is a message to the Egyptian Church from an Egyptian Muslim: By Allah! if you conspire and join ranks with the remnants of the Mubarak regime, in order to topple Mursi—things will be different between us. . . . I say to the Church: true, you are our brethren in this country, but we have our red lines. The legitimacy of Dr Mohammad Mursi is where we draw the line. If anyone splashes water on this legitimacy, we shall splash him with blood.

Other Muslim Brother figures had also issued threats against the Copts. One of them, Wagdi Ghoneim, produced a video in December 2012 titled: "A notice and warning to the Crusaders in Egypt," and it began with: "you are playing with fire in Egypt. I swear that the first people to be burned by the fire will be you." These ominous statements reminded people of the tense times at the end of Sadat's rule, as he particularly resented the term "Coptic nation," which was used by some militant Copts, and that implied that Egypt's unity, and consequently his authority as its president, was disputed. The "divisive" nature of Coptic "nationalism" was what incensed Sadat most. He was trying throughout his presidency to stress that Copts would be accepted and tolerated as equal citizens, but at the same time they should entertain no doubts as to who ruled the land, and should not challenge the predominance of Islam in the Egyptian polity. That message, which Sadat had hammered home on several occasions, was nothing new or surprising to the Copts, so they have become accustomed to maintaining a low profile, resigned to their status as a tolerated minority, and did their best not to arouse the wrath of the Muslim radicals, or provide them with any excuse to question the loyalty of the Copts to Egypt and to the Arabs. Thus,

---

25. See Israeli, *Man of Defiance: A Political Biography of Anwar Sadat*, 268–69.

26. The statement was posted on the internet on 13 December 2012 and reported by MEMRI No 3699 of 13 December 2012.

they usually succeeded in going about their business without attracting too much attention. As long as they were not pushed to the wall, and provided their basic freedom of worship was not menaced, they accepted humiliation, job discrimination, cultural slights, and sometimes open persecution.

The 1919 Revolution in Egypt had counted a disproportionate number of Copts among its heroes, and in 1922, towards the end of the formal British mandate, seven Copts had died for their patriotism. But the rise of Islamic radicalism in the 1970s, which in many ways had kindled Muslim-Coptic confrontations in Egypt, has contributed to the process of eliminating from the historical writings and records the prominent role of the Copts in the liberation of their country. But the submissive role of the Copts in Egyptian society and their often-heroic efforts to secure Egyptian independence had not diminished the suspicion and slur directed at them over generations. After the election of Pope Shenouda III in September 1972, Sadat suspected that the new opinionated spiritual Chief of the Copts was taking advantage of the weakness of the government in the pre-October 1973 period to press Coptic demands. But since he was absorbed with the preparations for the October War, he chose to placate them rather than launch the offensive against them, for he regarded national unity as paramount then. The Copts, while reiterating their unfailing loyalty to Egypt, of which they had been the original masters, insisted nonetheless on the independence of the Coptic Church, which they regarded as the way to express their identity.

In January-February 1977 the Copts launched a campaign of fasting and solidarity, which only exacerbated the suspicions of the Muslim radicals. When in September 1977 the government announced its intention of reinstating capital punishment for Christian converts to Islam who then reneged on their new faith and returned to Christianity, the standard punishment for heresy in Islam, a five-day fasting period was again declared by the Coptic Church in protest. Sadat, who had attempted during the October War to dismiss the vicious rumors about Coptic "traitors," made a great effort to renew contact with church leaders in order to avert escalation of inter-communal clashes. In October 1977, while pondering over his peace initiative, Sadat attended a Coptic wedding, and asked the Patriarch to join him in prayer as a gesture of reconciliation. The Copts responded with great excitement and gratitude. However, in 1978–79, the Muslim radicals' violence against the Copts escalated again and Sadat was unwilling or unable to crack down on them. The Copts felt again abandoned, as the burning of churches, the murder of priestly families, and the bombing of the Damshirieh Sanctuary in Cairo prompted new and vigorous protests by the Coptic community. Thereupon, the Pope canceled the Easter celebrations of 1980, suspended his participation in official ceremonies where members of the Egyptian government took part, and rejected the idea, spread by Sadat and his government, that Shari'a should be the basis for legislation in Egypt.

The protest of the Copts culminated in 1981, as Sadat's popularity was spiraling down to his demise and murder. In 1980, the Copts published in North American newspapers large adds blaming the Egyptian authorities for their plight, and that was countered by a large-scale government campaign against the Copts in the Egyptian media. In 1981, the Zawiya al-Hamra events broke out when Muslims took over a plot of land belonging to Copts and declared their decision to build a mosque there. The clash between the two communities generated an exchange of fire, resulting in dozens of deaths and injuries, and the burning and destruction of many houses and some churches. At the end of that three-day battle, the authorities that quelled it saw in the fact that the Copts had defended themselves an indication that they were stockpiling arms for rainy days, when they saw that there were no chances to claim their autonomy.

Mubarak's three-decades rule kept the same pattern of calming the emotions and preventing large-scale clashes. Under him, the most renowned Copt, Butrus Ghali, who had served as a Minister of State (not a full-fledged Minister) in Egypt's Foreign Ministry, was appointed as Secretary General of the UN, a nomination which greatly enhanced the community's prestige. But when Mubarak was dismissed by the January Revolution of the Arab "Spring," there was fear again among the Copts of new rampages of the Muslim radicals, which climaxed during the short tenure of President Mursi. But when President Sisi ousted him, the Copts did not hide their joy and expectation for a renewed improvement of their lot, in view of the prevailing confrontation between Sisi and the Muslim Brothers that he removed from power by a military *coup*.

Unfortunately, due to Obama's destructive and ill-fated support for Mursi and the Brothers during their short stint at government in Cairo (2012–13), he was by inference also backing the worst oppressors of the Copts. Indeed, while a large gathering of Egyptians was preparing in June 2013 to demonstrate against Mursi's rule, Coptic Pope Tawadros II was urged by Mursi to call upon his people not to join that protest, while the American Ambassador in Cairo was also trying to prevent Egyptians from protesting. Indeed, the 18th Edition of *Sadi al-Balad* reported that lawyer Ramsy Naggar, the Coptic Church Legal Counsel, during the June 17 meeting of the Ambassador with the Pope, asked him to urge the Copts not to participate in the demonstrations against Mursi and the Muslim Brothers. The Pope courteously answered that from his spiritual position he did not interfere in political matters. Many Egyptian civil activists indeed repeatedly condemned Ambassador Patterson for behaving like a "Muslim Brother

Stooge," or that she "showed a blatant bias in favor of Mursi," and that her remarks had earned the US administration the "enmity of the Egyptian people." Some Coptic activists openly counseled the Ambassador to "shut up and mind her own business," or that they wished to "be blessed with her silence." Patterson was also accused of revealing the US policy of supporting everyone in the Middle East who opposed his leaders: in Libya against Qaddafi, in Egypt against the thirty-year ally Mubarak, and in Syria against Assad, all under the pretext of human rights and freedom of the people against their dictatorial leaders.[27]

Ibrahim also argues in the same write-up that, in fact, Obama was asking the Copts not to act against the rulers who had stepped up Coptic persecution, making it almost legal, and creating a much worse situation than Mubarak's human rights violations during his thirty-year rule. Under Mursi, indeed, an unprecedented number of Christians had been arrested, often receiving more than double the maximum prison sentence under the charge that they "blasphemed" Islam. It was under Mursi that St. Mark's Cathedral, the holiest site of Coptic Christianity, and the Headquarters of Pope Tawadros himself, was besieged in broad daylight by Muslim rioters, aided by the very security forces that were sent to establish order. Coptic children were also targeted for abduction, ransom, rape, and forced conversion.[28] Ibrahim accused the American Administration of not only supporting the rapists who wage Jihad on secular rulers in Islamdom, but also urging the Christian victims to "know their place" and behave like *dhimmis,* namely to continue to live as second-rate citizens, but never complain. He also reported that in November 2012, during Mursi's tenure in office, Salafi Muslims invaded a Coptic church in Cairo after the Friday prayer, and hanged a sign declaring the place as *Masjid al Rahman* (the Mosque of the Merciful), claiming that the church did not have the necessary permit. The invaders occupied the place for twenty-four hours, asserting that since there was a small mosque at the end of that street, "the presence of a church was an offence."[29]

Ibrahim also reported that on 28th November 2012, a Cairo court sentenced to death seven Egyptian Copts, who were tried *in absentia* for allegedly participating in the creation of a YouTube movie, which had prompted violent demonstrations of protest in many Muslim countries. The seven were convicted for "insulting the Islamic religion through participating in a movie that insults Islam and its Prophet," Judge Suliman explained. Some of

27. Ibrahim, *FrontPageMagazine.com,* 25 June 2013.
28. See Ibrahim, *Crucified Again.*
29. Ibrahim, *Gatestone Institute,* 1 February 2013.

the seven denied that they had participated in the movie in the first place, and thought they were scapegoated for other reasons. This sort of sentence, usually also applies to Muslims, who either renege on Islam or show disrespect for it or for the Prophet Muhammad.

A thirteen-year old Christian girl, Maggie Fazez, while traveling by subway, had her hair shorn by a veiled Muslim women. The girl later said that when she entered the train, she inadvertently pushed the veiled Muslim, an act that is considered offensive by Muslims, and led to an exchange between the two. When the girl left the train she was shocked to discover that her hair had been cut off and left hanging on the collar of her jacket. Her father recounted that his daughter refused to take in any food when she came home, so struck she was psychologically. The same week, another Coptic girl in the first grade had also her hair cut off, thus moving a Coptic activist to write to the Minister of Interior to find the veiled woman who was suspected of both cases. It so happened that another veiled woman from Luxor was being tried for cutting the hair of two of her students a month earlier, as a punishment for not wearing the veil (*hijab*).

After faking prayer in a Coptic church in Egypt, Muslim eavesdroppers overheard a discussion about the meat slaughtered during the Islamic festival of 'Id al-Ad'ha (the Festival of Sacrifice, celebrated at the end of the Pilgrimage to Mecca). By the time the pastor reached home, he heard appeals on mosque loudspeakers by Muslim clerics to join hands to punish the infidel pastor for "prohibiting that Festival to Christians." The calls from the minarets said: "Pastor Patras is a blasphemer and an infidel liable to be killed." Thereupon, hundreds of Muslims attacked his house, beating and kicking him and destroying his home, before police could intervene and take him into custody. He was held and denied bail, due to his "grievous crime" of denigrating a Muslim festival, which amounted to blasphemy.

The case in point is of Philemon Semere, twenty-two, who escaped from Eritrea to Ethiopia in 2010, where he sang in the church choir of Adi Harish refugee camp. Early in 2012 he traveled to Sudan in an attempt to reach Israel, where thousands of his compatriots have sought refuge, but was abducted by the traffickers in the Sinai. He was abused and tortured and faced the choice of either providing $33,000 or losing his kidney forcefully. A BBC report specified that while it was impossible to ascertain Philemon's fate, Christian Solidarity Worldwide and other NGOs who have studied the case, say it bears the hallmarks of what has become a thriving business in that lawless region of the world. Hence, Philemon's call to the world to provide the money and save him from killing by his abductors.[30]

---

30. Ibrahim, *Gatestone Institute*, 1 February 2013.

Attacks on Christian children in the Muslim world have become a particularly sad aspect of Christian persecution and Muslim oppression, since it gives the impression that by singling out Christian children, they signal to them and to their society that it is dangerous to grow up in a Muslim society, therefore Christians had better either convert to the dominant culture, as many do, or migrate from the land, as many more tend to do when they have the opportunity.

In May 2013 a six-year-old Coptic boy, Cyril Sa'ad, was abducted and held for ransom. After his family paid the ransom to his Muslim abductor, Ahmed abdel Salam (ironically the "Servant of Peace"), he still murdered the child and threw his body in the sewer of his house. So, after paying £30,000 to the kidnappers, the family found itself bereaved. Some weeks later, ten-year-old Sameh George, who served as an altar boy in the St. Abdul Masih (Servant of Christ) Church in Minya, was kidnapped while on his way to church for prayers leading up to Orthodox Easter. His family reported that it was his custom to go to church and worship in the evening, but when he did not return and they started to worry, they received a call from the kidnappers threatening to execute the boy unless they got a £250,000 ransom for him. Briefly before that second incident, another Coptic boy, twelve-year-old Abanoub Ashraf, was kidnapped in front of the church St. Paul, in Shubra al-Khayma District. The four men who abducted him put a knife to his throat, dragged him to their car while opening fire on the church, and then sped away. Later, they called the family to demand an exorbitant amount of money as ransom.

In the lawless situation in which Egypt has found itself since the 25th January 2011 Revolution that toppled Mubarak, kidnapping Christians children is becoming a very attractive, lucrative, and almost risk-free business, and apart from the monetary gain, the attackers also saw in their acts an effective way to deter Copts from sending their children to church, thus responding to some of their clerics who have repeatedly declared that attending church worship was "worse than attending bars and brothels."

Particularly vulnerable have been Coptic girls, as an International Christian Concern described: "hundreds of Christian girls have been abducted, forced to convert into Islam and forced into marriage in Egypt. These incidents are often accompanied by acts of violence, beatings, and other forms of physical and mental abuse." In the summer of 2013, a Christian girl, Agape Girgis, went to school accompanied by a Muslim social worker and two teachers, one of whom was a Salafi, but she never returned. As reported, she was later returned to her family and to her priest after protests, and she stayed with them for some time due to the ordeal she experienced during her abduction, which according to a Coptic cleric was "heart breaking," for she was drugged and found herself in a secluded place with an elderly women, and Salafis who tried to convert her into Islam.[31]

A few weeks earlier, another fourteen-year-old Coptic girl, Sarah Abdelmalik, was also abducted on her way to school, and reported to have been smuggled across the border to Libya, where other Copts have been mistreated by the local ISIS branch, with the help of the Interior Ministry, which at the time was still under the Mursi administration. When the affair got to the Coptic Pope, he said that the kidnapping and forced conversion of Sarah were a disgrace for the whole of Egypt, emphasizing that no family can accept the abduction of their daughter and her forced conversion. Ibrahim concludes that in the past few years, 550 cases of abduction and forced conversion were documented in Egypt, and their rate had surged since the Muslim Brother rule had taken over in 2012.

This rule of the Muslim Brothers also occasioned a concomitant rise in sexual harassment of all Egyptian women, a notion that was dismissed as a "rumor" when President Mursi was questioned by foreign correspondents on his visit to Germany. Copts have charged that the collusion of Egypt's security as well and judiciary authorities in these horrors only shows the extent of the war of attrition against the Copts in the land where they used to be the master.[32] These horrific acts were echoed in far away New Jersey in the US, as authorities there charged a local Muslim with beheading two Coptic Christians. The murderer, twenty-eight-year-old Yussuf Ibrahim, killed the victims and buried their bodies in a backyard in Buena Vista, NJ. Authorities said the murderer was driving a Mercedes that belonged to one of the victims.[33]

Counter-claims by Muslims of the abduction of their girls by Copts have attempted to balance the picture in the eyes of world public opinion. The vast *New York Times* write-up on 11th June 2011,[34] just a few months after the 25th January Revolution which removed Mubarak, was the greatest epoch-making media event in the Muslim-Christian struggle for recognition of their mutual grievances. The headlines in Egypt's mainstream papers indeed screamed: "Copts Kidnapped Raghada," reference to a young Muslim who was allegedly abducted by Copts, who tattooed her with a cross. She claimed that they tied her with ropes, beat her with their shoes (a supreme humiliation for any Arab, whose culture abhors even to mention the word

---

31. Ibrahim, "Jihad on Egypt's Christian Children."
32. .Ibid.
33. Tracforamerica@gmail.com, 20 February 2013.
34. Kirkpatrick, "Egypt's Christians Feel More Peril with Revolution." *New York Times*, 1 June 2011, 5.

kundara, shoes, without accompanying it by an apology), and forced her to read some psalms from their Scriptures. This story, which could not be confirmed, nonetheless meant for the Christian Copts a validation of their fears that the post-revolution era augured less tolerance and more danger for the religious minorities. So, while at first the Christians welcomed the revolution, joining the call for tolerance and democracy that was shouted in Tahrir Square, they quickly realized that they were becoming its first victims. Indeed, within the five months following Mubarak's removal from power, the sectarian violence in Egypt had caused twenty-four fatalities, more than two hundred injured, and three churches torched.[35]

One of the basic problems facing Egypt's Christians, and other Christian minorities in Islamdom, is the fact that rising Islamic radical groups are demanding that Shari'a be the main, or only source of legislation in the country, which Christian minorities view as affecting their human rights and freedom of worship. In Egypt, even before Mursi's short-lived term in office, Muslim groups defended the article in the Egyptian constitution that stated that Egypt was a Muslim country that derived its laws from Islam, while Christians and liberals were by definition opposed to such a foundation of the country's rule, though they hardly dared to speak out against it. Instead, most civil politicians would add to that article that in matters of personal issues, non-Muslims should be subject to their own religious law, as is widely the case in many Middle Eastern countries where the Ottoman heritage had bequeathed the custom of the *millet*, where personal matters were left to the discretion of one's religious community and did not depend of the state judiciary. That is precisely what Christian minorities wish to preserve, because Muslim radicals want to Islamize it in accordance with *Shari'a* law. The most daring Christians and civil liberals dream of a Western-style separation of religion and state so that the state would have no say at all in matters of personal law, but it is hard to say how Muslim countries in the present situation could accept that amendment. In fact, in Egypt stricter regulations on building new churches are enforced than on building new mosques, and the Copts refuse to acquiesce in this state of affairs, although they circumvent it by building community centers that also encompass worship facilities.[36]

Another sensitive issue governs divorces. While the Coptic church, like the Vatican and Catholicism, enforces in Egypt today the near total ban on divorce, compared to the comparatively liberal position of Islam on ending marriages, often Christians who wish to divorce convert to Islam, just

35. Ibid.
36. Ibid.

to obtain their goal, and after that try to reconvert. But then they face the threat of "apostasy," which may cost them their lives. This stratagem was known to have triggered many cases of alleged "abductions" of women to abet or prevent such "conversions" and acts of "heresy," which have greatly contributed to the eruption of the Muslim-Coptic hostility and violence. But the custom of using this civic way to circumvent religious law has become so embedded that few are advocating for the change of the law. To show a smiling face to the liberals and Copts, the pre-Mursi Muslim Brothers have named a Christian as the deputy leader of a new joint political party, which called for a "civil state," but also indicated its aim to promote laws derived from Islamic law that are "common to other great religions," like freedom of worship and faith, equality between people, and human rights and human dignity.[37] But when these lofty ideas came to the practical test, under Mursi's tenure, they turned out to have been mere eyewash to calm the Copts' suspicions down and lure them into lending their votes to the Brothers, who were then in opposition to the Mubarak regime. Under revolutionary Muslim regimes, like Iran's and ISIS's, things have deteriorated even further.

No sooner had the removal from the helm of Husni Mubarak, who had symbolized the bastion of stability after his thirty-year rule,[38] taken place in March 2011 that order began to crumble and the military took over to prevent the slide to total chaos. On 5th March, Muslims attacked, plundered, and set ablaze an ancient Coptic church in Sool, a village north of Cairo. Afterwards, scores of Muslims gathered around the scorched building and pounded its walls with sledge hammers to cries of "Allahu Akbar!" The attackers played with the relics of the church's saints and martyrs and transformed the desecrated site into a mosque. Christian girls were being abducted and raped, and the overall terrorization of the Coptic community caused their massive flight from the village. A radical sheikh, who was charged to investigate the incident, later shared his findings on Egyptian TV. He unsurprisingly "found out" that Islam was a religion of peace, mercy, and justice, and he insisted that the Muslim youth who attacked the church never intended to do so; rather, they went there to search for a Coptic man. But after invading the church, they discovered there ancient liturgical books in the Coptic script and papers with the names of Muslims, which were interpreted as "sorcery," hence they destroyed the church. The truth of the matter, however, was that since some Muslims venerate St. Mary, they often submit their names to churches for intercession on their behalf. But the

37. Ibid

38. For the plight of the Copts under the Mubarak Regime, see Magdi Khalil, "How the Munarak Regime Enables the Persecution of Egypt's Copts," *Middle East Forum*, 4 March 2010.

venerable sheikh did not condemn the perpetrators. On the contrary, he directed his blame to the Coptic "dhimmis," a sign in their eyes of his intention to subject the Christians to jizya, as of old.[39]

Of equal concern was the *fatwa* issued by Sheikh Jum'a, the Mufti of Egypt, who is considered a moderate cleric, ostensibly condemning the eruption of violence against the Copts and their churches, but also raising new angles of interpretation that may turn out to aggravate the situation of the Christians. Fatwas are usually issued in response to specific rising questions, in our case asking what is the legitimate Islamic ruling concerning attacks on Christian places of worship, and on the worshippers, and whether an official pact of dhimmitude exists between the Muslim state and the Christian minority, affording it the state protection. Islamic law understands *dhimmis*, who include Christians and Jews, to be people who surrendered to the forces of Islam under certain conditions, including the payment of *jizyah* and acceptance of their inferior status as specified in the Qur'an.[40] The great and authoritative fourteenth-century commentator Ibn al-Kathir had explained that "reducing the stature" of the *dhimmis* meant paying *jizya*, which is a sign of infidelity and disgrace. He adds that non-Muslims living under Islamic rule are to be "subdued, miserable, humiliated, disgraced, and belittled." Classical Islamic law included other debilitating limitations on Christians, including the prohibition to build new churches or repairing old ones, bearing arms, riding horses, etc. The classical law considered that the *dhimmis* who paid the *jizya* were thereby purchasing their life and the protection of their property for the year ahead, which meant that the non-Muslim who paid this tax in fact submitted to Islamic law and secured his life, but when he failed to observe these humiliating and demeaning conditions, he forfeited his life and property, including his family, which could be lawfully confiscated. Hence the conclusion easily drawn by Muslim radicals, that since the present Christians in Islamdom are not protected by the dhimma pact, because they do not pay *jizya*, they forfeit their right for protection. The implications are direct, staggering, and immediate, and good reason for concern to any Christian in Islamdom.[41]

The year of the January Revolution (2011), which launched the Arab "Spring," prior to the elections that brought Mursi to power in 2012, had already augured ill enough to spawn the emigration of 100,000 Copts from Egypt. The Union of Egyptian Human Rights Organizations (UEHRO)

---

39. Ibrahim, *FrontPageMagazine*, 22 March 2011.

40. Sura 9:29.

41. Durie, "The Mufti of Egypt Stands up for Christians—Or does He?" and "The Dhimma Time Warp Returns for the Copts of Egypt," Markdurie.com.

estimated then that a quarter million more may flee abroad before the end of that year, due the chaos and military rule in the country, which did not inspire much confidence in the future. For it was feared that the Salafist preachers were fomenting threats and intimidation, attacks and insecurity to make Egypt *Christianrein*. Copts are among Egypt's most educated and productive elites, who contribute to the management of the country's economic infrastructure, and have well enough established communities in their diasporas of the US, Canada, Australia, and the EU to turn to for aid. According to their reports, there were already 16,000 of them settled in California, 10,000 in New Jersey, 8,000 in New York, and 8,000 in other American states. 14,000 of them had gone to Australia, 17,000 to Canada and another 20,000 to EU countries. The Coptic rate of emigration escalated since March 2011, after the constitutional amendments in Egypt and the increase in Salafist attacks, and their intention to impose *Hudud* laws, namely *Shari'a*-based punishments, including capital punishment, the severing of limbs, stoning, amputation, and flogging. On 12th September, Yasser Borhami, Head of the Alexandria Salafists, accused the Copts on a popular TV show of being "infidels, who live in darkness, because they are away from Islam." Enraged Copts regarded those words as incitement to killing, and were worried about the government's impassivity in the face of the mounting dangers.[42]

The attack on the *Qiddissin* (Saints) Church in Alexandria of January 2011—which took place two weeks prior to the launching of the Spring Revolution, proving that the Revolution was neither the reason nor the trigger for it—had occasioned a most scathing criticism of Egyptian society by a Coptic journalist, who took the occasion to settle historical accounts with Egypt, the Arabs, and Muslims, in the highly visible and influential *Al-Ahram Weekly*[43] of which he was the Managing Editor, under the significantly castigating title: *"J'accuse."* He accused the Egyptian regime of Mubarak of failing to combat Islamic radicalism, and even of nurturing Salafism in the hope of limiting and controlling the more menacing Muslim Brothers. He also accused the so-called "moderate" and civic Egyptians for having grown more bigoted towards the Copts, and the intellectuals and liberals of all creeds for keeping silent in the face of the violence against the Copts. He dismissed the chorus of condemnations of this Christianophobia coming from all sides, and the empty assurances of "unity" between Christians and Muslims in Egypt, as hypocrisy that could not cover up the heaps of narrow-minded prejudice and bigotry that hold in their grip many of the

---

42. Jerry Gordon, *The Iconoclast*, 27 September 2011.
43. *Al-Ahram Weekly*, Cited by MEMRI, Special Dispatch 3483, 3 January 2011.

participants in these condemnations. He claims that a *Christianrein* Egypt—which no one could imagine for the past millennium and a half, since the Muslim takeover—is no longer beyond imagining. He was incensed particularly by the "millions of moderate Muslims, who rose up in fury over the decision to halt the construction of an Islamic Center near ground zero in New York, but applaud the Egyptian police when they halt the construction of a staircase in a Coptic church in Cairo."[44]

That much ado, which caused a media outrage in Egypt, was not totally unjustifiable. The Alexandria attack was indeed the worst in recent memory of a series of assaults on Copts and their churches. In the preceding year of 2010 a shooting massacre took place outside the Nag Hamadi Cathedral on 7th January, on the eve of the Coptic Christmas.[45] Mark Durie, an Anglican priest from Melbourne, Australia, and human rights activist, deplored both the impassivity of the authorities and the complicity of Middle Eastern community leaders and media organization who inflamed a climate of incitement against indigenous Christians in Arab countries. The Alexandria massacre of January 2011 resulted in twenty-one dead and seventy-nine injured when a bomb exploded at the church on New Year's Eve. He singled out the interview of Muhammad Salim al-Awa by Ahmed Mansour on al-Jazeera TV, aired on September 15, 2010, which made outrageous and false allegations against the Coptic Church and its leaders, which have subsequently been invoked by al-Qa'ida in deadly attacks on Christians in the Middle East. He emphasized that the Copts were a direct continuation of the Christian community founded by St. Mark, and they had maintained their faithfulness to the apostolic creed despite two millennia of persecution and trials.[46]

Another hideous attack followed in March in the Imbaba area in Cairo, when throngs of thousands of Muslims fired guns and hurled Molotov cocktails at Coptic homes, churches, and businesses, killing dozens and injuring hundreds when three churches were set aflame, crying "Allahu Akbar!" According to eyewitnesses, it took security forces some seven hours to get to the spot after shooting had started. One priest said: "I called everyone but no one bothered to come," and he naively added that he now has to ask for international protection. A Muslim liberal writer, Nabil Sharaf al-Din, commenting on the large-scale attacks, courageously said that "either the army is incapable of stopping anti-Christian attacks or it is an accomplice

44. Ibid

45. For the entire story, see Guindi, "Symbolic Victims in a Socially Regressing Egypt."

46. Mark Durie, " Condolences for al Qiddisin Church in Alexandria and Copts Everywhere." mark@markdurie.com, 3 January 2011.

to the violence." Muslims said that the trigger was a Christian girl who had converted to Islam, but, they alleged, she was abducted by her community, which tortured her into renouncing Islam—hence the rampage was part of the "rescue effort." Usually, it is the counter-claim that one encounters in Egypt, of Christian women who are kidnapped by Muslims and forced into Islam. Before the rampage, thousands of Muslims marched in front of St. Mark's Cathedral, the residence of Pope Shenouda, demanding the release of other Christian women—two wives of clergy, who Muslims insist, were converted into Islam only to be abducted and tormented by the church to return to Christianity. While it is difficult to verify these claims and counter-claims, it does not stand to reason that an oppressed minority that fights for its survival would engage in such monstrous activities that would undermine its very existence.[47]

During the same post-Mubarak turmoil in the months following the January Revolution, Ayman Anwar Mitri's apartment in Qena was torched and he was beaten by a bunch of bearded Muslims. He was accused of having rented his place to "loose Muslim women." After the attackers beat him with the remnants of his charred furniture, they amputated his right ear, "an appropriate punishment under Islam," they claimed. During the beating, they kept repeating that they would not leave any Christian in the country. Blood still dripped from his unhealed wound into a plastic container when Mitri was interviewed two months later.

The Salafi vigilantes who brutalized Mitri ignited another rampage in the area of Qena on the Upper Nile, many of whose inhabitants are Copts. In April 2011, a Christian had been appointed as the new governor of that area, replacing another Christian who had held the post under Mubarak. The Salafis responded by demanding the appointment of a Salafi to the post and mounting mass protests to showcase their newly acquired political influence. Contrasted to the Muslim Brothers, who put a smiling face to the Christians at that point, by recognizing their contributions to society, the Salafis insisted that Islam does not permit them to fill any role. This was the reason why the Brothers participated in the elections under Mubarak and were perceived as "moderate," while the Salafis rejected the Western-style elections and the entire concept of Western democracy. But after the Revolution, they aligned with the Brothers to gain the leadership of the country through elections. Days after his ear's amputation, the Salafis threatened to kill Mitri's relatives, and police refused to help. Instead, the authorities pushed for *Sulha* (reconciliation), during which the Muslims declared that

---

47. Ibrahim, "Muslims' Inferiority Complex Kills Christians."

the ear amputation was an "error" and that the "young people did not mean it."[48]

The Salafi and other Muslims' negative attitude to Copts and their houses of worship had nothing extraordinary or new to it. That was standard medieval Islamic conduct, which was renewed and revalidated by Sheikh Damanhuri (1689–1764), who wrote an essay on the churches of Cairo, reaffirming the concept that church construction, or any display of non-Muslims symbols under Islam, was "emasculating" to Muslims, hence their violent reaction.[49] This is like in cases of "apostasy" of Muslims, or "insults to Islam and its Prophet" by non-Muslims, which are considered "humiliating" to Muslims, to the point of feeling "emasculated," the most oppressive sentiment imaginable for the supremacist Muslims. The luxury and splendor of many cathedrals, which mostly dwarfed the more modest mosques in the beginning of Islam, may have added to the feeling of inferiority and insecurity, which is at the base of this feeling of humiliation and emasculation. The text of Damanhuri, an eminent leader of al-Azhar University, who reacted to the construction of a church in Cairo, causing agitation among Muslims, under the title "The Presentation of the Clear Proof for the Obligatory Destruction of the Churches of Old and New Cairo," was translated by renowned Western Orientalist Moshe Perlman, and excerpted by Bostom and by Bat Ye'or:

> When I learned of the rise of this deplorable affair, and that in this Community no longer is the prophetic injunction heeded to deter the Infidels, the enemies of the faith, from their goal, I began to write the answer, by explaining the right path. . . . Areas demarcated and settled by Muslims, including Cairo, Kufa, Basra Baghdad, Wasit, as well as any village that was taken by force, and not returned by a Muslim Caliph to those vanquished and dispossessed, are subject to this verdict.
>
> These are Muslim cities in which the *dhimmis* may not display any of their religious symbols, for example, erect churches, bring out wine or pork, or sound the clapper of bells. No new synagogue, church, monk's cell, prayer assembly of theirs is allowed in these cities, by the consensus of the *'ulama* (doctors of the Holy Law). It has been mentioned above that our city, Cairo, is Islamic, started after the conquest of Egypt under the reign of the Fatimids. Therefore, no church, synagogue and the rest may be erected in it. . . .

---

48. Trofimov, "As Islamists Flex Muscle, Egypt's Christians Despair."
49. Bostom, "Coptic Church Construction and Egyptian Muslim Emasculation."

The Prophet, Peace and blessing upon Him, said: "No emasculation (*khisa*) and no church in Islam . . . ." The relation between emasculation and church is that the erection of a church in Muslim territory denotes the elimination of manliness in the people of the territory, just as emasculation, in reality, is the emasculation of virility in an animal. Though the sense of the world in our context in withdrawal from women by attachment to churches. The connection is evident. By "no church" the Prophet meant no construction thereof, a prohibition that is, that no church in Islamic territory signifies the elimination of virility in the people of the territory, which is not permissible, even as the elimination of man's virility by castration is not.[50]

Under President Mursi (June 2012–June 1013) things were expected to grow, and they indeed grew, worse. According to a report from April 2013,[51] police officers in Cairo, firing tear gas, joined with a rock-throwing crowd fighting a group of Christian mourners in a battle that escalated into an attack on Egypt's main Coptic Christian Cathedral that lasted for hours. That was the third day of sectarian violence that tested Mursi's pledge to protect the Christian minority. By the end of the day, one man died in the clashes, bringing the total toll of fatalities in that weekend to six. Mursi called the Coptic Pope and assured him that he considered any attack on the Cathedral as an aggression against him personally, ordered an investigation of the riots, and pledged to protect both Muslims and Christians. The violence had erupted in the town of Khusus in the outskirts of Cairo on the preceding Friday, and escalated into a gunfight that killed four Christians and one Muslim. Hundreds of Christians and sympathetic Muslims gathered in the Cathedral for the four Christians' funeral, chanting for the removal from power of Mursi and his radical Muslim allies who brought him to power. The crowd intoned the usual bombastic pledge one hears in any Arab demonstration: "with our blood and soul we will sacrifice ourselves for . . . ." This time it was for "the cross," on other occasions it is for "the Prophet," "the Galilee," and such. Then, clashes erupted after the service between the emerging mourners and a crowd outside the Cathedral. Dozens of riot police with armored vehicles and teargas canon entered the fray on the side of the crowds of young Muslim men who were pelting rocks and firebombs at the mourners.

During that epoch-making incident, teargas canisters fell inside the walls of the Cathedral compound, sending gas into the sanctuary and two

---

50. Ibid.

51. Kirckpatrick and Fahim, "Attack on Christians in Egypt comes after a Pledge: Egyptian Violence Raises Anxiety over Islamists' Rhetoric about Minorities."

nuns running for shelter. Later, some of the young civilians who had been attacking switched to taunts, making lewd gestures against the cross, with the policemen not only making no attempt to stop them, but even appearing to support and aid them. Many of the Christian defenders pulled back their sleeves at the iron entrance gate to display the cross that they tattoo on their wrists. Others stood on the Cathedral walls and rooftops nearby and threw firebombs at the riot police. The Interior Ministry issued a statement accusing the mourners of starting the violence, crediting the police for interfering to stop it, and condemning the Christian mourners for vandalizing cars, which led to the fights with the inhabitants of the area. Though these scenes of violence had been rife under Mubarak too, this time they were blamed on "foreign conspiracies," while the Copts blamed Mursi, asking "who is responsible for the surroundings of the Cathedral being unsecured for more than five hours today?" and contending that "if the security forces want to know who is behind these events, they will." To strengthen their case against Mursi, some quarters produced a video where Safwat Higazi, a popular speaker who had introduced Mursi during his presidential campaign, is telling the crowd at the delta city of Mahalla that Mursi would usher in "a United States of Arabs and an Islamic Caliphate with its Capital in Jerusalem."[52] He added that the Muslim Capital will move to Jerusalem, not Cairo or Mecca, and reiterated the war cry: "millions of Martyrs march to Jerusalem," thirty-five years after his country had signed a peace treaty with Israel. A popular singer was at hand to serenade the crowd, with Mursi present and approvingly smiling, with the refrain in support of the Hamas: "Banish sleep from the eyes of the Jews. Come, you lovers of martyrdom, you are all Hamas." Another video, which attacked the Copts, was produced showing the same Higazi pledging that "supporters of Mursi" would "spill the blood of anyone who challenged his legitimacy." The message was ominously clear.

Higazi continued to star in the coming pro-Mursi and anti-Coptic demonstrations, thus auguring the violently escalating clashes in the spring that would lead to Mursi's demise a few months later in June 2013. A violent clash took place outside the presidential palace in December 2012, where again Higazi turned his ire against the Christians, amidst the crowd of Mursi supporters. He told the cheering crowds that 60 percent of those engaged in the fighting outside the palace were Christians sent at the instigation of opposition leaders, and issued a warning to them: "We say and I say to the Church that you share this country with us, you are our brothers in this

---

52. Stack, "Egyptian Violence Raises Anxiety over Islamists' Rhetoric about Minorities."

nation, but there are red lines, and one redline is the legitimacy of Dr Mursi. Whoever splashes water on that, we will spill his blood." In an interview to a Brotherhood-linked satellite television channel, another prominent Muslim Brother, Muhammad al-Beltagy, who is popular with the Muslim Brothers' younger generation, repeated the claim that most of Mursi's opponents outside the palace were Christians. Even if this allegation is exaggerated, it is evident that the Copts were petrified when the Muslim Brothers, their persecutors for decades, came to power after the elections of 2012, and they naturally joined the coalition of the opponents of the Islamic rule of the country, and evidently were on the side of the Sisi counter-revolution of 2013, which ousted Mursi and his gang and ushered in a new era of civil government, much to the liking of the Copts. But it would be grossly hyperbolic to posit that the Christian minority of Egypt had caused or lent a direct hand to that counter-revolution, which was not welcomed by the US and the West due to its reversal of the democratic elections that had brought the Brothers to power.[53]

Naturally, Hegazi, Beltagy, and other leaders of the Muslim Brothers had been known before the Mursi revolution, though the emergence of a President from their midst had provided the opportunity to catapult them into national prominence and to lend to their statements such a significance as to make the Copts shiver from their influence. Already in 2009 Hegazi had used his television program on an Islamic network to urge his viewers to boycott Starbuck Coffee due to the alleged ethnic and religious background of the lady who was portrayed on its logo, who was ridiculously identified as Queen Esther, "the queen of the Jews of Persia." He said explicitly: "The girl you see is Esther, the Queen of the Jews of Persia. Can you believe that in Mecca, Medina, Cairo, Damascus, Kuwait, and all over the Islamic world hangs the picture of beautiful Queen Esther, with a crown on her head, and we buy her products?" The Copts were rightly concerned that this kind of absurd bigotry might extend to them too. That same year, Hegazi was blacklisted from entering Britain, but under Mursi his star rose and in September he was appointed to sit on Egypt's Human Rights Council, akin to appointing the head of the mafia to preside over public order. A Brotherhood website started to report on acts of "Christian trickery and sabotage at election time, during the presidential race and the referendum on a new constitution in December 2012. The Christians were accused, just like anti-Semites do to Jews around the world, of destroying ballot boxes, disguising themselves in Islamic headscarves to stump for Mursi's opponents, and transporting dozens of nuns to a polling station to try to swing the vote. Two days after

53. Ibid.

protests at the US Embassy in Cairo on 11th September 2012 and the attack on the American Consulate in Benghazi, where four American diplomats were killed, the Twitter account of the Muslim Brothers posted an update expressing relief that no diplomats in Cairo had been harmed, to which an account of the US Embassy responded with a sarcastic rebuke.[54]

When in 2010 a Christian man in Egypt was accused of dating a Muslim woman, twenty-two Christian homes were torched, to frantic Muslim cries of "Allahu Akbar!"[55] This was because that Coptic infidel had hurt the honor of the entire Muslim Umma, committing the unforgivable crime of luring a naïve and weak-minded Muslim woman into a relationship in which an infidel would "desecrate" her clean and unassailable body by conquering her and reducing her and her/his progeny to infidelity (due to the Arab/Muslim custom of identifying their children by the faith of their father). The reverse, of course, is permissible, for a Christian women who weds a Muslim man submits herself and her progeny to Islam.

When, on another occasion, Muslims made false accusations against a Copt, one Christian was killed and a dozen were hospitalized, while an old Christian lady was thrown out of her second-floor balcony. Other Christian homes, shops, fields, and livestock were plundered and burned to fanatic cries of "Allahu Akbar!" for it is easier to murder and rampage neighbors when it is done "in the name of Allah." Here were set the rudiments of collective punishment, which we hear so many Muslims complaining against when they are applied to them.

One of the most poignant documents of anti-Coptic hatred in Egypt was recorded in July 2010, a short time before the upheaval of the Arab Spring took over and made things immeasurably worse. It is a statement by Nagla al-Imam, a Christian lawyer converted from Islam, after she was detained and beaten by Egyptian security personnel.[56] Here are a few excerpts:

> I was standing peacefully in front of the Cathedral. I was with my children, we were carrying the Cross and a coffin. . . . According to the law of this country, we are apostates. . . . For a year now we have been under house arrest, jailed in my own house. . . . They have aborted all my attempts to speak about Christ, they threatened us, they accused us, they degraded us. I parked my car in front of the Cathedral, they told me that they needed me for a few seconds, I was holding my children's hands

54. Ibid.
55. Ibrahim, "Islam's Christian Scapegoats."
56. Broadcast on Al-Tarek TV, 8 July 2010. Translated and published in English by clergyman Mark Durie, http://markdurie.blogspot.com/2010/07/nagla-al-imams-statement.html.

when the two men called my name. I thought they were from the church. They insisted that they needed to talk to me on a small stroll.... One of my fellow Christians was there, he saw what happened and I asked him to take the children into the church....

After waiting for a few hours in an office, ... I experienced fear, anticipation, worrying, and many other things. Then came Sir Basha and asked me why I was making trouble, but I responded that I was a human rights activists, and I was restricted in my travels. He took hold of the Cross which hanged with a chain on my neck and asked who was that? I scolded him to take his hand off the Cross, because he did not know its worth. But he insisted that he did, and threateningly tightened it around Naga's neck.... She challenged him to hit her, if he were "a true man," and he in response held her hair and bashed her head against the desk. He slapped her repeatedly and punched her in the ribs and on her arms, causing her to bleed from the side of her mouth.... He warned me against delivering me to some women torturers, and I was supposed to know about them due to my legal profession. He threatened me: "Do not leave your house until you go out on a trolley to your grave...."

When she went home, her ribs, her shoulders, her neck and her entire body were hurting. She felt she was a "piece of flesh to them, an object of defamation and slander." I felt no safety except with the Christ, without work and threatened to be de-registered as a lawyer, without an income and far from my family.... I felt I was being taught how to be humble, ... what it meant to focus on Christ and not to depend on humans. ... Next day I did a medical report. I am keeping the name of that man for myself, I am a proud Egyptian citizen, and it is my right to follow the religion of my choice. I have harmed no one. Christianity does not seek to promote terrorism and killing. On the contrary, it is the religion of peace and love....[57]

An adjunct of Egyptian Christianity is its Libyan counterpart. The Christian minority there is much smaller than Egypt's, however, many Copts from Egypt sought to improve their fortune in neighboring Libya, when its petroleum industry functioned full speed and Gaddafi's absolute rule provided stability and predictability. But after the Arab Spring of 2010–11 and the collapse of the state apparatus, economic opportunities have dwindled and personal safety has all but disappeared. In February 2013 four Christian missionaries in Libya were placed under arrest, facing

57. Ibid.

indictment for proselytizing. Arab media also reported that about a hundred Copts from Egypt, who were working and living there, were arrested in Benghazi, on the same accusation. In one video made by one of the Islamic militias, most of the actors seemed like Salafi radicals, with long beards and clipped moustaches, showing the detained Copts in one large hall, hunched over on the floor, with all their hair shaven off, looking dejected or doomed, like concentration camp prisoners. Many of them were apparently tortured, some of them having the crosses tattooed on their wrists burned off with acid. The video also showed a table loaded with Bibles, Christian prayer books, pictures of Jesus, Mary and other saints, offered as "evidence" of their preaching plans. Across the rooms, cries of "Allahu Akbar!" reverberated.[58]

A few days later, a Coptic church in Benghazi was attacked by armed men, resulting in the injury of the priest, Fr. Paul Isaac, and his assistant. This was the second church to be attacked in Libya in two months, since December 2012, when a grenade was exploded in another church in Misrata. Again, loud cries of "Allahu Akbar" were heard, pretending to reflect Islamic supremacism. Libya's Muslim radicals had no problem arresting and torturing these Copts, and indeed boasting of their acts on video and the internet. Libyan law makes it illegal for Christians to display their Christianity or preach it. Therefore, those Muslim militants could not be chastised for implementing the law when abducting Christians and torturing them, since they had crosses, Bibles, and religious icons. Thus, whereas the Libyan government (when there is one) did not condemn the abuse of Christians for their alleged preaching, it can always claim that it was acting according to its own laws, but it has only "expressed regret" for these incidents. The Ministry of Foreign Affairs said that the attacks were "against the teachings of the Islamic faith, and against international covenants of human rights." But in fact, dhimmitude laws are part of the *Sharia* too, and any country abiding by them can be said to consider them superior to international law. For if the authorities consider Christianity a false religion, it is natural that they should ban its recognition, let alone its spread, thus making all the contradictory statements to this effect simply irrelevant. This is typical of the narrative of Christian subjugation, versus the narrative of freedom, suggested by Habib Malek.[59]

---

58. Ibrahim, "Mass Arrest and Torture of Christians in Libya."

59. Ibid. See also Malek, "Arab Christians between Thoughts of Subjugation and Freedom."

CHRISTIANOPHOBIA IN THE SUDAN

In 1998 Bin Laden, with the financial and political support of Iran, created the World Islamic Front against Jews and Crusaders, the precursor of al-Qaïda, designated to "kill Americans and their allies, civil and military." In the same year, two bombs, which exploded simultaneously, ripped through the two American Embassies in Kenya and Tanzania, killing three hundred people and injuring five thousand. The bombings were attributed to Bin Laden and his Sudanese connection. The US retaliated by destroying a chemical complex near Khartoum which belonged to Bin Laden, and also bombed a terrorist base in Afghanistan. Sudan and Iran continued meanwhile their activity in East Africa, in the Balkans and Kashmir, and also in Chechnya and as far away as the Philippines. After one decade of hyperintensive plots in Sudan, Islamic leader Hassan Turabi was removed from the helm by Omar Bashir in 1999, who also suspended the Parliament and declared an emergency. In 2000, Bin Laden's operatives were caught in Canada trying to cross into the US with car bombs, while others were seized while trying to blow up sites in Amman and in Moscow. Bin Laden was at the zenith of his power then, leading him to the Twin Tower horror in 2001, which pulled America into the fray and turned it into the major world power fighting Muslim terrorism.

Although a long string of events has characterized that period since 1989, there have been no periods similar to 1989 in the density of Islamic happenings. Nonetheless, one could point to major events like the fall of the Soviets, the victory of the Afghani Mujahideen, the Islamic coup in Sudan, the death of Khomeini, and the Rushdie Affair as the main events in that year. The other occurrences, like the rise of the Hamas and of the Israeli Muslims, the events in Algeria and Tunisia, were all contributing factors to making 1989 an axial year, all driven by the triangular engines of Iran, Sudan, and Bin Laden, and affecting the far reaches of the world like Central and Southeast Asia, the Horn of Africa, Russia, and eventually America too. So much so that the fears and suspicions in international relations became now focused on the Islamic threat. As it transpired, the American East African Embassies, the Twin Towers and the Pentagon, the Cole, and the attacks against Americans in Somalia, were all led by Iran and actively aided by Sudan and al-Qa'ida. Afghanistan, which joined those leaders during the decade of the Taliban, saw itself eclipsed since the US and NATO started to battle there in 2001. But, in view of the prospective debacle of the Western powers there, one can assume that Afghanistan will rejoin those engines of Islamic terrorism as soon as the Americans leave.

The persecution of Christians in Sudan has been closely connected with the rise of the diarchy there between Omar Bashir, the military commander and formal Head of State, and Hassan Turabi, the Muslim scholar and intellectual who held important functions in government and provided the ideological Islamic underpinnings to the military rule, which imposed the *Shari'a* laws devised by Turabi. There were many ups and down in the relations between these two men, and in consequence the fortunes of Christianophobia knew some fluctuations, but the main issue in our context has been the secession of the mostly Christian South Sudan into an independent state, to put an end to the long and bloody feud between north and south focusing on religious and tribal identity. While in South Sudan internal conflicts have inhibited a rapid development based on the wealth of oil in its territory, the North has never totally reconciled either to the idea that the vast country was split between two separate religion-based entities, or to the fact that the oil riches happened to be located mostly on the Christian side of the disputed border. Before the partition of the land, violent mobs surged once again in Khartoum, the Capital, a day after thirty-six people died in riots sparked by the death of Sudanese Christian Vice-President and former southern rebel leader, John Garang.[60]

The riots were unsurprisingly blamed by the Sudanese authorities on the Garang supporters, who in turn imputed the helicopter crash where he was killed to the Sudan Muslim government. It was reported that Arab-Muslims invaded some neighborhoods heavily populated by southerners in the outskirts of Khartoum, attacking people in the streets and raiding homes. William Ezekiel, the Managing Editor of the *Khartoum Monitor*, claimed that some people were shot to death by "Arabs who attacked them, who entered their houses and looked for southerners (Christians). Where is the government? Where is the police?" A senior UN official in Khartoum said angry southerners from camps outside the capital, for people displaced by the long war in the South, attacked the Omdurman area, and a Muslim imam was slain. He specified that the situation was getting dangerous due to the religious overtones of the clashes where thirty-six people were killed and three hundred injured before curfew was imposed on the city. Only following the rampage did the government and Garang's own Sudan People's Liberation Movement admit that Garang's death was accidental, and dismissed the rumor of a "plot," to keep alive the fragile north-south peace deal. Garang had just become the first Vice-President of the country as part of the US-sponsored deal between the warring parties that ended the two decade long civil war.

60. Smith, "Violence Breaks Out across Sudan Capital."

Thereupon, Salva Kir Mayardit, long-time deputy to Garang at the SPLM, was named to succeed him. Garang, who had been a colonel in the Sudanese army, had been dispatched to the south to quell a rebellion, but he deserted and formed his own rebel movement, which since 1983 dominated the scene in Southern Sudan and fought for resources and for a share of power. It is estimated that some two million people died in the riots and military operations mounted by both sides. A Christian compound in Khartoum was stormed by a throng of Muslims "armed with clubs, iron rods, a bulldozer, and fire," the day after a Muslim leader called on the Muslims to destroy the infidels' church. Shouting "Allahu Akbar!" and "No more Christianity from today on," the Jihadis stormed the Bible school bookstore, burning Bibles and threatening to kill anyone resisting them. "What happened could not be imagined, it was terrible," said an eyewitness. "They burned all the furniture of the school, and the church as well." As usual, he added, "Police at the compound stood back and did nothing to prevent the mob from vandalizing the compound."[61]

It is remarkable that the plight of the Sudanese Christians has gotten so much resonance in the world, that it become a topic discussed at the Human Rights Council of the UN in Geneva. David Littman, the accredited representative at the Council for the Association for World Education, raised the issue in August 2005. He paid tribute to John Garang, who had become Vice-President of Sudan after signing a new constitution with his old enemy, Omar al-Bashir, because time had come for peace, short of which the devastation of the south may have ended in a genocide like in Darfur. Of course, all concerned took that shaky alliance seriously, believing in Western terms, that a constitution was a holy document that obliged the signatories to behave accordingly, and it stood permanently in spite of the fortunes of time and politics. They should have understood that in the Muslim world, the often-changed and replaced "constitutions" were mere statements of policy that were sure to be annulled when the opportunity presented itself. In any case, Littman eulogized Garang, following his tragic death in an accident, who had appeared before the Council ("Commission," at that time—1999) and spoken of the long suffering Christians of Southern Sudan. It was Mr. Littman who introduced Garang and his wife to Mary Robinson, the Commissioner for Human Rights. John Garang made then a long harangue at the Commission about the genocide going on in Southern Sudan. He had said then:

> In 1992 the regime in Khartoum declared Jihad against the people of Southern Sudan and the Nuba mountains. Since then,

---

61. Ibrahim, "Muslim Persecution of Christians, April, 2012."

Jihad has been declared again and again. I ask this very important question: is the Jihad a religious right of those who declare and wage it, or is it a violation of the human rights of the people against whom it is declared and waged?[62]

* * * * * * *

Of all Arab countries, Lebanon was probably the only one designated as a Christian majority one, since under French colonial rule it was conceived and tailored to embrace a quota system regime that would ensure *sine diem,* that the presidency and the command of the military would remain in Maronite hands, while the Prime Ministership would go to the Sunnites, the Speakership of the Parliament to the Shi'ites, and some other perks to the Druze and other minorities. That system had begun to unravel in the 1970s when the Muslim majority, which commands both Lebanon and the adjoining Arab states, realized the growth of the Shi'ites and demanded changes in the system. The Maronite Christians, however, who were at the helm of power, refused the idea of a plebiscite which might confirm the demographic changes that the country had undergone, due both to rapid population growth among the Muslims, and the increased rate of Christian emigration to the West. It was not until the twenty-first century, and following the Lebanese War I (1982–83), which proved the impotence of the official Lebanese Army, and the second Lebanese War (2006), where the Shi'ite Hizbullah emerged as the most formidable armed force in the country, that the latter, backed by Syria and Iran, became the main power broker of the country, determining the rules of the game, and making the Christian official predominance of the country merely theoretical and edging towards a change. Once Hizbullah extricates itself from the Syrian civil war and takes the time to recalibrate anew the rapport of forces in the land their power will only grow.

In spite of the upsurge of Shi'ite Islam in Lebanese politics since 1975, most Lebanese seem still to agree that only a Maronite President can hold the helm of the state, and in fact most of the business, intellectual, and cultural elites hail from the Maronites, a reality that prevents the Christians of Lebanon from claiming official persecution or discrimination. The Maronites are the majority among the Lebanese Christians, but that faith comprises also Greek Orthodox, Catholics, Armenians, and others, and altogether they retain parity with the Muslims in parliament, despite their steady demographic decline in the country. However, despite their predominance,

---

62. David Littman, address to the Commission on Human Rights, Geneva, 9 August 2005.

the country cannot be confessionally partitioned, due to Maronite presence practically everywhere, which also constitutes the glue, in Nissan's[63] words for holding the hodgepodge of incompatible Lebanese groups together in one entity. As Nissan has amply illustrated and documented,[64] beginning from the 1970s the Maronites have engaged in destructive inter-denominational and civil wars that have eroded their standing and shifted the focus of power to others. For example, the Faranjieh family in Tripoli, which controlled the north of Lebanon for decades, pioneered the creation of local militias and private armies, which eliminated the authority of the national military commanded by a Maronite general, who on more than one occasion also became the President. Etienne Sakr, also known as "Abu Arz," referring to the cedar (Arz) tree which represents the identity of Lebanon, created another military force and also the Maronite orientation of association with Israel, a source of antagonism for the Muslim components of the Lebanese population, who are sponsored by what remains of Syrian power, and by the Iranians, at a time when Palestinians and Syrians were wrecking havoc on the country and subjecting its civilian population to destruction, mayhem, massacres, mutilations, and rapes all over the land.

In 2002, amidst the turmoil in Lebanon, the enmity between the Muslim-majority community and evangelists, who represented the dwindling demography and power of Christians, came to fore when with hymns and prayers, fellow missionaries of slain Bonnie Witherall, a thirty-year-old American who was killed by a gunman, eulogized her at the clinic where she worked. Her senseless murder was not only in response to the anti-Americanism that was raging across the country at that time, but was also attributed to the renewed effort by evangelical missionaries from the West to spread the Christian gospel to Muslims in the Middle East. Since in Lebanon, like in many other countries, faith defined not only religious affiliation, but also political power, with specific posts reserved to the once-dominant Maronites under the 1943 arrangements, but since the 1960s Muslims had emerged as the majority and the question of converting across one's religious affiliation became very sensitive. It was Bishop George Kwaiter of the Roman Catholic diocese who remarked that Bonnie was murdered because she was preaching to Muslims. Indeed, she used to gather the Muslim children of a neighborhood and preaching the gospel to them, while dispensing food and toys and all manner of social assistance, an activity that upset Sidon's Muslim hierarchy.[65]

63. Nissan, *Politics and War in Lebanon*, 64.
64. Ibid, especially chapter 4 on the Maronites.
65. MacFarquar, "Killing Underscores Enmity of Evangelists and Muslims."

As is the wont of Lebanese politics, that murder was not an isolated case of shaking the delicate balance in the country, due to the controversy it raised. For example, Rev. Sami Dagher, the area leader of the Christian Missionary Alliance, played on that thin line that divides between proselytizing and plain free speech, when he denied that Witherall was trying to spread the faith outside the pre-natal clinic where she volunteered, but on the other hand, he did not deny that she was preaching within the clinic, and merely admitted that she sought to "expose people to the idea that Jesus Christ was their savior, and let them decide for themselves." What is that if not evangelizing? According to missionary sources, nearly six hundred women had received pre-natal care and heard "the good news of our compassionate healer, Jesus Christ," meaning that while getting pre-natal care, those women were exposed to proselytizing. Those Christian sources also stressed that "dramatic conversions were being reported," and that "local religious leaders have written about us falsely in the newspapers and preached against us in the city mosques." The husband of the slain missionary indeed admitted in public that they "had come to Lebanon in order to spread the love and hope of knowing Jesus," adding that "this is a message worth laying down our lives for."[66]

Especially since the end of the twentieth century, American missionary work in Lebanon grew more assertive, and by the 1990s American fundamentalist Christians put a renewed emphasis on sending in young missionaries to spread the message. Before the civil war broke out in 1975, Lebanon was home to hundreds, if not thousands of missionaries. Both the proclaimed freedom of religion and the Maronite domination of politics gave them a wide range of activities to operate in, but after the war, when Christian dominance dwindled, and Muslim Sunnites and Shi'ites demanded an increasing share in the leadership of the country, the Christian population of the southern city of Sidon, which was 10 percent before the war, has shrunk to a few hundred families. Israel's incursion into southern Lebanon in 1982, and its lingering occupation of the area also raised suspicions of American missionaries, especcisely when Christians set up a Christian TV station, earmarked specifically for evangelization, which Muslims took as undermining Lebanon and denigrating Islam, and in collaboration with Israel to boot. So when the US Embassy in Beirut invited Muslim leaders to an *Iftar* celebration, the Sidon Muslim notables courteously declined to participate. It is thought that Muslim leaders became wary of missionary activities because they combined evangelizing with such attractive items

---

66. Ibid.

as computers, English instruction, and toys and candies in Sunday school classes, for hundreds of Muslim children.[67]

The major families of Maronite elites of Lebanon, like Faranjieh, Chamoun, and Gemayel, were themselves locked in personal and political vendettas that made the appearance of a unified Maronite front illusory, and helped defeat the dominance of the old guard of the Christian elites. In 1990, the Lebanese Phalangists of Pierre Gemayel, led by that infamous arch-murderer, Samir Geagea, fought against the Lebanese Army commanded by Michel Aoun, and even Patriarch Sfeir failed to establish peace between them. But the Ta'if Agreement of 1989, signed in Saudi Arabia and imposed by Syria, had already reduced the powers of the Maronite President, diminished Christian parliamentary representation, and defined Lebanon as "Arab," with an obligation to share a special relationship with Syria, which practically ran the country. The result was that the Maronites—who were the one and only case of Christians in the Islamic world to reject dhimmitude and defy Islam, and were courageous enough to take arms against their Muslim persecutors—ended up pointing their weapons against each other and losing for good their privileged status among the political actors in their country. In 2002, Hizbullah murdered Elie Hubeika, one of the leaders of the Lebanese Forces and the deadly rival of Samir Geagea. Hubeika had been "credited" with the massacre of hundreds of Palestinians in the Sabra and Shatilla refugee camps, of which Israel was charged as "responsible." The vicissitudes of the rocky Lebanese politics came to a climax in 2005, when Rafiq Hariri—the wealthy Sunnite businessman who, since he took office in 1992, had been committed to the reconstruction of his destroyed country—was murdered by Hizbullah (at the instigation of its masters in Damascus and Tehran), which became impatient with the anti-Syrian and pro-Western policies of that popular and effective leader.

The unprecedented collaboration of Maronite President Emile Lahoud with the Shi'ite assassins of Sunnite Hariri, which transpired post-factum, did not make, of course, inter denominational relations in Lebanon any easier, demonstrating that inter-personal hatreds, interests, and jealousies were more important than confessional loyalties, a situation that could only lead to the dethroning of the Christians from their privileged role in Lebanese politics, and their consequent marginalization and ultimate persecution by the hateful Muslim majority.

Maybe the political power of the Christians, when united and purposeful, during their sane period, was the only one capable of stopping Lebanon, and Christianity in Lebanon, from sliding into the abyss; short of

---

67. Ibid.

it, Hizbullah became the only competent power, sustained by the Iranians and supported by (and supporting) Syria, which was able not only to hold the country together, but also contained in the long run the real potential to extirpate Christianity from the land altogether, as its patrons had done in Iran, under the passive and treacherous eyes of the Western powers, which had engineered Christian-dominated Lebanon in the first place. For, as Nissan himself concludes, the consequences of the self-destructive policy followed by the Maronite leadership were that Tony Franjieh, Bashir Jumayel, and Dany Chamoun were murdered, not necessarily by their confessional rivals; and Raymond Edde, Michel Aoun, and Amin Jumayel (the brother of murdered Bashir) were exiled. This is hardly the way to enhance Maronite prestige and hold on power by the Christians of Lebanon, and certainly the road to facilitate their decline and eventual extinction.

In the Lebanese context, we cannot overlook the tremendous ideological effect of Hizbullah on Lebanese attitudes toward the West and Israel specifically, and towards Christians and Jews in general. Sheikh Hussein Fadlallah, the spiritual leader of the movement and an affiliate of the Shi'ite Revolution in Iran, was open to the world, including to Christians, and sided with a dialogue with them. He asserted that while the Westerner was still secular, due to the separation between church and state, Christianity was part of his humane feelings, although he was no longer Christian in the full sense of the word. He contends, like the moderate revolutionaries in Iran such as moderate Khatami, that if Muslim theologians had presented social, economic, and constitutional aspects of Islam in a way that enabled the Westerners to better understand Islam, he could have opened up to Islam. He gave the examples of [Holocaust denier] Roger Garaudy and Bernard Shaw, who exhibited much optimism, claiming that the future belonged to Islam. However, since many Muslim clerics are incapable of presenting Islam to the Western world, the existing problems of information, politics, and culture turn Islam into a scarecrow for the Westerner.[68] Fadlallah's disciple, and Secretary General of the militant Hizbullah, which has embraced the more intransigent line of Khamena'i, thinks more assertively, although he ominously warns Christians in soft words. He said to the Christians of Lebanon, in response to their demand to question the legitimacy of Hizbullah:

> I say to you on this day: We [Hizbullah] are men of patience, men of sacrifice, men of steadfastness. We cannot be provoked,

---

68. Sheikh Hussein Fadlallah, "Interview," *Al Mushahid al-Siyassi*, *BBC Arabic Weekly*, 30 May 1999; cited by MEMRI, Special Dispatch No 35, 17 June 1999.

and we will not be ensnared by the provocation of some of the political forces in the domestic Lebanese arena....

We understand the background and the circumstances.... In the past, they wanted to attack Syria and the Lebanese opposition, and also attacked the Resistance [namely Hizbullah].... But today they cannot attack Syria, for Allah be Praised, we have entered a new phase in relations with it. Attacking the opposition in general is also somewhat difficult, since the ministers of both the opposition and the coalition are in a single government. Therefore, the only remaining option for them is to attack the Resistance and its arms....

I want to address the Christians in Lebanon.... I call on the Christians in Lebanon to conduct a calm discussion, far from the inflammatory speeches, inciting declarations, and the like. I mean a calm discussion among themselves regarding the options for this stage and for the future. They should benefit from past experience, to consider the experience of past decades, and the outcome of the bets some of them placed... on Israel. Where did these bets lead Lebanon, particularly the Lebanese Christians? They must examine also the outcome of the bets some of them placed on the US administration, and where these bets led Lebanon, particularly Lebanon's Christians.[69]

IRAQ AND SYRIA

These two countries, which were both ruled by two branches of the Ba'ath Party, until Saddam Hussein's demise in 2002 and Assad's struggle to survive his civil war, under the protection of the Iranians and the Russians, both with a long record of Christian persecution, have now become the highest ranking in the Arab world (place 3 and 4, and scoring 86/100 and 83/100 respectively) in terms of Christianophobia. In the past, before both lost their tyrannical Ba'ath leaders, they had protected their Christian minorities by their mere regime of fear, which deterred anyone from violence, save by the ruler. After they are gone or have lost their central power, the devolution of authority and the tribal competition, which have thrown those countries into chaos, where no one calls the rules, the Muslim radicals have assumed the rule of terror inherited from their former tyrants (e.g., ISIS, Jabhat al-Nusra) and are exerting it over the Christian minorities to murder or exile them. In Iraq, the dwindling Christian community (Assyrian and

---

69. *Al-Safir,* 23 December 2009; Reported by MEMRI, Special Dispatch No 2718, 29 December 2009.

Chaldean) marked Christmas of 2011, the year of the Arab "Spring," with bomb attacks across Baghdad that killed dozens of them. That was the year when the American forces completed their retreat from Iraq and the departure of the Christians was accelerated mostly at the pace of their absorption in the West. The Chaldean Bishop, Shlemon Warduni complained then that "our faithful in Iraq live in fear . . . they fear there is no peace, no security, so they go where they can live in peace. The government cannot ensure their lives." One ought to remember that before the American incursion into Iraq, and despite the harsh Saddam regime, there were some two million Christians there, of whom 80 percent or more had left by 2013. Even before they left, the Americans did little to protect them, and in fact in October 2010 an attack on a Baghdad church left forty-four Christian worshippers, two priests, and seven security force members, dead. According to Louis Sako, the Chaldean Archbishop of Kirkuk, the Iraqi security forces had not been well enough prepared to ensure the protection of Christians, for fifty-seven churches and other houses of prayer in Iraq had been attacked since the American incursion, with a thousand Christians killed and six thousand injured.[70]

Better to recall, that all those lands the Muslim radicals wish to cleanse from infidel presence, had been conquered by Islam at a time when they were almost totally Christian. Even when the Ottomans took over in the sixteenth century, there was still a Christian plurality there, while in Palestine and Lebanon a Christian majority still prevailed. The sad history of their dwindling under the pressure of oppressive Islam has been told by Bat Ye'or,[71] to remind us that those who now seek the "purification" of their Islamic lands from infidels had themselves invaded and desecrated a Christian land that was not theirs. In Syria, where a quarter million people have lost their lives in four years of conflict, averaging a hundred fatalities daily, murder and destruction have become so frequent and matter-of-course as to be seen as a banality in the general atmosphere of lawlessness, chaos, and utter unconcern for human life. Therefore, the thousands of Christians who have perished do not attract any special attention or sympathy, especially given that the Christians in Syria, like other minorities, depend for survival on the tyrannical regime of Assad and are among its supporters and defenders, together with Iran and Hizbullah, who paradoxically persecute Christians in their own respective domains.

Iraq has been the Islamic manifestation of the ancient Mesopotamian cultures of Babylonia, where the ancient religions of Judaism and

---

70. See Trifkovic, "A Grim Christmas," 4.
71. See Bat Ye'or, *The Dhimmi*.

Christianity found refuge and flourished before the Islamic age. Thus, since the rapid evacuation of the ancient Jewish community in the early 1950s, the entire persecutory attention of the Muslim Iraqis has focused on the vestiges of the various Christian denominations that are extant, especially in the north of the country. Many of their churches were burned down and their congregants murdered, often by state instigation. But since ISIS has taken over those regions of the country and led its rampages against the non-Muslim populations, the Christians have been fleeing to the West whenever they can.

In the decade between 2002 and 2014, thirteen cases of harsh persecution were recorded against Christian individuals and congregations. Of course, the question stands whether the increased degree of Christianophobia and the increased pace of persecution accords with the identification of the Iraqi Christians with the American incursion into Iraq since 2002, or was it the more intensive presence of al-Qa'ida in Iraq, with its legendary commander Zarqawi commanding its troops in the Anbar Province, which vigorously defied the Americans, that heightened the phobia towards Christians. For, at that time, although al-Qa'ida did not officially take responsibility for the anti-Christian acts of terror, it was the primary culprit in public opinion every time a car-bomb exploded near a church during the Sunday Mass, as it happened in Baghdad and Kirkuk in 2005; or when Muslim terrorists threatened, and then destroyed, in 2005, the most ancient Christian church in the country and even took hostage for a day, as a warning, the Archbishop of Mosul. Before then, in 2004, twelve churches were blown up within three months in Baghdad and Mosul, and eleven Christians were murdered by passing hostile vehicles that shot at churches and Christian neighborhoods. Often, the police stood by and did nothing to establish order, due to their fear of the terrorists. Thus, persecution in the Arab world against Christians did not begin with the Arab "Spring," nor was it the fruit of the resulting chaos. In 2006, the Archbishop of Jazirah and the Euphrates for the Syriac Orthodox Church of Antioch, sent the following poignant appeal to Christians at large:

> Brothers and Sisters in Christ,
>
> I am writing you from Damascus [four years before Assad's throne began crumbling], where I am attending the Holy Synod meetings. This evening we were shocked with very sad news from Mossul, Iraq. Our priest, Father Boulos Iskander was killed by shooting. Three days ago he was kidnapped by a fanatic group as a consequence of Pope Benedict's recent speech [perceived to be "denigrating" Islam and its Prophet]. They

forced the community in Mosul to write thirty large posters denying what His Holiness [the Pope] has cited in respect of Muhammad, the Prophet of Islam. Although their request was done, the fanatics killed the priest. The Bishop of Mosul, Saliba Chamoun, received the tragic news during the evening session of the Holy Synod. He immediately left the meeting, returning to Mosul to be with the faithful in this difficult time.

I wanted to share this news with you in order to convey to you the image of the hard time Christians are facing in the region. I kindly ask you to mention the martyr Father Boulos in your prayers, please include all our churches, especially in Iraq, in your prayers.[72]

During the Syrian civil war, where most groups of rebels target the government, when not busy with their infighting, the Christians became the victims of the Islamic opposition, such as Jabhat al-Nusra and ISIS, as both an abhorred minority creed and as allies of the hated government. So, *whatever* the outcome of that struggle, they will end up suffering. That is the reason why while twenty years ago the Christians totaled about a million souls, only a fraction of that, some 200,000, have remained, the rest have migrated or poured into the refugee camps of adjoining Turkey, Lebanon, Jordan, and Iraq.

Paradoxically, the worst persecutors of the remaining Christians are the Jihadi opposition groups who are supported by the US, which allegedly stands for human rights and civil rights. For example, a bomb exploded near a Syriac Orthodox church in half-ruined Aleppo, killing between twenty and eighty people and maiming many more. The bomb also destroyed a school and the French hospital, as well as a nursing home. Also, the Arabic Evangelical Church of Aleppo was mined with explosives and blown up. Its pastor, Ibrahim Nasir, said that "this day, we cry to the Christ to say: my God, forgive them, for they do not know what they are doing." Another bomb exploded in front of the Orthodox Church of the Annunciation in the city of Raqqa, the capital of the ISIS Islamic state, which has decreed that Christians would be made henceforth to pay the *jizya* like the *dhimmi*s of old. That explosion caused two deaths, injured a woman, and spread terror among the vestiges of the Christian population.[73]

In another case, at least three Christians were kidnapped in the context of the US-supported Jihad against Assad. The kidnappers demanded $100,000 in ransom for each. One of the three, a seventeen-year-old girl

---

72. Sent on 17 October 2006 to all churches in the Middle East.
73. Ibrahim, *Gatestone Institute*, 1 February 2013.

had been abducted from the street by four men, after they assaulted her sixteen-year-old brother, knocked him to the ground, and drove off with her. That was part of the rising violence against Assyrian Christians during the Syrian civil war, much of it perpetrated by the rebel militias, especially the rebels against the regime among them. As Ibrahim shows in his report, attacks against Christians in the Muslim world have reached pandemic proportions, therefore it has become necessary to issue a monthly report which collates such events in various parts of the globe, as to show both their frequency and severity, and to indicate the worldwide context and the proportionality between the various Muslim centers of the world, each in its context, style of action, and overall obedience to *Sharia* requirements.[74]

Many analysts of the Syrian civil war contend that the main reason Christians are generally not participating in demonstrations against Assad's rule is because they fear reprisals at the hands of the Sunni Arab majority if the Alawite-dominated regime falls. The Alawites, who have incorporated Christian practices, like celebrating Christmas, into their faith, apparently feel an affinity with the Christians, which serves as the basis for the coalition of minorities on which the regime rests, and therefore Christians under the secular Assad regime feel protected. However, the same cannot be said of another estranged minority, the Kurds, who are Sunnites. *Wikileaks* have revealed that 2009 US diplomatic cables claim that the Christians in northeast Syria consider the Kurds to be recent intruders, and fear the potential creation of a greater Kurdistan. That emanates from the 2005 Kurdish rebellion, which had caused much damage to public property. The Christians also claim that mass immigration of Kurds, from adjoining Iraq, Turkey, and Iran, and their high birthrate, have transformed al-Jazirah from a Christian-majority region of 80 percent to a now Kurdish-dominated zone, with only 35 percent Christians. This suggests to the Christians in Syria that the Kurds of al-Jazira are striving for an autonomous region similar to Iraqi Kurdistan. They know from experience that since 1991, after the Gulf War, the Kurdistan Regional Government (KRG) has engaged in an active campaign of discrimination against the Assyrian Christians, as well as against Yazidis and others who are not recognized as separate ethnic groups within the Kurdish autonomy, and that problem has intensified since the American incursion into Iraq in 2003.[75]

According to those reports, Peshmerga militias have confiscated Assyrian land and a resolution was passed by the autonomous authorities to legalize these thefts. It is also claimed that the Iraqi Kurds have attempted to

74. Ibid.
75. al-Tamimi, "Kurdish-Christian Rivalries."

marginalize the Assyrian Democratic Movement, which is the representative of the Assyrians in Iraq, and when Kurdish authorities were tasked with delivering ballot boxes to Assyrian districts in the north of the country, they failed to do so as part of blocking them from voting, while Assyrian election workers were fired or even killed. A 2007 report by the US Commission on International Religious Freedom was cited as accusing the Kurds of having diverted water and vital resources from Christian to Kurdish communities, leading to vast emigration of Christians, followed by seizure of Christian land and property by the Kurdish population. To lend credibility to their claims, Kurds have been re-writing history, in the same way that Palestinians have been denying Jewish historical roots in Palestine; for example, they claim that they are the true indigenous inhabitants of northern Mesopotamia and Anatolia, and that Kirkuk was a Kurdish city founded by their kin, while in fact that ancient city had been created some four millennia BC, well before the arrival there of the Kurds some three thousand years later, and had been in the heartland of ancient Assyria. In view of this rocky history, which the Syrian Christians have been scrutinizing very closely, they have little reason to believe in Kurdish designs as they encroach upon territory that the Christians consider theirs.[76]

In Iraq, the Christians are persecuted in part due to their religious ties with the West. In the 2010 large Baghdad church attack, which left more than fifty dead, it was said by the perpetrators to have been in retaliation for accusations hurled elsewhere by the Coptic church. The al-Qa'ida suspects of that tragedy went further by threatening Christians around the world as being "legitimate targets" of Muslim *Mujahideen* wherever they encounter them. This relates to the recurrent theme of the Muslim Umma as one universal world community that functions like a living organic body, and which hurts all over whenever part of it is injured anywhere, and retaliates in consequence, as a sign to its vitality. Therefore, since the Christian minorities in Islamdom are the most readily accessible, they are the first victims to be targeted. Mark Durie, the Australian Priest and Islamic scholar, notices in his book:

> Even a breach by a single individual dhimmi could result in Jihad being enacted against the whole community. Muslim jurists have made this principle explicit, for example, the Yemeni scholar, al Murtada wrote that the "[dhimmi] agreement will be canceled if all or some of them break it," and the Moroccan al-Maghili taught "the fact that one individual, or one group,

---

76. Ibid.

among them has broken the statute is enough to invalidate it for all of them."[77]

In November 2010, a spate of early-morning bomb and mortar attacks on homes of Christians in Baghdad left at least three people dead and twenty-six wounded. All in all, forty-four worshippers, two priests, and two security officers died during the seizure of the Baghdad Cathedral by radical Muslims, and the ensuing shootout. More specifically, two mortar shells and ten homemade bombs targeted the homes of Christians in various neighborhoods of the Iraqi capital between 6:00 and 8:00 AM of the 10th of November. That came just ten days after the deaths during the seizure of the Baghdad Cathedral. One day before, three Christian homes in the Mansur District in West Baghdad were firebombed, while one week before (3 November), al-Qa'ida claimed responsibility for the Baghdad Cathedral slaughter and warned that it would step-up attacks on Christians. The perpetrators said that they carried out the church attack to force the release of Christian converts to Islam who were allegedly being detained by the Coptic church in Egypt, but days later they announced that Christians everywhere were "legitimate targets." Christians in Iraq were threatened by al-Qaida that they should either leave the country or will be killed. Archbishop Athanasios Dawood confirmed that "if they stay they will be finished one by one."[78]

While in Syria the large-scale persecution of Christians is linked to the civil war and to the determination of the rebels to totter the Assad rule together with his "coalition of minorities," which comprises the Christians, Iraq's Christianophobia relates back to the beginnings of the Islamic state of the Abbasids that made its capital in Baghdad. The Assyrians, for example, regard themselves as the descendants of the biblical indigenous people of Mesopotamia, when the prophet Jonah preached to the people of Nineveh, and which came down crumbling when Nineveh fell in 612 BCE, a few decades before the Jewish First Temple in Jerusalem. Nowadays it is the location of Mosul in northern Iraq, one the first cities occupied by ISIS, and rampaged for its antiquities and its non-Muslim minorities. In 630 CE, that land was subjugated by the conquering Muslims, followed by Kurds, who invaded from the Anatolian Plateau in the thirteenth century, evicting the Assyrians from their homes and massacring many of them. In 1933, with the establishment of the modern Iraqi state, the Assyrians of northern Iraq were almost totally eliminated once again, but they survived and that event has shaped their identity ever since. In Saddam's absolute dictatorship,

---

77. Mark Durie, *The Third Choice*, self-published, cited by Ibrahim, ibid.
78. *Egyptian Gazette*, 10 November 2010.

although ostensibly a secular one, Assyrians suffered under his Arabization policy. By the census of 1977, the regime referred to the Assyrians as Arabs or Kurds, until they became "Christian Arabs" by fiat of the regime. Under this Arabization under pressure, one of the mainstays of the regime, Tariq Aziz, changed his name from Yuhana (John) into the Arabic Tariq upon joining the Ba'ath, and acceding to a high position in Saddam's government. Together with seeming tolerance towards Assyrians, he forbade them nonetheless from any religious activities that linked them to coreligionists abroad. In the Iran-Iraq War (1980–88), many Assyrians were drafted and sent to the frontlines, which resulted in a high rate of fatalities among them. At this time, and after the Gulf War of 1991, many Assyrians left for Australia, Canada, and the USA. Those who found asylum in the Kurdish Autonomous region after 1991 have also been discriminated against by the Kurds, though they became immeasurably freer than under the Saddam regime or what happened to them after the departure of the Americans in 2012.[79]

After Saddam was removed by the American incursion into Iraq, his seeming protection of Christians was taken up by Muslim fanatics and transformed into open persecution. On 22nd March, an elderly Assyrian couple was murdered in their district, the wife being beaten to death and the husband had his throat cut. On 7th June 2004 four masked men drove into the Assyrian Headquarters in Baghdad and opened fire on Christians going to work, killing four and injuring others. On the same day, three Christian women were killed in another drive-by shooting as they returned home from work. All cases, the Christians believed, were religiously motivated, at a time when Christians and their churches received letters in Arabic threatening them that if they did not follow Islamic practices and also follow the "resistance" (to the "US occupiers"), they will face consequences like "torture and burning and blowing up houses with the families in them." Mandaeans, who follow the teachings of John the Baptist, have received the same threats and suffered the same kind of violence.[80] Most of the 1.5 million Assyrians had been concentrated in Baghdad, Mosul, and other northern towns. Most of them belonged to the Assyrian-Nestorian and to the Chaldean (Catholic) churches. The latter is a splinter group of the Assyrians that seceded in the sixteenth century from the Nestorian Assyrians and adopted Catholicism. Although they share the same Assyrian roots, the patriarch of the Chaldeans, Mar Raphael, has stated that "Assyrian" is an ethnic identity, implying that Chaldean is a religious one. Both groups insist they are not Arabs and castigated Arab institutions that encompass them in the Arab identity.

79. Lewis, "Iraqi Assyrians: Barometer of Pluralism."
80. "Iraq Christians Killed, Christians are Fleeing."

So, during World War I, as the Young Turks promoted their aggressive Turkish nationalism, many Christians were decimated by the Turks, just like the Armenians, another persecuted Christian denomination, and the few survivors found refuge in Lebanon and northern Iraq. The Assyrians formed a political movement, the Assyrian Democratic Party, raising some suspicions, since only patently undemocratic parties or governments (like the Romanian Democratic Republic or the National Democratic Party of Mubarak) resort to that ornamental epithet.[81]

Christians were targeted by Muslim radicals after the American incursion of 2003 on suspicion that they "collaborated with the invading Crusader army," so their businesses were destroyed and Christian university students were harassed, while Christian women were forced to wear the veil. Since Christians teach foreign languages at their schools, it is understood that American occupation forces employed Christians as local help in translations and office work, thus raising the accusations of "collaboration." At some point, "Brigades for the Liquidation of Christian Agents and Spies" have threatened to liquidate those who worked for the occupiers, that they would be pursued into their homes and churches. Placards posted in the Christians areas ominously warned that:

> The Christian minority enjoys peace and security in the land of the Muslims and in our country in particular. Its members have held senior positions in the State. But their malevolence toward Muslims became evident when the occupier entered our country. He found great support among them in the form of translators and agents who acted as informers against Muslims. Their churches receive evangelist groups. They spread moral corruption and pornography in our streets. Muslims have been arrested, women raped, and houses destroyed as a result of Christians being agents of the occupiers.[82]

Even if only a fraction of these accusations is true, and there is no doubt that in all appearance the Iraqi terrorists believed it was, one can understand the wave of anti-Christian fury that blew up after the American incursion, on the part of Sunnite radicals, who had ruled the country and sustained Saddam, but now felt that the marginalized Shi'ite majority, aided by the Americans and their suspected collaborators, the Assyrians, was being groomed to take over the rule of the country. In August 2004, five churches in Mosul and Baghdad were hit in one day in a coordinated

---

81. Lewis, "Iraqi Assyrians: Barometer of Pluralism."

82. Cited by Nimrod Raphaeli, "The Plight of Iraqi Christians," MEMRI, *Inquiry and Analysis, No 213*, 22 March 2005.

attack that killed twelve people. On 10th September, mortar attacks were mounted on the Assyrian town of Bakheda (Qarqosh) in the Nineveh area. In October, five churches in Baghdad were hit on the first day of Ramadan, a time of religious extremism in the entire Muslim world, and in the following month of November, eight more Christians were killed in two more church bombings. As the military and public sectors were closed to them in the post-Saddam era, Christians have focused on business and on illegal alcohol trade among Muslims, which had been limited before, except for Saddam and his family and cronies, in whose cellars a great quantity of expensive alcoholic beverages was found. Thereafter, attacks on Christian liquor businesses ensued. These was joined in the Shi'ite southern city of Basra by such fanatic groups as the "The Revenge of Allah" or "Hizbullah" or the "Organization of Islamic Doctrines," who roamed the streets and meted out "Islamic punishments" on traders of liquor as well as on prostitution. As a result, four hundred Christian stores were forced to close, while the rampaging attackers were rewarded for "martyrdom and for being designated by Allah to uproot vice." Is there any doubt why in this nefarious and dangerous ambience, and lack of protection by the authorities, Christians would elect, indeed be forced, to run away for their lives, what we call "emigrate"?[83]

An interesting angle has been expressed by Syrian refugees abroad, who are no longer terrorized by the government they had just fled from, in this case to Amman and the refugee camps in northern Jordan, which had traditionally evinced tolerance towards its Christian minorities. Martin Janssen, a Dutch reporter, attended in Amman in May 2013, a prayer for the two abducted Syrian Christian clergy, Greek Orthodox Archbishop Paul Yazigi and Syriac Orthodox Archbishop Yohanna Ibrahim, captured by Syrian rebels. After the prayer he met with refugees who told how they fled from their villages after they were told by rebels, presumably Islamic groups, that they were now under an Islamic emirate and were subject to *Sharia* Law. They said they were offered four choices: either to renounce the Christian "idolatry" and convert to Islam; or to pay a heavy tribute to Muslims (*jizya*) for the privilege of keeping their heads and their Christian faith; or be killed; or flee for their lives, leaving all their belongings behind, the option that they obviously chose, while other Christians left behind were either killed, or tried to pay the tribute but found it too heavy, after the rebels kept increasing its rate, and some were unable to pay the fee so they converted into Islam to save their lives.[84] Despite the plight of these refugees, they

---

83. Ibid. See also Kaplan, "The Plight of Iraqi Christians"; Fadel and al-Qeisi, "Iraqi Christians Flee after Violence"; and Myers, "With New Violence, More Christians are Fleeing Iraq."

84. Martin Janssen from Amman, translated by Rev. Mark Durie, himself an

are always welcome in the adjoining Islamic countries where they sought refuge, like Lebanon, Jordan, Iraq, and Turkey. Nonetheless, in Jordan for example, some parliamentarians have been calling on the government to expel all Syrian refugees, because they pose a security risk. Some Jordanian Christians reported that a few weeks earlier the Jordanian security services had managed to thwart an assassination attempt on King Abdallah, that was planned and orchestrated by a sleeper cell of the Syrian al-Qa'ida-affiliated Jabhat al-Nusra movement. It was precisely to escape such radical Muslim movements that Syrian Christians have fled to Jordan.

Janssen's Christian refugees interlocutors were all from northern Syria, from the cities of Idlib and Aleppo and the villages in between. For example, one of them, the elderly Jamil, had lived peacefully with another thirty Christian families in a village near Idlib, together with two hundred Sunni families. But in the summer of 2012 things changed suddenly. One Friday, trucks appeared in the village with heavily armed and bearded strangers who knew no one in the village. They began to drive with a loudspeaker broadcasting the massage that the village was now part of an Islamic emirate, and Muslim women were henceforth to dress in accordance with the provisions of the *Shari'a*. They could convert to Islam and renounce their "idolatry," or remain and pay the *jizya*. For those Christians who did neither, they could leave behind their property and depart, or they would be slaughtered and their throats cut. He said that his own family had initially opted for the *jizya*, but when the amount kept rising, almost all Christians fled, and their lands and farms were lost. Some who were either unable to pay the tax or unable to run away, converted to Islam. In neighboring villages all Christians who elected neither option were murdered. Aleppo came under the same wave of plundering and looting, everything from wheat, diesel, bread, school equipment, businesses, and factories, and any factory owners who protested were mercilessly executed. Miryam, an Armenian woman who remained in Aleppo, learned from her relatives who fled to Turkey that the armed militias were selling there their booty at bargain basement prices. She had to live without water or electricity for days, and even became accustomed to the sound of explosives and gunfire that tore them from sleep every night.[85]

Beyond this suffering and deprivation, the most crucial factor which determines the uprooting of these millions from their ancestral lands and their rushed exit from their countries into the uncertain arms of wandering and misery, has been the constant terror that paralyzes one who lives in

---

Anglican pastor in Melbourne, Australia, "The Dhimma Returns to Syria," markdurie.com blog, 2 June 2013.

85. Ibid.

lawlessness and chaos, and can hope for no protection in his country nor for a welcoming asylum to start a new life. It is the daily fear that the bus transporting his children to school would be targeted and blown up; the psychological terror of going to church on Sunday, when you know that Muslim neighbors are determined to kill you because you are a Christian; or when you do not dare to go to bed at night, knowing that your relatives and acquaintances were surprised by rocket attacks which crashed into their property as they slept; or when one spends hours every day in the queues of the remaining bakeries that still make bread; in short a life which in its simplest form has become too dangerous. Things got so bad, that even churches that were proudly lit up at night, now hide in darkness with their congregants taking turns to night-watch them from prospective attackers.[86]

In another report from Homs, the third largest city in Syria, almost the entire Christian population of fifty thousand seems to have run for its life under the prevailing cross-fire between the regime and the threatening rebels, with paradoxically fears growing not from Assad, the ally of Christians and other minorities, but from the radical Muslim groups who demand immediate submission to *Shari'a* rules whenever they take over any piece of territory. Most of the Christian refugees have fled to neighboring villages, or other major Syrian cities where it is easier to melt undetected, or to Lebanon. Since some rebel forces did occupy Christian institutions, like schools, homes of the elderly, and even churches, all those became targets of the Assad loyal forces and were destroyed beyond recognition or restoration. In this situation, even Muslim neighbors have turned on Christians because they have attracted government retaliation, which hurts them too. Christians have also suffered abductions and gruesome murders, and some families which were unable to pay the high ransom for the release of their relatives, and fearing that they might be tortured, have been driven to ask the kidnappers to kill their loved ones immediately. Church leaders hesitate to travel at night, fearing that as symbols of Christians they may be the target of assassination. The authorities have warned congregations not to gather in large numbers over the Easter period in case their meetings are bombed.[87]

SAUDI ARABIA AND GULF STATES

Saudi Arabia, which ranks 12th in the world list of Christianophobia, and has itself scored 77/100, in the World Watch list, putting her in the fourth

---

86. Janssen, "The Dhimma Returns to Syria."

87. *Barnabas Fund*, "Syrian Christians in Desperate Straits: Will the Churches Survive?"

place in the Islamic world after Iraq, Syria, and Sudan, has been the most severe in its implementation of the Wahhabi brand of puritan Islam. In fact, it is the only Islamic nation which, due to the location there of the two holiest sites of Islam, Mecca and Medina, does not even permit Christians to visit, much less to build houses of prayer, and the few Christians that dwell there are either foreign workers or visitors.

There have been some voices since 2008 that have lamented the departure of non-Muslims in general from the Arab world, an exodus that has negatively affected the social and economic standing of Arab states; Saudi Arabia, for instance, cannot project its self-image of moderation and tolerance of the other while the steady departure of the Christians remains unrelenting.

Saudi Arabia has, until recently during the American-Iranian nuclear talks, also been the closest client of the USA in the region, and depended on America's military umbrella, as was demonstrated in 1990–91 during the Kuwait crisis and the Gulf War of those years, so it could not sustain American criticism if the rights of Christians were not respected. At the same time, there was no dearth of public callings in Saudi mosques for the elimination of Christians (and Jews). In 2004, for example, a guest worker of Indian descent and Christian creed was arrested for "propagating Christianity," which is punishable by death. His family claimed that he was pressured by his prison wardens to convert to Islam if he wished to escape the capital punishment. All in all, there were eleven known cases of Islamic persecution of Christians in Saudi Arabia, accompanied by threats of death, in the years 2002–12.

In Saudi Arabia there are no churches, in spite of the fact that foreign workers make up one third of the population, many of whom are Christians. They are forbidden to display any sign of their faith, and some have seen their Bibles shredded by the authorities upon their entrance to the Kingdom. An official cleric, Sheikh al-Buraik, has recently said in a mosque in the capital Riyadh: "People should know that the battle that we are going through . . . is also with those who believe that Allah in a Third in a Trinity, and those who say that Jesus is the son of Allah, and Allah is Jesus, the son of Mary."[88] Following the conversion to Christianity and subsequent escape of a Saudi woman, the country introduced a monitoring system that tracks any cross-border movements by female Saudis. Using SMS technology, the tracking device alerts a women's male guardian (father, husband, or other male relatives) by text message when she leaves the country, even when they

---

88. "Muslim Countries Becoming Bolder in Persecuting Christians"; and "Saudi Telethon Host Calls for Enslaving Jewish Women."

travel together. This move shows how women are held under a state of semi-slavery in the Kingdom.[89]

In other Gulf states, there are many expatriate workers, some of them are Christian. In those places, governments do not understand the role of the church hierarchy, since in Sunnite Islam it is absent, therefore they believe that the guest Christians there can exercise their religious duties without the interference of their clergy. This approach deprives Christians of their spiritual guidance and affects their faith. Government also prevents Christians from building churches. Some Muslims fear that close cooperation with Christians would result in revitalizing Christianity at the expense of Islam, therefore they advocate additional curbs on displaying Christian symbols within Arab societies. These restrictions also include, not only the erection of churches but also the abolition of parochial schools. Conversely, some Christians fear that too close a cooperation with the Muslim majority and integration in it might encourage assimilation and run the risk of eventual dissolution.[90]

The most fascinating (or cynical, if one is less generous) aspect of Christianiphobia in the Muslim world is revealed when the most fundamentalist Muslims, who have no tolerance for Christianity in their countries, attack "Christian extremists" in Western lands, which evince the most generous tolerance toward Islam within their boundaries. The case in point is the orchestrated onslaught of the Saudi press against Christian fundamentalism in the USA. *Al-Watan* (the Nation) even went as far as claiming that Christian fundamentalism was no less dangerous to international peace than other forms of religious extremism. That was the organized response of the Saudis against a reported Pentagon briefing that described Saudi Arabia as a "kernel of evil" in the Middle East. Obviously, that was an exchange of name-calling between two ideological rivals, who instead of providing evidence to sustain their accusations, they exacerbated the tension by cursing and abusing each other. Except, that while America, the West, and Christians can exhibit a record of openness to others, legality and democracy at home, and fairness toward other faiths, Muslim radicals have only lawlessness, murder, limb severing, and chaos to show for their record. Of course, the Saudis are not pleased by the way they are depicted in the West, especially after 11th September, when the perpetrators and Osama Bin-Laden, their ideologue and financier, turned out to be Saudis. Disregarding the cataract of hatred poured daily on America and the West in the Muslim

---

89. Ibrahim, Gatestone Institute, 1 February 2013.
90. Kashan, "Arab Christians as Symbols."

press, the Saudi papers described Christian fundamentalism as supportive of Israel and dangerously influencing American foreign policy.[91]

One is not surprised by this sort of xenophobic and imbalanced eruption toward other creeds, if one bears in mind the Saudi educational system, which not only follows the radical teachings of Wahhabism according the strictest Hanbali school of law, which consecrates Jihad and hold Mujahedeen in the highest esteem, but also shows contempt to Jews and Christians. A textbook for 8th Grade,[92] for example, explains why Jews and Christians were cursed by Allah and turned into apes and pigs. Quoting Surat al-Ma'ida,[93] the lesson explains that Jews and Christians have sinned by accepting polytheism and therefore they incurred Allah's wrath. To punish them, Allah has turned them into apes and pigs. The book further states that the struggle between Muslims and Jews will continue until the Day of Judgment; that the Muslims shall ultimately be victorious; and that Jews and Christians are the enemies of the believers. They will not be favorably disposed toward Muslims and it is necessary to be cautious in dealing with them. The book also asks questions for class discussion: Who will be victorious in the Day of Judgment?; With what types of weapons should Muslims arm themselves against the Jews?; Name four factors leading to the victory of Muslims over their enemies. With this kind of indoctrination to their children, is there any wonder that Muslims grew up despising non-Muslims and seeking ultimate victory, no less, over them? These themes are spread throughout the world, at great expense, in 1,500 mosques, 202 colleges and 2,000 schools for educating Muslim children in non-Islamic countries in Europe, the Americas, Australia, and Asia.[94]

This indoctrination is followed by oral messages that are hammered in by members of the royal family, high officials, and preachers of the regime, who miss no opportunity to reiterate those messages. Sheikh Majid al-Firian, stated in a mosque in Riyadh: "Muslims must educate their children to Jihad . . . and to hatred of the Jews, the Christians and the Infidels . . . ."[95] In an interview to the daily *al-Sharq al-Awsat*, Prince Na'if reiterated that: "we do believe in the soundness of our school curricula, especially on

91. Abdelhadi, "Saudis Lash US Christian Extremists," BBC News, 8 August 2002.

92. *Sharh KItab al-Tawhid* (Explaining the Book of the Unity of Allah), for 8th Grade (2001), 43.

93. Qur'an, Al-Maida, verse 60.

94. Stalinsky, " Saudi Arabia's Educational System: Preliminary Overview," *MEMRI, Special Report,* No 12, 20 December 2002.

95. "Friday Sermons in Saudi Mosques: Review and Analysis," MEMRI, Special Report,
   www.memri.org/bin/articles.cgi?Page=archives&Area=sr&ID=SR01002

subjects relating to Jihad; . . . we do not change our system on demands of others."[96] In those years following the September 11 events, where most perpetrators were Saudis, a major debate erupted in the Islamic world as to whether it was the Islamic educational system, which included curses against Jews and Christians, which raised this kind of new terrorist generations. For in the Friday sermons in the mosques, supplications are voiced, which include curses against Jews and Christians, and beg Allah to "shake the earth under their feet," "paint the White House with black color," "destroy the Jews and Christians," or "drain the blood from their veins." Due to repeated Western complaints against these methods, some preachers and officials have tried to exonerate themselves by belittling the significance of the curses. Abd al-Aziz Amar, the deputy Head of Islamic Affairs in Saudi Arabia said to the Sharq al-Awsat:

> These supplications are at the heart of our ritual, and are directed only to Allah. . . . But the supplications targeting the People of the Book (Christians and Jews) have not been voiced against them in general, but only against those among them who have oppressed others. . . . Even Christians and Jews who lived in proximity of the Prophet were not all lumped together, and only oppressors among them were targeted.[97]

Another Saudi, Abdallah al-Ghamidi, from al Damam, wrote to the Editor of *al-Watan*, candidly admitting to the faulty custom of cursing infidels. He said:

> Why did we deviate from the customs of our ancestors who used to behave gently with Infidels, and we have elected to curse them on Fridays in the mosques? We prayed that Allah should wipe them out, dissolve them, turn their wives into widows and their children orphans? It is noteworthy that these annihilationist and grinding curses are all directed toward Christians and Jews only. Why do not we include also Buddhists, pagans, calf and river worshippers, who are even greater sinners? I believe that it would be more worthwhile for us Muslims and for all humanity, to pray to Allah that he should direct them to the right path, for the call to Allah to wipe them out holds no benefit to us, quite the contrary, it will only create an abysmal hatred. Imagine how we would react if the Pope would pray every day in the Vatican for the destruction of all Muslims. . . . If we want a

---

96. 'Ayn al-Yaqin, 20 September 2002
97. *Al-Sharq al-Awsat*, 29 December 2002

good relationship with the people of the world, we have to show them that we wish them good and not annihilation . . . .[98]

No less instructive was the reaction of other readers, who resented the "columnists and intellectuals" who want our preachers to abstain from cursing Jews and Christians. "This hurts our feelings," they said, "because Christians and Jews have described the Qur'an as satanic, and have demanded that it be cleansed from the verses that incite to Jihad or reveal the immorality of the Jews." They also rationalized their rejection of Ghamdi's plea to desist from cursing the people of the book, by claiming that they heard the cries of Palestinians and saw the children who were being murdered in Israeli jails, and the young prisoners who were being held in the Guantanamo jails. "Did they respect our feelings, when they wished to attack Mecca and Medina, in order to punish Muslims?" they asked. They conclude by assuring that "our needs do not permit us to surrender or to be weak, on the contrary, we must strengthen ourselves.[99]

The same sort of debate took place in neighboring Kuwait. When the minister of Holy Endowments demanded that preachers should refrain from cursing Jews and Christians, Sheikh Nasser Shams al-Din reacted: "It is permissible to curse Jews and Christians. Allah has termed them polytheists. We do not deny that there are some good Christians and Jews, but that does not mean that we should prohibit cursing them." Other Kuwaiti media argued that in the situation of turmoil in the Muslim world, where they fight each other, they should first achieve peace among themselves before they seek to curse others, Christians and Jews, exactly as Muslims would not countenance being cursed by others. It is unreasonable, they contended, that while Muslims turn the world upside down when someone dishonors their faith, that they should keep cursing and dishonoring others. Those moderate voices reminded their brethren that it was Christians (i.e., Americans) who protected Muslims from another Muslim—Saddam Hussein, so it would be absurd to curse them, as long as those who do curse are unable to protect Muslims from that murderous Saddam. Kuwaiti media nonetheless reported that despite these rational voices, many preachers continued to curse Jews and Christians right and left, for it was the Qur'an that urged Muslims to curse them, as in the opening Sura of the Holy Book, which is repeated in all daily prayers, with regard to those that Allah's wrath has come down on (the Jews) and those who have been led astray (Christians).[100]

---

98. *Al-Watan* (Saudi Arabia) 24 June 2002.

99. Ibid. 27 June 2002.

100. *Al-Watan* (Kuwait), 18 May 2002.

In other parts of the Gulf and the Islamic world, including Jihadi sites, the demand to desist from cursing Jews and Christians was rejected out of hand. Sheikh Qaradawi, the most significant Sunnite Muslim spiritual leader, who dwells in Qatar, said in his weekly column in *al-Jazeera TV*:

> It is not rational to just attack Jews and Christians in general. We are just castigating the aggressors among them. In many Islamic countries there are Christians and Jews who dwell there and are citizens. So it is not reasonable to provoke them by cursing them. Thus, when I preach at the mosque I am specific: "Allah, tackle the Jews who aggress the chicks." I do not curse Jews in general, but those who have robbed the lands, spilled blood, and permitted the prohibited. I do not curse Christians either, but only the hateful Crusaders who deploy traps against us . . . .[101]

---

101. *Al-Jazeera TV*, 22 December 2002.

CHAPTER TWO

Christian Minorities under African Islam

Islam has been making big strides in Africa since the Middle Ages, where in addition to its rule and the many Muslim sultanates it established from Morocco to the Horn of Africa, it also seeped gradually to Sub-Saharan countries, overtaking entire areas in the East and West Africa, or establishing itself as a large minority, as in Kenya, and undoing many efforts of the colonial inroads to evangelize Black Africa. Ever since, Islam has confronted competing Christianity on what it considers its turf and area of cultural influence.

Mali, for example, that isolated, remote, and scorched land at the edge of the Sahara, which had known glorious days when Timbuktu was a famous commercial and study center on the fringes of the Islamic world, has been shaken up by the Islamic Spring of the 2010s in rather odd ways. In Sudan, it is the breakdown of the alliance between Omar Bashir of the military arm and Hassan Turabi, the spiritual head, that has caused the unrest in general and so permitted the unleashing of the wave of anti-Christianity. One of the powerful figures of the Anglican church in Africa, Archbishop Nicholas Okoh, believes that Africa is under attack from Islam, and that Muslims are mass-producing children to take over communities on the continent. Okoh was elected the Primate of Nigeria in 2009. There are about seventeen million practicing Anglicans in Nigeria, but they face persecution in the north, while Islam and Christianity are vying for supremacy in the rest of the country. He said that the Islamic attack in Africa was determined in Uganda, Kenya, and Rwanda, spending money where they do not even have congregations, building mosques and hospitals, luring Africans away from Christianity by promising them four wives, instead on the one that Christianity permits. That would permit them to have many children, and for every extended family to become a village.[1]

Abu Hifz al-Mauritani,[2] who was accused by the US for masterminding the attacks against American Embassies in East Africa in 1998, and was notorious enough to be included in President Bush's list of "wanted," had met Bin Laden in the Sudan and became one of his underlings. After September 11, he gave an interview to *al-Jazeera* Television where he said that as no al-Qa'ida member had been convicted at that point, he had to deny any connection between the organization and those events. But he also emphasized that an accusing finger should be pointed to the US, due to her "oppression, tyranny, travesty of justice, and aggression against the Arab, Muslim, and other oppressed people." He said that the US ought to be blamed, because the perpetrators of the attack were trained in the US, not in Afghanistan, and that the US people should take their country to task for having spent billions of dollars on maintaining its security, military, and intelligence apparatus, but in vain, due to their dismal failure to prevent the attacks. He claimed that while his organization did not perpetrate that horror, "hundreds of millions of Muslims could not contain their joy at the sight of America tasting in one stroke some of the pain and bitterness she had inflicted on Arabs and Muslims over the years." He insisted that though his group was not the author of that disaster, the results thereof were "good for us and fit in with our interests."[3]

With this kind of attitude towards America and the West in general, it is obvious why Muslim radicals would entertain their antagonism towards the culture of the West, essentialized in the Christian faith, and requiring consequently a systematic persecution of its representatives in their midst. For al-Mauritani was complaining in his interview against the US which was hitting mainly civilians in Afghanistan ("which proved Western cultural and moral values"), killed and maimed children in their mothers' bosom, destroyed mosques and burned Qur'an books, and wiped out entire villages. He dubbed the US counter-Attack in Afghanistan a "Crusade," which added a religious dimension to the war, and said that his group's support for the

1. *The Times*, 21 September 2009.

2. Not to confuse with Abu-HIfz al-Masri, who fought for the Taliban in Afghanistan. Abu-Hifz (the Keeper or Guardian) is a common *nom de guerre* in al-Qa'ida, and the fact that they are differentiated by their country of origin (the one is Mauritanian, the other Egyptian) is indicative of the truly international nature of that organization.

3. *Al-Jazeera* Television from its correspondent in Qandahar, Yussuf al-Shuli, published in *al-Sharq al-Awsat* (London) 27 September 2001.

Taliban stemmed from the Qur'anic injunction to support the Truth, since the Taliban government was the only one that ruled according to the Qur'an, the Sunna of the Prophet, and the great doctors of the Holy Law of Islam. He also asserted that it had become incumbent upon Muslims to fight Jihad in Palestine due to the "Crusader-Jewish alliance," and that was the reason why al-Qa'ida struck at Christians and Jews wherever they can find them. That implied, of course, that since the most helpless Christians are to be found in Islamdom, it was easier and more obvious that they should persecute and eliminate them there, be it in Africa or anywhere else.

There are nine countries in Africa (not counting the Arab countries of North Africa, Sudan, and Mauritania, which figure in the Arab world count), that are listed in the World Watch list of Open Door USA cited above. Their international rankings among all states which persecute Christians are: Somalia (90/100), which ranks 2nd overall; Eritrea (79/100), which ranks 9th overall; followed by Nigeria, with the largest Christian population (78/100); Central African Republic (67/100) in the 17th spot; Kenya (63/100), which is a Christian majority state living in the proximity of the Islamic terrorism of Somalia, in 19th place; Ethiopia(61/100) in 22nd spot; Djibouti (60/100) in 24th place; Tanzania (56/100) in 33rd spot; and Mali (52/100) in 40th place. Like in previous chapters, we will bring here the most illustrative examples of persecution, regardless of majorities and minorities, either on the national level or on a local level. For instance, the northern Nigerian states, which are populated mainly by Muslims, are also the most violent and virulent against their local Christian minorities, while in the Christian south the situation is more peaceful. In Kenya and Tanzania, which are Christian majority, the major acts of terror, like the blowing of American embassies there in 1998, were perpetrated by fanatical Muslims from neighboring Somalia.

THE CHRISTIAN MASSACRE IN NIGERIA

The series of horrors that have grabbed the world's attention during the Islamic Spring have been the rampages of ISIS in Iraq and Syria and the Boko Haram in Nigeria. Here the large-scale killing of Christians, the destruction of their entire communities and culture, and often their forced conversion into Islam, or expulsion, or imposition of the revived *dhimmi* status, including the *jizya* poll-tax, have become the order of the day wherever the Muslim groups took over new territory in the face of helpless, corrupt, and weak local tyrants.

In summer 2014, following the precedent of ISIS in the Middle East, Boko Haram declared the Muslim-majority north Nigerian provinces, that it had taken over, as an independent "Islamic state." The month of September 2013 in particular will be remembered as a bloody season when three hundred Christians were murdered by Muslim terrorists all over their controlled territory. Worth also remembering is October 2012 when Boko Haram terrorists took over a state technological college, where they sorted out the Christians from the Muslims and slaughtered thirty of them. For them it was simply a matter of obeying their holy laws, which prescribed the elimination of unbelievers, so they did not regard the horror as a crime, just like the perpetrators of September 11, but as the fulfillment of Islamic tenets, just like their "elder sister in Syria and Iraq."

But a decade before there was any Boko Haram, Islamic anti-Christian rampages were noted by the media and reported worldwide. In May 2004, riots were reported from Kano, the most important Muslim-majority city in northern Nigeria. It was then said that Muslim mobs, brandishing machetes and clubs, attacked Christians in the streets of the city, which triggered a counter-rampage by Christians, followed by retaliation to avenge a massacre of hundreds of Nigerian Muslims. The result was that thousands of Christians had to hide in army barracks and police stations, as mobs attacked them outside, where dozens lost their lives. Barry Owoyemi, a Christian, said of his dead neighbor: "I saw them put an old tire on his neck and set him ablaze." The witness was himself taken to safety by police, who had to fire their guns in the air to deter the attackers. That rampage exploded after thousands of Muslims protested the killing of six hundred Muslims in Yelwa, a town in central Nigeria, where ethnic Hausa-speaking Muslims were the majority. In retaliation, Muslims were blamed for the killing of fifty Christians in town. In 1999, President Obasanjo had been elected, after fifteen years of an oppressive military government, and the simmering inter-ethnic tensions, which had killed some ten thousand people, exploded to the surface. The new President, himself a Christian, and a former military junta leader, ordered the security forces to put an end to the riots, at a time when Kano was burning, thirty people were dead in the clashes, and the rioters were burning buildings and blocking residents from escaping. Things got so bad that the leader of the Ibo-speaking Christian minority, Boniface Ibekwe, asked the police publicly, in the presence of journalists: "stop this killing today or give us 6 months to leave Kano peacefully."[4]

Unsurprisingly, while international media, like the Associated Press, gave a more balanced picture on killings on both side of the Muslim-Christian divide, the strictly Christian or pro-Christian advocacy outlets spoke

---

4. "Muslim Mobs, Seeking Vengeance, Attack Christians in Nigeria," *Associated Press* (AP), 13 May 2004.

mainly of the plight of Christians under Islam, it being understood that in most cases it was a Christian minority that faced persecution and discrimination on the part of the Muslim ruling majority. In fact, the Christian Association of Nigeria (CAN) spoke of the Kano riots in terms of the "600 Christians who have been killed and of the 12 churches that were torched." Bodies were still discovered a few days after the rampages, only because the hospital mortuaries were full, and there were many cases where families buried their dead without informing the authorities that kept the statistics. The harrowing cases of killed children and of pregnant women who were ripped open and their babies shot, little by little came to light to make clear that these were not passing episodes, and that the brewing hatreds between the communities went so deep that there was no chance of healing them any time soon. There were reports that despite the curfew imposed by police, Muslim mobs moved from one house to the other looking for Christian victims, then torched the houses, trapping their occupants inside. There was also a report that the chief Muslim cleric of the city, Umar Ibrahim Kabo, ordered all Christians to leave by 14th May, and that thirty thousand of them heeded the call.[5]

Tragically, the Boko Haram movement of Muslim radicals has so overwhelmingly taken the limelight of the media by its infamous horrors against other Muslims, and especially against Christians, that it has overshadowed and pushed to the sidelines the much older, yet still unresolved, Biafra crisis, which concerned the massive oppression by the Nigerian federal government of the Igbo people, precisely in proximity to the northeastern region of Nigeria where the Boko Haram is now operating. The Biafran crisis, which lasted from 1967 to 1970, was in fact a movement of secession by the Igbo from Nigeria due to economic, ethnic, cultural, and religious tensions among the various peoples of the country. The creation of the new dissident state, which was pushing for recognition, was among the causes of the Nigerian Civil War, also known as the Nigerian-Biafran War. But that state was formally recognized by only five countries, while other nations which did not give official recognition did provide humanitarian support and assistance to the splitting country. After two-and-a-half years of war, during which a million civilians had died in fighting and from famine, Biafran forces agreed to a ceasefire with the Nigerian Federal Military Government (FMG), and Biafra was reintegrated into Nigeria. Now the Movement for the Actualization of the Sovereign State of Biafra (MASSOB), which advocates a separate country for the Igbo people of south-eastern Nigeria has

---

5. "Hundreds of Christians Die in Bloody Massacres in Kano," *FreedomNowNews@aol.com*, 14 May 2004.

been revived, accusing the state of marginalizing the Igbo people. MASSOB says it is a peaceful group and advertises a 25-stage plan to achieve its goal peacefully.[6]

Boko Haram means literally the "Forbidden Book," a reference to the Western books, culture, and education that are prohibited by this radical Muslim group in northern Nigeria, the most populated African country (ca 175 million people), which is split between the Muslim north and the Christian south. Like in other Western colonies in Asia and Africa, when international boundaries were drawn between the colonial powers towards apportioning territories that were due to become independent, little consideration was accorded to ethnic, linguistic, tribal, or religious differences, so as to found more or less homogeneous political entities, and resulted in a hopeless mixture of peoples and cultures, which have been for the most part spending more energy and wasting more resources to disengage from the groups and entities forced upon them, than to integrate and form a joint national unity held together by a social contract acceptable to all. The religious clash between the Muslim radical Boko Haram and the rest of the population, especially the Christians, is one such an outcome, though here it assumes a fanaticism that is nurtured by religious hostility, unlike the ethnic enmities between Tutsi and Hutu in East Africa, or the Congo and Katanga controversy at the center of the Continent.

Officially, the group calls itself *Jama'at Ahl al-Sunna Lidda'wa Wal-Jihad* (People Committed to the Prophet's Teachings for Propagation and Jihad), and it is a militant Islamic movement based in northeast Nigeria. The group numbers a few thousands at the most, and was designated by the United States as a terrorist organization in November 2013. It may have killed in its terrorist activities, which are focused against local Christians, more than five thousand civilians between July 2009 and June 2014—perhaps more victims than its own membership—in attacks occurring mainly in northeast, north-central, and central states of Nigeria. Since 2009 Boko Haram have abducted more than five hundred women and children, including the kidnapping of 276 schoolgirls from Chibok in April 2014. 650,000 people had fled the conflict zone by August 2014, an increase of 200,000 compared to the year before.

After its founding in 2002, Boko Haram's increasing radicalization led to a violent uprising in July 2009 in which its leader was executed. The government's declaration of a state of emergency at the beginning of 2012, extended in the following year to cover the entire northeast of the country,

---

6. Estelle Shirbon. "Dream of free Biafra revives in southeast Nigeria." *Reuter* 12 July 2006.

resulted in a marked increase in both security force abuses and militant attacks. It proved ineffective in countering the insurgency, hampered by an entrenched culture of official corruption. Since mid-2014, the militants have been in control of swathes of territory in and around their home state of Borno, but have not captured the capital of the state, Maiduguri, where the group was originally based. The uncompromising hostility of the northern Nigerian Muslims towards anything remotely perceived as foreign—a mindset of *boko haram* that has in the past been applied even towards vocal recitation of the Qur'an—has historically been a source of friction with the other Muslims from the middle of the country. Thus, Boko Haram has also been translated as "non-Moslem education is forbidden," "Western influence is a sin," and "Westernization is sacrilege."

Mohammed Yusuf founded the sect that became known as *Boko Haram* in 2002 in Maiduguri, the capital of the northeastern state of Borno, establishing a religious complex with a school that attracted poor Muslim families from across Nigeria and neighboring countries. The center had the political goal of creating an Islamic state, and became a recruiting ground for Jihadis. By denouncing the police and state corruption, Yusuf attracted followers from unemployed youths. He is reported to have used the existing infrastructure in Borno of the *Izala Society*, a popular conservative Islamic sect, to recruit members. The *Izala* were originally welcomed into government, along with people sympathetic to Yusuf. The Council of Ulama of Nigeria advised the government and the Nigerian Television Authority not to broadcast Yusuf's preaching, but their warnings were ignored. Yusuf's arrests elevated him to hero status. Boko Haram was founded as a Sunni Islamic fundamentalist sect advocating a strict form of *Shari'a* law, and developed into a Salafist-Jihadi group in 2009, influenced by the Saudi Wahhabi movement. It seeks the establishment of an Islamic state in Nigeria, and opposes the Westernizing of Nigerian society that has concentrated the wealth of the country among a small political elite, mainly in the Christian south of the country. Nigeria is Africa's biggest economy; 60 percent of its population of 173 million (2013) live on less than $1 per day. The *Shari'a* law imposed by local authorities, beginning with Zamfara State in January 2000, and covering twelve northern states by late 2002, may have promoted links between Boko Haram and political leaders, but was considered by the group to have been corrupted.

Boko Haram kill people who engage in practices seen as un-Islamic, such as drinking alcohol. In a 2009 BBC interview with Mohammed Yusuf, the founder of Boko Haram, he claimed that Western education "spoils the belief in one God." He also said, "Like rain. We believe it is a creation of God rather than an evaporation caused by the sun that condenses and becomes rain.... Like saying the world is a sphere. If it runs contrary to the teachings of Allah, we reject it. We also reject the theory of Darwinism." Boko Haram conducted its operations more or less peacefully during the first seven years of its existence, withdrawing from society into remote northeastern areas, somewhat similar to the *Takfir wal-Hijra* groups in Egypt in the 1960s and 1970s. The government repeatedly ignored warnings about the increasingly militant character of the organization. In 2009 police began an investigation into the group, code-named "Operation Flush." On 26th July, security forces arrested nine Boko Haram members and confiscated weapons and bomb-making equipment. Either this, or a clash with police during a funeral procession, led to revenge attacks on police, and widespread rioting. The federal government in response launched a Joint Military Task Force operation, and by 30th July more than seven hundred people had been killed, mostly Boko Haram members, and police stations, prisons, government offices, schools, and churches had been destroyed. Yusuf was arrested, and died in custody "while trying to escape." He was succeeded as leader by Abubakar Shekau, formerly his second-in-command and interestingly enough carrying the same prestigious name of the first seventh-century Caliph of Islam, Abu Bakr, like the head of IS in Syria and Iraq.

Boko Haram has maintained a steady rate of attacks since 2011, striking a wide range of targets, multiple times per week. They have attacked politicians, religious leaders, security forces, and civilian targets. The tactic of *Islamikaze*[7] was introduced by the organization in the two attacks in the capital on the police and UN HQs. In Africa as a whole, it had only been used by *Al-Shabaab in* Somalia and, to a lesser extent, AQIM, the North African branch of al-Qai'da.

Since early 2013, Boko Haram have increasingly operated in Northern Cameroon, and have been involved in skirmishes along the borders of Chad and Niger. They have been linked to a number of kidnappings, often reportedly in association with the splinter group *Ansaru*, which won them a higher level of international attention.

Beginning in August 2014, they changed their "hit-and-run" tactics, instead occupying swathes of territory in northeast Nigeria from which the increasingly beleaguered Nigerian military were unable or unwilling to expel them. President Goodluck Jonathan was elected in 2011, and immediately after his inauguration in May, Boko Haram initiated a series of bombings, including in the Capital Abuja. The most "successful" of these was the attack on the army barracks in Bauchi. A spokesman for the group

---

7. For a clarification of this term, which is wrongly dubbed in common parlance "suicide bombing," see this author's *Islamikaze: Manifestations of Islamic Martyrology*.

told BBC Hausa that the attack had been carried out, as a test of loyalty, by serving members of the military hoping to join the group. This charge was later refuted by an army spokesman, who claimed, "This is not a banana republic." However, on 8th January 2012 the President would announce that Boko Haram had in reality infiltrated both the army and the police, as well as the executive, parliamentary, and legislative branches of government. Boko Haram's spokesman also claimed responsibility for the killing outside his home in Maiduguri of the politician Abba Anas Ibn Umar Garbai, the younger brother of the Shehu of Borno, who was the second most prominent Muslim in the country after the Sultan of Sokoto. He added, "We are doing what we are doing to fight injustice; if they stop their satanic ways of doing things and their injustices, we would stop what we are doing."

Due to the spread of Boko Haram to adjoining countries like Cameroon, an agreement was signed between it and Nigeria in February 2012 to establish a joint border security committee, geared to coordinate border patrols between the parties to try to seal the border to hostile operations of the Boko Haram.

In 2014 Boko Haram continued to increase its presence in northern Cameroon; in May, it abducted ten Chinese workers and in July, the Vice-President's home village was attacked by around two hundred militants; his wife was kidnapped, along with the Sultan of Kolofata and his family. At least fifteen people, including soldiers and police, were killed in the raid. In a separate attack, nine bus passengers and a soldier were shot dead and the son of a local chief was kidnapped. Hundreds of local youths are suspected to have been recruited. In August, the remote Nigerian border town of Gwoza was overrun and held by the group. In April 2014, Boko Haram kidnapped 276 female students from Chibok, Borno. More than fifty of them soon escaped, but the remainder have not been released. Instead, Shekau—who has a reward of $7 million offered by the US DOS since June 2013 for information leading to his capture—announced his intention of selling them into slavery. The state of emergency was extended in May 2013 to cover the whole of the three northeastern states of Borno, Adamawa, and Yobe, raising tensions in the region. In the twelve months following the announcement, 250,000 fled the three states, followed by a further 180,000 between May and August 2014. 210,000 fled from bordering states, bringing the total displaced by the conflict to 650,000. The US Bureau of Counterterrorism provided a summary of Boko Haram's 2013 foreign operations:

> In February 2013, Boko Haram was responsible for kidnapping seven French tourists in the far north of Cameroon. In November 2013, Boko Haram members kidnapped a French priest in

Cameroon. In December 2013, Boko Haram gunmen reportedly attacked civilians in several areas of northern Cameroon. Security forces from Chad and Niger also reportedly partook in skirmishes against suspected Boko Haram members along Nigeria's borders. In 2013, the group also kidnapped eight French citizens in northern Cameroon and obtained ransom payments for their release. The US State Department listed Boko Haram as a terrorist organization in November 2013, citing various reasons including links with AQIM, "thousands of deaths in northeast and central Nigeria over the last several years, including targeted killings of civilians."

The State Department currently believes Boko Haram is affiliated to al Qa'ida. The Nigerian government claims that Boko Haram is "the West Africa branch of the world-wide Al-Qa'ida movement with connections with Al-Shabaab in Somalia and AQIM in Mali."

Boko Haram gets funding from bank robberies and kidnapping ransoms. Equipment captured from fleeing soldiers keeps the group constantly well-supplied. In February 2012, recently arrested officials revealed that while the organization initially relied on donations from members, its links with AQIM opened it up to funding from groups in Saudi Arabia and the UK. The group also extorts local governments. In the past, Nigerian officials have been criticized for being unable to trace much of the funding that Boko Haram has received. Boko Haram has occasionally been connected in media reports with cocaine trafficking; however, there appears to be a lack of evidence regarding its means of funding. The Nigerian military is, in the words of a former British military attaché speaking in 2014, "a shadow of what it's reputed to have once been. It's fallen apart." They are short of basic equipment, including radios and armored vehicles. Morale is said to be low.

The country's defense budget accounts for more than a third of the security budget of $5.8 billion, but only 10 percent is allocated to capital spending. In a 2014 US DOD assessment, funds are being "skimmed off the top," troops are "showing signs of real fear," and are "afraid to even engage." In July 2014, Nigeria was estimated to have had the highest number of terrorist killings in the world over the past year—3,477, killed in 146 attacks. "Boko Haram are better armed and are better motivated than our own troops. Given the present state of affairs, it is absolutely impossible for us to defeat Boko Haram," admitted an official.

An interesting comparison between Boko and ISIS was offered by author Joannis Mantzikos,[8] suggesting that while Boko voiced an informal

---

8. Ioannis Mantzikos, "Boko Haram and ISIS: The Same Coin?" in *Research on Islam and Muslims in Africa*, 3 November 2014.

support for ISIS, Abu Bakr's leadership springs directly from Zarqawi, former al-Qa'ida strongman in Iraq, while Shekau's relationship with al-Qa'ida's affiliates is rather strained. At the same time, since al-Qa'ida has supported Boko financially, the author doubts whether the group would risk alienating its informal relationship with al-Qa'ida. This is a crucial point because while ISIS has been financially self-sustaining, Boko is still dependent on outside funding. Boko also occasionally attacks Muslims, while the present head of al-Qa'ida, Zawahiri, has shown concern about that, as he has also done regarding Zarqawi previously and ISIS now. Another major difference is that al-Qa'ida has been interested in global Jihad, more than in the conquest of territory, while Boko Haram, following the model of ISIS, is more inclined to expand the territory it controls. In fact, Boko has been taking advantage of the lawlessness in neighboring countries to expand its control of the border areas of Cameroon, Niger, and Chad, despite the fact that it lacks the good training, equipment, and command and control abilities that ISIS possesses. Also, while ISIS enjoys a steady flow of volunteers from abroad, Boko relies solely on its own local human resources.

Joannis Mantzikos also identifies Boko Haram as a political insurgency, implying that ISIS is a religious rebellion, an assumption that is questionable, in view of the manifest political aspirations of Baghdadi in handling the revolution and building the Caliphate on the one hand, and the enforcement of religious puritanism in Boko-controlled territory on the other. Both organizations are similar, at any rate, in considering any non-Sunnis, including Christians and Shi'as, as infidels who must pay the *jizya* poll tax to their Muslim masters or face death or expulsion. But in Nigeria the religious conflict is mainly concentrated in the tensions between the Christian south and the Muslim north, and the treatment of the Igbos and Yorubas is made on a tribal basis, while the annihilation of the Yazidis, Westerners, and Shi'as in Iraq is done on a religious basis. If that is the case, it would be understandable why the highest Muslim authorities in the world, which represent "true and tolerant Islam," in their parlance, have condemned the abduction of three hundred female students by Boko in Nigeria, most of them Christians, some of whom were converted to Islam in their captivity.[9] In any case, Boko murderous attacks against Christian communities and colleges, and kidnappings and abuse of Christian females, have become routine in Muslim-majority northern Nigeria.

25th November 2012 was yet another bloody Sunday for church goers. Eleven people were killed when the Protestant Church of St. Andrew was attacked by two *islamikaze* terrorists. Shortly after the Mass, one of the

---

9. Memri Report, 15 May 2014.

terrorists drove a minibus loaded with explosives into the church, and after soldiers and civilians gathered in the spot, another Jihadi detonated another car bomb that caused the eleven deaths and thirty injuries, mainly among the members of the church choir. Another three Christians were ambushed when traveling to the Mass and murdered.

On 29th September 2013, Muslim terrorists dressed in Nigerian military uniforms invaded an agricultural college, shooting interns as they slept in their dorms, killing some fifty students, altogether with the attack the previous weekend in Kenya, totaling a staggering two hundred dead and hundreds more injured, mostly Christians. The day before the college attack, Muslim herdsmen in Kaduna State in Nigeria slaughtered another fifteen Christians. One day prior to that, Muslims killed a Christian pastor and his son, torched their church in Dorawa, and murdered another twenty-eight people. In effect, the murders of Christians in Nigeria have become such a routine affair as to make evident once again the banality of evil.[10]

All in all, in the two years 2012–13 alone, Boko has killed, bombed, torched, or attacked fifty churches in Nigeria, slaughtering 366 people, mostly Christians, though sometimes Muslims too are hurt as collateral damage, in these church attacks. In addition, thirty-one separate attacks were launched on Christian individuals, killing 166 persons; twenty-one attacks were focused on clerics or senior Muslims figures critical of Boko, killing at least sixty persons; and twenty-one more attacks were mounted against "un-Islamic" institutions or persons engaged in "un-Islamic behavior," killing seventy-four more people.

Concrete examples out of these impersonal statistics are horrifying: in the month of July 2013 alone, Muslim terrorists set off four bombs near three Protestant churches in Kano, killing forty-five people; at least twenty-eight people were killed in a series of explosions throughout a Christian neighborhood of Kano, when people were out to enjoy the night life of the city; thirty Christian men, women, and children were slain in three villages, and one hundred homes were torched; another village was raided a Sunday morning just before church services and six Christians were slain. And above all, the number of abducted Christian girls grew, who were held in the house of Muslim leaders until they were convinced/compelled to alter their faith. Boko had declared that it was a way to "strike fear in the hearts of Christians," a familiar quotation from the Holy Book.[11]

---

10. Ibrahim, "Nigeria: Where Jihad and Christian Persecution Run Rampant," 1 October 2013.

11. Ibid.

The violent persecution of Christians in Nigeria has had significant implications for radical Islamists in neighboring Mali, who draw inspiration from it. While Islamists in Mali have not been targeting Christians, their aggressive tactics have shaken the country to its very core.

EAST AFRICA (SOMALIA, KENYA, TANZANIA)

As to Somalia, it was thanks to the research of Nancy Kobrin—an American psychologist who did work with the émigré Somali community in the Twin Cities (St. Paul and Minneapolis), which has grown into the largest Somali community outside Somalia—that we can reconstruct some of the links between fundamentalist Muslim trends in Somalia, some of which are linked to the Yemenite and Palestinian contexts. In a specialized article in *Family Security Matters*[12] she describes several cases she dealt with that are instructive to our theme here. Somalia, a poor and chaotic Muslim country that did not settle into any pattern of rule since the end of its colonial period, which did not turn out to be its worst, has been the home of unruly tribal lawlessness and international piracy, a practically non-existent central government, and the predominance through the barrels of their guns of Muslim fundamentalist groups who naturally identify with Arab and Islamic causes and find common grounds with the Palestinians, who, like them, engage in revolution as a way of life and appear to have elected Islam as their solution. One of those groups that vie for power in the midst of the chaos is *Al-Shabaab* (the Youth), believed to be an affiliate of al-Qa'ida in East Africa, which has acquired its name in infamy since it blew up the American embassies in Dar al-Salam and Nairobi in 1998, causing hundreds of casualties, some Americans and mostly locals. President Clinton thought about a swift retaliation in Somalia, where the perpetrators had found asylum. But in view of the botched operation and the many casualties, he renounced the whole affair, and it was not until September 11, 2001, and President Bush, that the Americans would begin to take seriously and consistently the battle against world terrorism. It was with some of those affiliates that Nancy Kobrin has worked and collected data.

A young man of twenty-four, a member of *Al-Shabaab*, was re-arrested in London after having violated his ban not to trespass the Olympic Park there while wearing his court-ordered electronic tracking device. He was reportedly doing reconnaissance as a "suicide bomber" for the Olympic

---

12. Nancy Kobrin, who is also the author of *The Banality of Suicide Terrorism: The Naked Truth About the Psychology of Islamic Suicide Bombing.* https://www.facebook.com/

Games. He had tried to carry out a "suicide bombing," (which I prefer to dub *islamikaze*, the combination of Islam and *kamikaze*) against British troops in Afghanistan. He reportedly went to Somalia after that. He comes from a large family, suggesting emotional deprivation. Two more Swiss Jordanians were also found to have joined the foreign-fighter wing of *Al-Shabaab*. When charged with terrorism in Kenya, they were denied the right of extradition to Switzerland. The facility to move between nationalities and countries is what gives to these terrorist mercenaries the international aspect of their activity, just like Zarqawi in Iraq, who was Jordanian by nationality, Palestinian by birth and identity, but al-Qa'ida leader in Iraq to fight the Shi'a and the Americans until he was gunned down in a gun battle in Western Iraq; he had as mentor the Palestinian arch-terrorist Abdallah Azzam, the spiritual guide of Bin Laden. The other member, nineteen years old, also of Jordanian origin, grew up in Biel, Switzerland, and disappeared in February 2011. He was apprehended in Kenya, thus showing that neutral Switzerland has a similar problem concerning the radicalization of Islam as the other European countries, Britain, and America. Just as the Somali families of Minnesota were shocked to find out that their youth were being recruited to *Al-Shabaab*, so were the families in Biel. The Swiss authorities fear a Mohammed Merah-type incident (in Toulouse, where a Muslim terrorist attacked Jewish worshippers in 2012 and killed some of them). In Somaliland, a Portuguese man was arrested with ties to *Al-Shabaab*. This was the first time that an *Al-Shabaab* terrorist had been apprehended by the Somaliland authorities. The country has endured more than twenty years of chaos, famine, and bloodshed with virtually little functioning infrastructure. While it is true that *Al-Shabaab* has been ousted from Adgoye, a town en route to Mogadishu, Somalia still remains the number one failed state worldwide. They continue to carry out acts of piracy and kidnapping of aid workers with this criminality flowing into neighboring Kenya, as in the attack against the mall in Nairobi, which occasioned dozens of fatalities. Both types of criminal acts bring in significant revenue as well as a "warped" prestige to shame-riddled *Al-Shabaab*.

The UN reported in 2006 during the Lebanon War that there were 720 *Al-Shabaab* fighting there. While the report has been disputed, the former Israeli ambassador to the UN, Dan Gillerman, confirmed that he knew of the Somali Jihadis. One wonders now how many Somalis have been able to infiltrate Israel hiding among the Sudanese and Eritrean illegal infiltrators, who are posing as shelter seekers, making their way to Eilat, South Tel Aviv, and other destinations, where their total numbers have already amounted to tens of thousands? We hear nothing about this from the press or government. Fewer know too that the Somali extremists identify themselves as the "poor Palestinians," and the Ethiopians as their cruel occupier "Israelis." This was communicated by the last young Somali Jew born and raised in Mogadishu, who was forced to flee the country along with his mother. Somalia is now *Judenrein*. It once had a thriving Jewish community of about six thousand. The Somali Jewish community traced many of their ancestors to Yemen. In Minneapolis, which has the largest diaspora of Somalis outside of Mogadishu, it was common to see bumper stickers saying "Ethiopia get out of Somalia," reminiscent too of the Palestinian part in the Arab-Israeli conflict.

Why is it important to understand this group's identification with the Palestinians? First and foremost, Israel and Jews will continue to be targeted. Second, such hatred and relentless attacks cause an identification with the aggressor, *Al-Shabaab*, which in turn precipitate underestimating what this terrorist organization is capable of doing. Third, the West continues to fail to factor in Somali clan dynamics, the level of rage of their male youth, the hatred toward their own females, and the lack of capacity for empathy for others. Nothing will change, estimates Kobrin, until such naïveté as symbolized by placing an electronic monitor tag on such a hardened criminal, as in the case cited above, is reconsidered. Why was that suspect not in prison in the first place? The "Terrorism Prevention and Investigation Measures" undertaken by the British, while well intended, prove to be inadequate and naive. There remain many more unanswered questions as the Somali saga continues.

Whatever turn Somalian policies may take, the ideological tendency to watch is that of Seyyid Muhammad Abdullah Hassan (1864–1920), a leader and poet, who is considered the father of Somali nationalism for his inspiration of the Dervish Resistance Movement in the twenty-year Jihad (1898–1920) against European and Ethiopian expansion into his country, in particular against the administration of British Somaliland and their Somali allies. This holy war had devastated Somalia and resulted in the death on one third of northern Somalia's population and the near destruction of its economy. Already after his return from his trip to Saudi Arabia in 1895, where he had joined the fanatical sect of Muhammad Saleh, whose tenets were of a harsh and uncompromising nature, as compared with those of the Qadariyya Sufi order, which was predominant in Somalia then, he began to condemn all excessive indulgences and luxuries and exhorted the people to return to a strict path of Muslim devotion. During his contacts with Catholic missionaries and colonial officials, he became convinced that Christians sought to destroy the Islamic faith of the Somalis, and that the Somali faith could never be realized unless his nation were free, so he enjoined his people to remove the European infidels. His qualities as a poet also enhanced his reputation, so that by the turn of the century he had thousands of followers whom he termed "dervishes." His followers believed in his supernatural powers, others were attracted by the promises of the wealth to be gained by raiding the stocks of the tribes that espoused the infidels' cause.

In 1899 he declared himself a Mahdi, inspired by the model of the famous Sudanese Mahdi who acted around those years. But a combination of Italian and British offensive against him and his dervishes, forced him to withdraw to Ethiopia where he died in 1920. Today, he is still seen as one in a long line of Muslim zealots who had revolted against any foreign infidel presence or against any perceived corruption in contemporary Islam. His dervish resistance serves as an inspiration to the actions of contemporary Muslim radicals in Somalia, such as the *Ittihad Islami* (the Islamic Union), which also toes the line of the Wahhabis of Saudi Arabia, where he himself had drawn his Islamic zealotry. We can also see that the patterns of raids against collaborators with the West for the booty they gain, which the West regards as piracy, the anti-Western hatred that often explodes into violence, and the puritanical Islam that movements like *Al-Shabaab* try to impose on the entire population, are all rooted in the example and precedents set by Seyyid Muhammad Abdullah Hassan.[13]

The sudden and unexpected death of the Shabaab "Emir," Ahmed Abdi Godane, in a US airstrike at the end of 2014, which was judged to have a "great strategic significance," may also have a great impact on the movement and the fate of Islamic radicalism in East Africa. He served in his perilous position only since 2008, following his election by the Shura Council after another air strike killed his predecessor, Aden Hashi Ayro. Godane's death saw the swift election by the Shura of Ahmad Umar aby Ubaidah to that post. The present transfer of power is significant because under the departed leader *Al-Shabaab* had merged with al-Qa'ida's East African branch, thereby extending its radius of operation, for example, the twin Ugandan bombings of 2010 and the 2013 Westgate Shopping Mall in Nairobi, which had resulted in the murder of sixty-seven people. Godane had improved command and control among his followers and created a special operations directorate, which resulted in Islamikaze killings and lent more sophistication to his insurgency movement. His departure might have an effect of these new avenues of development, and only time will tell how his little-known successor might influence the course of event.[14]

In Kenya and Tanzania, apart from the horrific blast of the two American Embassies in 1998, which cost the lives of two hundred victims, and

13. See Terdman, "Islam in Africa Newsletter."
14. Solomon, "Death of a Somali Jihadi," 2014.

despite the fact that these countries maintain a clear Christian majority, the presence of so large a Muslim minority, and the close proximity to radical Muslim Somalia, necessarily link all three countries in one complex of radical Islam, led by *Al-Shabaab* of predominant-Muslim Somalia.

In Kenya, a blast at a church in November 2012, inside a police compound in the town of Garissa, killed a police officer who also officiated as the local pastor, and wounded thirteen other people. *Al-Shabaab*, who were later to take responsibility for the blast at a mall in Nairobi which claimed dozens of victims, were believed to have initiated this bombing too. It was believed that their latest strategy was to lure poor youth "from Christian background" and use them to bomb Kenya's churches. Using naïve Christian youth, who are more difficult to identify and arrest beforehand, since they blend into the local Christian congregation, has proved a deadly *Jihad* strategy indeed. In Tanzania, as of May 2012, twenty-five churches and convents have been destroyed, almost all in the semi-autonomous island of Zanzibar, whose population is overwhelmingly Muslim, and openly hostile to Christians. One of the latest incidents revolved around a Muslim boy challenging a Christian to urinate on a copy of the Qur'an, and claiming that whoever did would be transformed into an animal. After the Christian boy took up the challenge, word spread and Muslims began to riot, and demands were heard that the Christian boy ought to be beheaded, after at least five churches were destroyed, including the Seven Day Church, the Anglican Church, and the Assemblies of God Church. Since no arrests were made connected with those violent riots, Christians were asking themselves whether the local government condoned these activities.[15]

Two separate grenade attacks on churches occurred in 2012. The first was when Muslims threw grenades into an open-air Christian church gathering, killing a woman and a boy and injuring fifty other Christians. In this event, Muslims had been holding their own gathering nearby, and the Christian congregants could hear the Muslim preachers railing against Christianity right before the attack took place. In the second instance, a Muslim man, pretending to be a worshipper at a church, threw three grenades during service, killing a twenty-seven-year-old student and injuring sixteen. The terrorist, who according to eyewitnesses, appeared to be of Somali origin, "looked uncomfortable and always looked down. He threw three hand grenades and only one exploded. He took off while firing in the air three gunshots."[16]

---

15. Raymond Ibrahim, *Gatestone Institute*, 1 February 2013.
16. "Muslim Persecution of Christians," *Gatestone Institute*, 18 May 2012.

On the island of Zanzibar, a semi-autonomous Muslim part of the Tanzania, which also includes a tiny Hindu and Christian minority, things have usually been quiet due to the local secular government that wishes to encourage peace and tourism into the country. However, the presence of Wahhabi preachers and Jihad recruiters has encouraged a mounting Islamic zeal. Six bomb blasts in March 2004 have shaken the existing state of affairs and raised concerns about the radicalization of Zanzibari youth. Youth demonstrations were set against Western influence in general, coming through tourism and the appointment of a Mufti, who himself did not believe that the government should appoint candidates to that post. On 10th March, a Roman Catholic church in central Zanzibar was set ablaze, which was described by police as a deliberate act aiming at inciting religious hostilities. One week later, a petrol bomb destroyed a school bus belonging to the Catholic church while it was parked in the school's grounds, and the next day five Muslim members of a radical group were arrested as suspects. Then, on 19th March, the house of the newly-appointed Mufti was attacked with explosives. The next day a grenade was tossed into a restaurant frequented by foreign diners. It landed on the table of a British diplomat but fortunately did not explode. A Western journalist reported missionaries from Saudi Arabia, Pakistan, and Kuwait, were going from mosque to mosque spouting sermons of hatred, based on Saudi scriptures. After the sermon the missionaries began recruiting for al-Qa'ida. Sometimes they use a local to recruit the youth, in order to avoid being caught by police, being more easily identifiable if they are strangers. The preachers are paid by Saudi "charities," which provide both the preachers and their texts.[17]

On the eastern side of the continent, in Somalia, a twenty-five-year-old, Farhan Haji Mose, who had converted to Christianity, was attacked and executed by Muslims from the *Al-Shabaab* group of terrorists. A crowd had assembled on a Friday to watch the slaughter of a Muslim who had embraced Christianity. His body was split into two, then carried away, only to be dumped near the beach of Barawa city. Friends and family did not risk recovering the body immediately, fearing that the perpetrators would consider them guilty by association and kill them as well. In general, Shabaab rebels have killed dozens of Christian converts from Islam, since they had embarked on a vigorous campaign to rid Somalia of Christianity. That group sought to impose a stricter version of *Shari'a* in the country than that

---

17. "Zanzibar: Church Attacked as Islamist Zeal and Anger Rises," FreedomNews2@aol.com, 26 March 2004.

meekly enforced by the chaotic government of Mogadishu, which was so "moderate" as to mandate the death penalty for apostates.[18]

As a "sideshow" to the horrors of radical Muslims in Africa, even in the Muslim island of the Maldives, in the Indian Ocean, off the coast of the black continent, officials at the international airport seized eleven books about Christianity from a Bangladeshi expatriate, who came to the Island from Sri Lanka. He was arrested, spent twenty-three days in jail, and was then deported. According to his story, the authorities mistreated him as if he were intent on destroying their nation by bringing in Christian books. They stripped him almost naked, to verify whether he was carrying anything else. Customs and police questioned him very intensely and denied him food. On that occasion, another Christian, an American, who was accused of links with the Bangladeshi, was also arrested and deported.[19]

---

18. Raymond Ibrahim, *Gatestone Institute*, 1 February 2013.
19. Ibid.

CHAPTER THREE

Christian Minorities under Asian Islam

The prototype of Asian Islamic treatment of Christians is the Taliban regime in Kabul, which held for some five years before it was destroyed by the American incursion in 2001. The Taliban got closest to establish a durable Muslim state, which though not widely recognized, had endured for five years (1996–2001) before it was crushed by American intervention. In this kind of state in the making, the persecution of Christians was so harsh as to place Afghanistan (81/100) in the 5th place in the world ranking for persecution of Christians and the first among the Muslims of Asia, before Iran (80/100), Pakistan (79/100), Uzbekistan (69/100), Turkmenistan (63/100), and Turkey (52/100). The other Muslim-majority countries, like Indonesia (50/100), Malaysia (55/100), Azerbaijan (50/100), Bangladesh (51/100), Kazakhstan (51/100), Brunei (58/100), and Tajikistan (50/100), though they have scored high enough (over 50/100), have been much less in the sights of international attention, each for its own reasons. India, which boasts the 4th or 5th largest Muslim population in the world (some 180 million), and has scored high in the world ranking for persecution of Christians (62/100), will not be covered here due the overwhelming Hindu majority that rules India, unlike Pakistan and Bangladesh, which used to be part of the large Indian entity.

THE CHRISTIAN MISFORTUNE IN AFGHANISTAN

Afghanistan's tragedy has been that it is so divided tribally, that only aggression from the outside can unify its intrepid fighters and lead them to victory against any outsider. But the problem is that they have been eaten up by so much internal conflict for years, that it is hard to see how this unfortunate country, which is the land of the brave, can emerge into modernity, peace, and reconciliation.[1] Strictly speaking, there has been no permanent settlement in this ill-fated land of scorched earth and snowy mountain crests, but it is evident that in the past decades, since the Soviet invasion of Afghanistan on Christmas 1979, and up until now, the most successful fighters for their cause have been the Muslim Jihadists, who first fought against the Soviets and defeated them, then unified the country under the Taliban after years of civil war. But that rough and cruel regime, which wanted to enforce Islamic law without regard to any other legal or moral code, ended up allying with al-Qa'ida which challenged the US in its home, and precipitated a costly American retaliation whose outcome it is still hard to tally. Muslim triumph will certainly entitle the courageous Afghanis to their full share in their Islamic statehood, and perhaps will even enable them to claim a pioneering role in the Islamic Revolution together with their Iranian neighbor.

Afghanistan has a long history of foreign intervention, due to the centrality of its position in Central Asia, between China and India, and during the Cold War between the Soviet Superpower and the vast Muslim hinterland, part of which was under direct Soviet tutorship in the six Muslim Republics of Central Asia (Kazaskhstan, Uzbekistan, Turkemenistan, Kirgyzstan, and Tadjikistan) and the Caucasus (Azerbaijan), and half-way into her Arab allies of the Middle East. The watershed in the affairs of the Islamic world and the international arena was the Khomeini Islamic Revolution in Iran in February 1979, which was patently intended for exportation, just a few months prior to the Soviet invasion. This means that beyond all the Shi'ite-Sunnite controversies, doctrinal and political, the deep divide between tyrannical monarchies, one of which he had toppled, and revolutionary regimes like his, and the inter-Superpower differences and tensions, Khomeini was determined to bring the revolution to the doorstep of the rest of the Islamic world. The Soviets, justifiably worried lest their Central Asian Muslim states be "contaminated" by the fabulously popular Khomeini's revolution, decided to preempt by invading next-door Afghanistan and adding it to the scope of the Brezhnev Doctrine, which had automatically triggered a Soviet intervention in any "East-bloc" country which faced either internal

---

1. See Barfield, *Afghanistan: A Cultural and Political History*.

or external "aggression." The decade-long bloody history of the Soviets in the quagmire of Afghanistan, which turned into their "Vietnam," was brought to an end only when they could no longer sustain their losses in the battlefield, and instead of pre-empting an Islamic revolution coming from the outside, they in fact precipitated an Islamic revolution from within their own Muslim republics, which turned into an all-out Soviet collapse in 1989–90, of which the dishonorable retreat from Kabul was only the trigger.

It was the remarkable unity of purpose amidst tribal and ideological differences among the tribes of Afghanistan (Pashtun, Tadjik, Uzbek, Hazara), each of which was supported by another outside power, that produced victory for the Afghans. The victory was remarkably facilitated by the "stinger" shoulder air missiles, provided by the CIA, which downed an unsustainably large quantity of Soviet airplanes and helicopters, and caused such a huge euphoria among the fighters that until the Soviet withdrawal there was only feast and contentment among the *mujahedeen*, and ironically, alliance with and praise of America.

However, as soon as the Soviets left, the battle for hegemony between the various tribes and factions began raging, which turned Kabul, the capital, into rubble, with increasing numbers of intrepid fighters shooting and destroying each other in an orgy of madness. Among the fighters who had began to withdraw since the holy Jihad was terminated, were the tens of thousands of volunteers who came from all over the Muslim world, with CIA and Saudi financing, to participate in the blessings of Jihad. Battle-hardened, and sensing that they were filling a holy duty of indefinite duration, they had to return abruptly to their countries of origin (mainly Saudi Arabia, Pakistan, Egypt, Jordan, and even Chechnya), where they were dubbed the "Afghanis." One of them was Osama Bin Laden, who had left behind his riches and went to dip his hands, soul, and body in the harsh but thrilling world of Jihad. When at home he tried to turn his Jihad energies against his own corrupt government, he was evicted from his country, then deprived of his Saudi nationality and condemned to exile, first in Sudan and finally in Afghanistan and Pakistan.

It was in the killing fields of Afghanistan that Bin Laden encountered the two men who would change his life and much of world history: Abdallah Azzam, his Palestinian spiritual and religious mentor, and Mullah 'Umar, the Head of the Taliban faction, who gave him shelter in his country, after he conquered it from all the fighting factions in order to establish in it an Islamic state to his taste, based on the Taliban. *Taliban*, which mean literally students, grew in the hot houses of the thousands of *madrasas* of Pakistan, from which millions of students from all over the Islamic world graduate every year, all indoctrinated about Jihad war and the rewards that await them after they are killed (*shahid*) in battle, much in the vein that Hassan al-Banna had taught at the beginning to the twentieth-century. When their leader saw that Jihad had turned in the hands of the Afghani factions into a ruthless battle to the end, for power and dominion, he realized that his student supporters, the Taliban, who were young, fresh, enthusiastic, devoted, and impartial, would be the best suitable to unify the country behind them and rescue it from total ruin. From his base in Qandahar he launched the battle at the end of 1995, and in September 1996 he took Kabul and installed his Taliban regime.

Almost united under the Taliban, except for a northern enclave, the theocratic regime of the Taliban in Kabul enforced perhaps the most rigid and puritanical Islamic regime ever seen in the modern Islamic world, even more so than the Saudi or the Iranian systems, which inspire fear, disgust, and contempt in the West. With Mullah 'Umar at the head of the system as some sort of spiritual leader, the like of that of Iran, and enforced obscurantist politics such as: forcing people to attend prayers and lashing out at late-comers or foot-draggers, as during the times of 'Umar ibn-al-Khattab, the second Righteous Caliph (634–44), who used to prod passers-by with his whip, to join public prayers; banning women totally from the public square, including education, and when in public they were forced to wear those mobile tents that covered them from head to toe, including their faces; enforcing Islamic morality in the streets, banning music altogether; overhauling the educational system so as to eradicate non-Islamic studies and expanding the Qur'anic ones; and finally eliminating all the manifestations of non-Islamic art, which culminated in the abominable blowing up of the giant Buddha statues at Bamyan, despite all the protestations of world leaders, including some civilized and enlightened Muslims among them. Many guesses circulated in the market of ideas as to the possible longevity of such a regime, where visibly many people, certainly the women, who had been enthused by, and supportive of the Taliban while they were liberating the country and uniting it with a view of bringing peace and tranquility to it, gradually turned to resentment and bitterness when they realized the harshness and inapplicability in the twenty-first century of such medieval concepts.

Backward Afghanistan, which had begun during the five years of Taliban rule to re-Islamize its society, did not abstain from meddling also in international, especially Islamic, affairs. Inter alia, it gave shelter and a base of action to Osama Bin Ladin and his entourage, and permitted him to build training camps in its territory, when it recognized the value of his work for the cause of Islam and against the West. Bin Laden, who had been evicted from his native Saudi Arabia for his subversive activities against the monarchy, found refuge in Omar Bashir's and Hassan Turabi's Sudan where he based his terrorist activities, trained terrorists, and spent large parts of his personal fortune for both world terrorism and local development. When hounded by the US there, and following several American retaliatory acts that Khartoum could not sustain, he was compelled to depart, and his choice fell, naturally, on newly constituted Taliban Afghanistan, where he found a very supportive leadership to his cause, and ideal ground conditions (mountains and deserts for hideouts and inaccessibility). One has to admit that Bin Laden made a great use of the terrain for his purposes, and launched world terrorist activities that had much resonance, like the bombings of the two American Embassies in East Africa in 1998, and the attack against the *USS Cole* in 2000, sending out the message that the USA and the world were in for a new era of terror, which the Clinton Administration had underestimated, and in any case proved inadequate to resist and to counter-attack.

Encouraged by his invincibility and the cover he was given by Mullah Omar, Bin Ladin had the daring to plan leisurely from his base in Afghanistan the September 11 attacks against New York and Washington, as President Bush was still a novice in world affairs. The disastrous consequences prompted Bush to prepare for a large-scale retaliation, not before he attempted to persuade the Taliban government to extradite the chief perpetrator to American justice. 'Omar's loyalty and courage, as he defied the US and stood by his protégé, were truly remarkable and could only be the fruit of a deep religious faith in the cause, whereupon America reacted massively and with determination, so that in a matter of weeks almost all Afghanistan, including 'Omar's stronghold in Qandahar, were in American hands, and the Taliban regime collapsed. It was relatively easy to conquer the country and to install the illegitimate, unpopular, and corrupt government of Hamid Karzai, hand-picked by the Americans, to rule the country, but he was not any better or more accepted than Mubarak in Egypt or the Shah in Iran.

The Afghani history of contemporary times is marked by the Americans, with a symbolic and reluctant participation of NATO, attempting for a dozen years to reinforce Karzai's regime, strengthen the national forces of the country to stand on their own, and help build, as in Iraq, a civil society base that can sustain some sort of stability and participatory order, if not a total democracy, when the Americans left in 2014. However, since the date of Western withdrawal was announced, the Taliban went back to control much of the countryside, in the face of the Western weakening grip (both ideological and physical) on the land. Sometimes, Karzai seemed to control not much territory beyond Kabul, and often even the capital was shaken by explosions of terror triggered by his many enemies and rivals. It seemed that, like elsewhere, the Islamic fundamentalist alternative was building confidently and patiently for the long run, and that the West, which is tired of more than a decade of unpopular war at home, might be the first to blink.

Worse, as we learn from some experts, the economic prospects for Afghanistan, on which hinges the entire plan for the country's rehabilitation after the war (if it ever ends after a few consecutive decades), were not very bright either. Ahmed Rashid and Alexis Crow[2] have claimed on that the projected foreign aid, designed to redress the country and its economy, will simply not be sufficient. They say that as of July 2012, seventy nations and institutions pledged $16 billion for Afghanistan's development over the next four years. Sadly, the money is likely to be wasted, just as the vast sums already invested since the US-led intervention have made little progress in creating a self-sustaining Afghan economy. After Western forces depart, Afghanistan will be a fragile state, threatened by the Taliban and other warlords and unable to create jobs. During the Western presence (which they term "occupation"), Western governments and development agencies have failed to invest enough in local people to enable them to earn lasting livelihoods. The result is that what has emerged in Afghanistan is an inefficient system that fails to motivate or educate local people in economic development, but reinforces dependence on foreign aid. Two-thirds of the population are under twenty-five and there will be no jobs for most of them once servicing foreign troops comes to an end. The government has never had the capacity to produce jobs, while the private sector is too small and has not been encouraged sufficiently to do so. Yet, only by enabling local people to share in their own profit can stability and growth last, while as happens all too often in the developing world, there is a tension between the foreign ownership of many projects and public services, and Afghans' desire to design and implement such projects themselves. But Western institutional aid has such difficult monitoring and accounting rules that most Afghans cannot benefit from it. Western state-driven development agencies are ill equipped for encouraging the local private sector.

The UN diplomat Lakhdar Brahimi, who later got involved in Syria, tried to forge a new way of negotiating in Afghanistan during the creation of a new government after the US invasion in 2001. He assembled a group of civilian scholars and journalists who knew the region far better than diplomats. They formed a core advisory group that declined to treat any side as loser or victor, and approached peacemaking as locals would. The group worked with Afghans from all social sectors to create both political and

---

2. http://www.ft.com/intl/cms/s/0/f5508056-da2f-11e00144feab49a.html#axzz228uvUSU6. 30 July 2012.

economic incentives for all groups to back peace negotiations. Mr. Brahimi regretted being unable to include the Taliban then. To negotiate with the Taliban now, the US needs a similar team of civilian experts, perhaps led by a US official. Peace will come only, argue the authors, by mobilizing all sectors of society for national reconciliation. Stability and growth will follow only by enabling local people to share the profits and by encouraging private sector solutions. Two years before NATO withdrew from Afghanistan, it was still not too late for the US to change strategy—but throwing billions of dollars of aid at the problem was not the answer.

Compared to the disunity and chaos that prevailed before, the Taliban regime brought a relief to many Afghanis; though for others it constituted an unbearable entity of repression and backwardness. Left to itself, with its enforced *Shari'a* law, the executions of violators of the law, the strict alienation of their women from any open social activity, and the prohibition of music, dance, and any sort of entertainment, they would have lasted much longer, exactly as their counterparts in Saudi Arabia have endured. But in view of the massive American incursion in December 2001, in retaliation for September 11, which precisely targeted the regime that had given shelter to Bin Laden, the terrorist behind the horrors of the Pentagon and the Twin Towers, the rule of Mullah Omar collapsed. But there is no telling what the future of the regime will be, if one takes into account the flimsy "democracy" the US has established upon departing and the Taliban forces that are waiting in the aisles for the opportunity to step in again and revive their Islamic radical state where persecution of Christians will be the mainstay of their policy. At any rate, the Taliban regime has become a model among Muslim radicals for enforcing an Islamic rule amidst war and controversy, and it is regarded as so exemplary that they blame the US for interfering militarily to destroy it, calling for an easy parallel to the ISIS, which is also a state in the making, where America is deeply involved in its demise.

A case in point, regarding the persecution of Christians was reported in 2006 by the *New York Times*,[3] about a case of an Afghani who converted to Christianity during the American presence there. Abdul Rahman, forty-one years had in fact converted to the Evangelical Protestant faith. However, according to the *Shari'a* law, apostates from the Islamic faith faced death penalty in the *Shari'a* court of Kabul. The court officials and the defendant had counted on "mental illness" (why else would a happy Muslims convert?) although the prosecutors vowed to pursue the trial of this new apostate from Islam to Christianity. This case was considered a great challenge to the

---

3. Munadi, "Afghan Case against Christian Convert Falters." *The New York Times*, 26 March 2006.

Afghan government because it symbolized the tension between the appearances of democracy and liberal reforms that Karzai was trying to display to the world, and the Islamic *Shari'a* laws in this Muslim-dominated country. The American Bush administration pushed President Hamid Karzai to resolve the case, but he resisted, citing "separation of executive and judicial powers." (It was convenient to invoke democracy when expedient.) The relatives of the defendant, namely his daughter and cousin, told the court that he suffered from mental illness; that he had been travelling to Europe, in Greece, Belgium, and Germany, and that if he acquired a foreign European nationality, this could help him to avoid the death penalty in Kabul. In the court the defendant claimed that he had converted to Christianity fifteen years earlier, and that the contradiction is between Islam and democracy and could be solved by the Afghan criminal code, which did not specifically forbid or prevent the conversion to Christianity of Afghan Muslim citizens. However, since according to Islamic laws, apostasy was the biggest crime and sin, and a real threat to Islam's existence, it is punishable by death. President Bush finally intervened, and calling upon the Afghan officials "to honor the universal principle of freedom," so the court allowed Abdul Rahman to leave Afghanistan after the Afghan President, who was completely dependent on the Americans for his survival at his post, expressed his intention to allow him to escape the death penalty.

An important offshoot of the Afghanistan experiment in Muslim statehood is the universal "Afghani" movement of volunteers, which again reminds us very much of the hordes of young Muslims from all over the globe, who are flocking to the killing fields of Syria and Iraq to fight for ISIS. Indeed, following the war in Afghanistan, where tens of thousands of young Muslim volunteers helped decide the war against the Soviets, most of those battle-hardened Jihad fighters, including Bin Laden, returned to their countries where they became troublemakers and security risks. That pool of fighters, which included also Muslim youth who reside in Western countries, has found its way to other foci of conflict where Muslims took part, like Palestine, Kashmir, Bosnia, Chechniya, the Syrian civil war, and now ISIS.

An open letter from the Afghani Christian community, passionately and desperately pleading for help, was issued by the exiled Christian Afghans in India, in response to a recent wave of arrests, torture, and imprisonment of Christians in Afghanistan, after an Afghani member of Parliament had called for Afghani Christians to be executed publicly, so bad the campaign of hatred against them had turned.[4]

4. "An Open Letter from the Afghan Christian Community: An Urgent Plea for

That letter lists a long litany of complaints by the desperate Christians of Afghanistan, many of them exiles in other lands. Maybe it is not so ironic if we remember that those waiting in the aisles to take over violently after the Westerners depart, cannot wait to get rid of the Westerners who have barred their way to absolute rule of the country, and of their Christian allies at home. Already, the new "constitution" that was adopted while Westerners were present, speaks of the *Sharia* as the basis for law. If so, that law would permit the authorities to kill infidels and apostates. Thus, even if constitutions in the Islamic world, given as it is to the whim of transient rulers, are not the rock-solid documents we know in the West, any Muslim takeover will necessitate a reversion to the real constitution, the Qur'an, and to the supreme Sovereign, Allah.

The letter addresses events following an inflammatory showing of photos and videos of "secret Afghan Christian converts," aired on *Noorin TV*, an independent station based in Kabul. That broadcast was incendiary, because the country considers itself 100 percent Muslim, and any harm to that self-image provokes subterranean streams of hatred and xenophobia, that were crystallized and hardened by forty years of civil wars and foreign invasions.[5]

After those broadcasts, no incitement was needed to kindle the explosions of hatred and calls of vengeance against Christians. According to an online report of the Associated Press on 1st June 2010, Abdul Sattar Khawasi, Deputy Speaker of the Afghani Parliament, called for the execution of the Christian converts, claiming that the Afghans who appeared on the broadcast video should be executed in public, and that the House should order the Attorney General and the Intelligence Agency to arrest those Afghans and execute them. On another occasion, Qazi Nazir Ahmed, a lawmaker from Heart, declared that killing a Muslim who converts to Christianity was "not a crime." Waheed Omar, the spokesman for the president, told reporters that President Karzai was personally taking interest in the case and had ordered his Home Minister and the Head of the national Spy Agency to conduct a full investigation and to take immediate action to prevent recurrence of that phenomenon. Other reports from the hinterland of the country attest to many arrests and frequent searches of homes and businesses, as well as to claims of torture by those under arrest, in an effort to extract from them the names of other Afghans Christian converts and the location of secret Christian churches and underground fellowships in the country.[6]

Help," markdurie.com blog, June 17, 2010.

5. Ibid.
6. Ibid.

The 150-member Christian Afghan community of New Delhi, also wrote about its torments while seeking refuge in India. They said that they left their country due to death sentences on account of the conversion to Christianity, for Afghanistan is a formally all-Muslim country where Christians are considered pagans and criminals, conversion is a crime, and infidels are sentenced to death. They feared that since all state organs in Afghanistan had made incendiary statements against Christians, as evidenced in that video, and Christian organizations and NGOs had to dissolve, and even student organizations have protested against Christianity, things have grown worse. Mr. Mujajdi, the Chairman of the Afghan Senate, has said that the government did not take serious enough action, therefore he and other leaders will call on the Afghan people directly to kill Christians. The Afghan home Minister told Parliament that four Christian individuals and one family were arrested and are under investigation, thirteen NGOs have been suspended, and Afghani Intelligence has been trying to arrest all listed Christians in the country. Two church organizations, by the acronyms ACA and NCA, have been closed down. Even the relatives and families of the converts, who remained Muslim, are being arrested and investigated, to account for their deviant family members. The letter writers could not understand how the Christian world which was fighting for a tyrannical regime in order to help it reach freedom and democracy, and prevent it from falling again into the arms of the Taliban, could keep silent while watching helplessly their coreligionists in Afghanistan being murdered, arrested, persecuted, and discriminated against.

THE CHRISTIAN PLIGHT IN IRAN AND PAKISTAN

Iran and Pakistan come right after Afghanistan and Sudan in the Islamic persecution of Christians, and they are listed 7 and 8 in the World Watch list, with rankings of 80/100 and 79/100 respectively. Iran, due to its Shi'ite regime, which is like the Sunnite in its fanaticism, only more so, has oppressed and extirpated Christianity and other minorities like the Baha'is from its midst, while in Pakistan, where Christianity had come much later, the few Pakistani converts into Christianity have known much persecution and misery. According to he Gatestone Institute's report by Raymond Ibrahim,[7] Pakistan's authorities have been mercilessly enforcing their "blasphemy laws," especially on non-Muslims. Aasiya Noreen, or "Asia Bibi," a fifty-year-old Christian woman and mother of five, has been on death row

7.. Ibrahim, "Islamist 'Justice': Slow Painful Death for Christian Mother in Pakistan," in *Muslim Persecution of Christians*, 26 July 2015.

for six years for allegedly insulting Muhammad, an "offense" that nowhere in the civilized world deserves capital punishment. The frightening prospects in these two countries are generated by the nuclear capacities of these two champions of the "Islamic bomb," who due to their destructive capacities are much more unlikely to be pressured, threatened, or called to order, if and when the West finally wakes up from its torpor and decides to put more value on human life and freedom of conscience, than on commercial and diplomatic interest. And so the lives of the half a million Christians in Iran (mostly Armenian and Assyrian) will be kept in suspense, even though the *Shari'a* law of dhimmitude protects them as long as they are subordinates of the Islamic state. In Pakistan, the tiny Christian minority is constantly threatened by the blasphemy law, which had already led to the murder or incarceration of some Muslim government officials and some Christians, or to their execution.[8]

In Iran, the printing of Christian literature is illegal. Converts from Islam—who are heretics (*murtaddun*) in the eyes of Muslims—are punished by death, while Muslims will usually parrot that for Islam "there is no compulsion in religion." Christians are not allowed to testify in an Islamic court when the case involves a Muslim, and they are discriminated against in employment. A 1992 UN report cited cases of imprisonment and torture of Muslims who converted into Christianity, and of Assyrian and Armenian pastors, the dissolution of the Iranian Biblical Society, the closure of Christian libraries, and the confiscation of Christian books, including 20,000 copies of the New Testament in Persian language.[9]

British Christian legislators expressed concern about the serious and growing persecution of Iranian Christians, and said that at least a dozen of them remained incarcerated while the crackdown against Christian converts continued. Britain's All-Party Parliamentary Group (APPG) said the British government should pressure Iran to "uphold the fundamental right of religious freedom for all Iranian people," and urged the release of imprisoned Christians, including Pastor Farshid Fat'hi, who has been held in the infamous Evin jail since December 2010.[10] But, as Britain, together with the other 5+1 powers caved in and signed the controversial nuclear agreement with Iran in July 2015, there seems to be no reason for the Iranians to yield to any Western pressure. Furthermore, Britain has rushed to reestablish diplomatic relations with Iran, and Foreign Secretary Hammond was at hand in Tehran on 23 August 2015 to re-hoist the desecrated British flag, which

---

8. Sanders, "Time for a Christian Mobilization," 2015.
9. Bat Ye'or, *Islam and Dhimmitude: Where Civilizations Collide*, 41.
10. Ibrahim, *Gatestone Institute Report*, 1 February 2013.

had been burned by Iranian mobs four years earlier, in a disgraceful show of obsequiously electing trade over principles. This time, the nuclear deal with Iran was compared to Munich 1938, but it seems to be even worse. In 1938, at least Hitler pledged to those naïve believers in peace, which included again Britain and France, that if the Sudeten land was yielded to him, peace will prevail in Europe, and they cringingly believed him. Now, Iran is pledging openly never to yield to anyone on her aggressive policy of destroying Israel and supporting her allies in the Middle East: Syria, Hizbullah, and Yemen, against Western interests, but the naïve and fawning Western signatories refuse to believe in Khamena'i's stated murderous intentions! Or worse, in their manifestation of their cringing *dhimmi* spirit, they submit to the contempt Iran is showing them, and instead of resisting it and standing up to it, they prefer to pretend that it only means well. He spits to their face and they prefer to pretend it is raining.

In Pakistan, a Christian pastor, Karama Patras, was arrested after a Muslim crowd assaulted his home, accusing him of committing blasphemy. When blasphemy, which is punishable by death, is applied domestically against Muslims who have reneged on their faith, one could say that as much as it is inhuman for a faith that declares in its Holy Scripture that "there is no compulsion in religion," it is the business of the Islamic countries themselves to rule themselves as they choose, exactly as it is vain to protest against the Saudi verdicts of severing limbs for theft or stoning convicts of "adultery." But Muslims are so unsure of their faith and perhaps so embarrassed to enforce its inhuman punishments on their own nationals, that they have been universalizing their *Shari'a* and seeking to enforce it on foreigners too. The result is that while Buddhism, Christianity, Judaism, and other creeds hold only their faithful responsible for the implementation of their laws, and none of them would persecute anyone who desecrates Jesus, Moses, or Buddha, diffident Muslims are demanding that disrespecting Islam or its Prophet, much more so defecting to another creed, should be universally criminalized and punished accordingly. That approach has caused "heresy" or "blasphemy" to be recognized as capital offenses in many Islamic lands, thus exposing Christians and other minorities to prosecution and death penalty.

Christians are constantly harassed in the streets of Pakistani cities by Muslim youth and are often indicted for "blasphemous" violations of the local law. According to a Fox News report, that anti-Christian persecution is often exacerbated by anti-Americanism. For example, Christians are targeted for persecution due to the American drone attacks on Islamic militants hiding on the border with Afghanistan. Christians account for only 1 percent of the 170 million population, but whenever a clash with America occurs, they watch the blame thrown at them, under the pretext that they "belong to America," since Muslim tradition holds that "all infidels are one religion." In a process of displaced aggression current in the Muslim world, Muslims everywhere believe they avenge themselves on the strong infidel they fail to challenge directly by attacking the weak infidel, like the Christian minorities living (if one could call that life) under Islam. For example, when years back Pope Benedict XVI made a speech that seemed unflattering to Islam, Muslim anti-Christian riots erupted, churches were torched, and a nun was murdered in Somalia. Some time later, when an American fringe pastor burned a Qur'an in Florida, dozen of UN aid workers, who were assisting unfortunate Muslims, were murdered in Afghanistan, some of them beheaded. These eruptions of violence throughout the Muslim world, once again brings to bear the clear Muslim priority they attach to slights to their "honor" over human lives, as if they were not certain of their faith, and stood ready at any time to react violently to anyone who dared to voice slurs against it, as in the cases of the Cartoon Crisis in 2006, the *Charlie Hebdo* in Paris in 2014, the Rushdie Affair in 1989, or the many executions of Muslim "apostates" who had dared to quit the "Faith of Allah."[11] Only Muslims are allowed denigrate others' creeds with impunity.

Two incidents of "blasphemy" charges occurred in Pakistan in early 2012. In the first instance, a Christian man was arrested and charged with blasphemy for rescuing his eight-year-old nephew from a beating at the hands of Muslim boys who sought to force the boy to convert to Islam. Watching the attack from a distance, his uncle rushed to the scene, rescued his nephew, and then went to his work as a painter. Soon after the incident, a Muslim mob of about fifty people, led by the village prayer leader, besieged the house of the uncle, demanding that the "blasphemer" be turned over to them. He was jailed, but eventually released after being threatened and harassed by jail inmates and prison wardens. In the second instance, the twenty-six-year-old mother of a newborn baby was jailed for a month, but after the authorities failed to provide a charge sheet within the mandatory fourteen days, in spite of her being accused by her neighbors of "uttering remarks against Muhammad," she was released.

In neighboring Iran, historical Christian monuments, including churches and Christian cemeteries, continue to be destroyed or allowed to fall into decay, as the Islamic authorities try to wipe out the country's Christian heritage. "It seems that the Islamic Republic Officials, unsuccessful in stopping the growth of Christianity among the people by pressuring them, arresting them, and banning Christian converts from attending church

---

11. Ibrahim, "Islam's Christian Scapegoats," *FrontPageMagazine*, 29 April 2011.

services, want to destroy historical Christian monuments in order to totally wipe their heritage from the face of Iran," says the report.[12]

Asia Bibi, a mother of six in the Punjab, was on Christmas 2011 one of a dozen Christians awaiting appeal of execution under Pakistan's blasphemy laws. On that day, after a year in jail, where she was not able to see her children and husband, because she was held in isolation, and was not allowed to bathe for two months, she could no longer even stand unsupported. Punjab Governor, Salman Taseer, had been assassinated the January before, and the Federal Minister of Minorities, Shahbaz Bhatti, was killed the previous March for defending Asia Bibi and criticizing their country's blasphemy laws. Pakistan is supposed to have a constitution that guarantees religious freedom, but murders, discrimination, and violent harassment of its small Christian minority persist. Any individual dispute with a Muslim, usually over land ownership, can grow into an inter-communal religious confrontation. In these rifts, Christians are often accused of blasphemy, a serious offense carrying capital punishment, and every angry exchange of words between the rival parties can always produce enough Muslim "witnesses" who would swear in court that they heard the unfortunate Christians insult the Prophet, Islam, or their Holy Scriptures, in which case the Christian's fate is sealed. The ease with which blasphemy charges are made to stick has led to a spate of malicious complaints, motivated by personal rivalry and greed, especially for the Christians' land. On many occasions, charged Christians were murdered before their cases reached the courts.[13]

Pastor Youcef Nadarkhani marked his thousandth day of incarceration in Lakan, the notorious prison in northern Iran, in July 2012. He was charged with the crime of "apostasy," which may cost him his life, for refusing to renege the Christian faith that he had embraced as a child. His many supporters, who crowd Twitter and other social media, have been trying to alert the world to his plight, for he symbolizes the emergency that church leaders say is facing 100 million Christians around the world.[14] This is a blatant example of the indifference within the Christian world toward the fate of Christian minorities in Islamdom, while in Europe itself people speak bitterly about "formerly Christian" Europe, which is so preoccupied with bowing to secularism that it avoids any expression of recognition of Christianity in general, and any manifestation of sympathy towards suffering Christian minorities in the world. Conversely, the lands of Islam, as well

12. Ibrahim, "Muslim Persecution of Christians, April, 2012," *Gatestone Institute*, 18 May 2012.

13. Trifkovic, "A Grim Christmas," 2011.

14. Cohen and Roderick, "The Religious Silence on Christian Persecution," *The Wall Street Journal*, 30 July 2012.

as Muslim minorities in the West, take their religion very seriously, so much so that Muslims—watching their mosques fill to capacity on Fridays while churches in Paris, London, and Amsterdam are depleted of worshippers on Sundays—have come to believe, and they declare openly, that Islam has become the religion of the future, while dwindling Christianity is doomed to disappear. It is only natural, then, that while the Muslim core takes an increasing interest in the Muslim minorities in the world, sustains them, reinforces them, and strengthens them economically and culturally, Christendom remains silent when their coreligionist minorities in Islamdom are crushed under oppression, discrimination, and murder.

According to Christian Freedom International,[15] the Christian minority in Pakistan is in danger of extinction, like the other Christian minorities in the Arab World and the Middle East. In fact, Christian persecution in Pakistan is growing and the Muslim-Christian tensions and problems are soaring in this country due to the imposed Islamic Shari'a laws, which have engendered reports on several anti-Christian attacks on girls, churches, and other Christian Pakistani believers as well. The Islamization of Pakistan and the increased persecution of Pakistani Christians are a real threat to Christianity. It is expressed, for instance, by the forced conversion to Islam of women who were kidnapped and were forced to marry Muslim Pakistani men, while the Pakistani Christian community is not protected by law. There were 700 girls that were abducted from their Pakistani Christian families in recent years who were forced to convert to Islam; and once converted, these Christian women *cannot* renege, even though they were *forced* to convert, because according to the *Shari'a*, an apostate is exposed to death sentence.

In Pakistan, there is even an Islamist militant terrorist group called *Lashkar e-Tayiba* that is collaborating with the authorities for Christian Persecution. It is responsible for the Christian threat of extinction and annihilation in the coming years, as more and more Pakistani Christians are fleeing to the West, and especially to Europe and America.

Christian persecution, or Christianophobia, in this Muslim-majority non-Arab country, is also characterized by rape and sexual harassment, as Mr. Jonathan Racho of the International Christian Concern claims: "rape has been used as a weapon of persecution against Christian girls in Pakistan, where Christians are treated as third-class citizens. In this Muslim-majority country, Christian girls are particularly vulnerable to these types of crimes because Muslim authorities are reluctant to protect them when their rights are being violated by Muslims." Moreover, according to Mr. Nazir Bhati, a

---

15. http://www.christianfreedom.org/the-christian-winter/persecution-in-pakistan.

Pakistani Christian that is a President of the Pakistani Christian Congress, most rape and sexual harassment cases in Pakistan are perpetrated against Christian Pakistani women.

Although nearby India is not a Muslim-majority country, it is worthwhile to consider its Christian minority, both because it shelters Christian converts from Pakistan and Afghanistan, and because of the immense Muslim minority of over 150 million, which in itself constitutes a threat on the much smaller and more vulnerable Christian minority. According to a Jose Kavi report,[16] though India's Hindu culture coexists with minorities such as the Sikh, the Buddhists, and the Brahmanis, the Christians are often singled out as the most suffering of persecution, maybe due to their small numbers compared to others, and to the suspicions of their identification with colonial times where all Indians were under the British boot. In this news report of the *National Catholic Reporter* newspaper, it is explained how attackers of an Indian Catholic church broke the Image, the Catholic Icon, in disregard of the sentiment of the Christian community. Fr. Eugene Moon Lazarus, the Priest of St. Mary's Church in Agra, a city in Uttar Pradesh state, which is famous for the Taj Mahal, claims that such anti-Christian incidents frequently occurr and are reported. For example, in April 2015, when a seventy-year-old Catholic nun was gang-raped and her monastery looted in Ranaghat town in Bengal State. Before these incidents were reported, five churches and a convent school were targeted in New Delhi, the Indian capital city. The first incident was a mysterious fire on the St. Sebastian Church that occurred in Dilshad Garden, an eastern suburb. A statement from the Catholic Bishops Conference of India, following the attack on Agra, argued that it was no "mere act of Vandalism, but well planned dastardly acts, aimed at deeply wounding the religious sentiments of Christians, and creating a feeling of insecurity among the minorities." The attackers, the bishops said, had intended to inflict "maximum shame and disgrace" on Christians. Thus, the bishops demanded swift action against the culprits. In India, Christianophobic acts against the Christian minority are usually committed by Muslims, so it was not a surprise that in that same week the Indian police arrested three suspicious Muslims for attacking the Agra Catholic Church in the name of Allah. These three assailants argued that they had attacked the church because of a romantic relationship between a Muslim man and a Christian Catholic girl. Those arrested in the nun's gang rape case were also Indian Muslims, but that caused some Christian leaders to say that the incident was carried out by Hindu radical groups attempting to pit India's two

---

16. Kavi. "India's Minority Christians Struggle against Violence and Persecution." *National Catholic Reporter*, 29 May 2015.

prominent religious minority groups (Muslims and Christians) against each other by blaming Muslims. According to John Dayal, a Catholic lay leader and former member of the prime minister's National Advisory Council, the police seemed to take special care not to identify any Hindu as a suspect. That means that beyond the inter-communal bigotry that these incidents involve, one has also to take into account the politicking and intrigues that hide behind these events.

Moving back to Iran: in 2005, an Iranian convert to Christianity was kidnapped from his home in the Northeast and stabbed to death. The murderers who took him tossed his bleeding body in front of his home a few hours later, a stark warning to others who would dare to follow his way. Within hours of the murder on 22nd November, secret police officers arrived to the murdered pastor's home, searching for Bibles and other banned Christian books that he had been distributing in Persian translations. News of the murder was broadcast by *Compass Direct*, an organ of persecuted Christians around the world, while no print or broadcast medium in the US even bothered to report it, despite the fact that Iranian security services had arrested and tortured other Christians in other cities, including Tehran the capital. Those officials also visited the homes of well-known Christian leaders and warned them to inform their flock in "secret houses of prayer" that they will be next when their turn comes. It was noted then that the murdered Protestant pastor was the fifth in the preceding eleven years, three of them having been former Muslims, thus deserving of death for "apostasy." A few days earlier, radical President Ahmadinejad, had called upon the thirty provincial governors of the country to crack down on the burgeoning movement of "house churches" across the country. Nina Nevisa, another convert from Islam, had been forced in the 1980s to flee Iran after members of her house church were arrested, tortured, and executed. She had fled to Virginia in the US.[17]

THE MALAY WORLD

The Malay world, which consists mainly of Indonesia, the largest Islamic country in the world, with over 200 million believers, but also of Malaysia and Muslim minorities in the Philippines and South-East Asia, like Thailand and Myanmar, has a reputation of tolerance and moderation, due to the long tradition of pluralism in those societies. Nonetheless, alarming reports of anti-Christian riots and persecution, and even acts of killing against foreign tourists who come to Bali and other tourist sites from Christian countries,

17. Timmerman "Iran's Christians Have a High Price to Pay," 2005.

indicate that the rise of Muslim radicalism there has also been affected by what is going on in the rest of Islamdom. Particularly noteworthy is the flow of boat people by droves, who try to make their way to wealthy and prosperous Australia, but are very often turned back, raising discontent against the reluctant country of shelter, much as the Muslims of the Middle East and Africa are unhappy with the countries of southern Europe and Israel, which turn many of them back and frustrate their dream to find a new life in new host countries.

In Indonesia, the local authorities in Java, the main island of the archipelago, have sealed the worship building of a Christian congregation, which had been meeting there for twenty years, after prominent Muslims had withdrawn their signatures approving that church's existence. According to the *Shari'a* law, which is applicable in Indonesia, sixty Muslim signatures are needed to approve the existence of a church. Other churches in west Java have faced loud demonstrations from Muslims who want to close them down. In one case, hundreds of Indonesians gathered under an Islamic banner and surrounded two separate churches, threatening the use of force if those Christian congregations continued to build new structures in their compounds, but two hundred policeman and military held them at bay. As a "sideshow" on the island of Mindanao, one of Muslim-majority islands in the Philippines, a Christian student and his Muslim girlfriend were shot by two motorcycle assassins. The twenty-one-year-old man died and the woman was in a serious condition. Police were investigating whether the ambush was connected to the personal relationship of the couple, as if there were any doubt about the traditional hostility in this Islamic land, which viewed the relations of a Muslim woman with a Christian man as an act of supreme sin (*haram*). It was considered even an act of "treason," while the reverse was considered "normal," since any non-Muslim female who married a Muslim man was *ipso facto* considered a Muslim convert in that patriarchal system.[18]

In the northern tip of Sumatra, one the main islands in the Indonesian archipelago, is located Banda Aceh, one of the most virulent bastions of radical Islam in Indonesia. The old wooden building of a Protestant church dating back to the first half of the twentieth-century, near Simpang Lima, was burned down in 1990, and the congregation sought permission to rebuild another in its place, which is no easy task in Islamic Aceh, pending which the worshippers met in sub-standard conditions in a garage. Ten years later, an agreement was signed by Christians in southern Aceh to destroy some of their old places of worship, while other makeshift temporary places were

18. Ibid.

permitted to function as "a sign of Islamic tolerance." The agreement rested, according to its wording, "with all sincerity and a sense of brotherhood, on the atmosphere of living in harmony between the religious communities." In a larger context, in all the Muslim Shari'a-compliant countries, Christians have great difficulties to obtain permission to build or renovate churches, and can face violent reprisals if they are caught building without a permit. In Egypt, building a church requires presidential approval. In Saudi Arabia, despite the presence of thousands of Christian foreign workers, no place of worship is permitted to exist at all. The root of this intolerance is the laws of dhimmitude that are applied on all territories conquered by Islam, and which specify that Christians (and Jews) must accept that limitation. This contrasts with the freedoms enjoyed by Muslims in Western nations, where mosques have been springing up in the thousands.[19]

In 2006, seven suspected Islamic terrorists confessed to beheading three Christian schoolgirls on Sulawesi Island in Indonesia. The seven detained suspects admitted that they planned and carried out these October beheadings in the town of Poso, according to Colonel Rudi in a statement to the Associated Press, while another girl was wounded and spared by the killers. Two of the suspects were found to have ties to Noordin Top, the key leader of the al-Qa'ida-affiliated *Jemaah Islamiya*, according to the Chief of Sulawesi police, General Oegroseno. The suspects are only a few of the scores of Islamic militants linked to this group, who have been arrested in the beginning years of the 2000s, following the Bali bombings of 2002, which were directed against Western tourists, or were perhaps a domestic affair aimed at hurting government income from foreign tourism. The worldwide publicity accorded to these unfortunate events, especially when the Bali killers were arrested and prosecuted, has raised much apologetic and sarcastic response from world Jihadi groups. One of them wrote:

> These benighted misunderstanders of Islam were evidently foolish enough to think that when the Qur'an says "strike the necks of Unbelievers,"[20] that it actually means "strike the necks" of the Unbelievers. The fools! They have probably been listening to Islamophobic rhetoric, or watching *United 33*! Don't they realize that the Qur'an is a document of staggering complexity, and that it can only be properly understood by Saudi-funded American professors who spend years in concentrated study, enabling them to determine that "strike the necks" actually means "hug the necks"? You have to read it in the original Arabic, you see

19. Durie "Church Construction and the Dhimma Pact: The Case of the Diocese of Maghagha and Edwah," Mark Durie's Blog, 30 July 2010.

20. Sura 47:4; and Sura 8:12.

and use your secret Arabic decoder ring, which likewise renders "beat her,"[21] as "tell her how much you love her."[22]

In Indonesia, which is reputed for its tolerance (though there were occasional eruptions of violence against Christians, especially in the island of Ambon), specialists of Malay Islam, like Ran Shauli and Giora Eliraz,[23] believe that the Bali bombings had nothing to do with Christianophobia of the kind found in the rest of Islamdom. Unlike human rights fighters, such as Mark Durie and Raymond Ibrahim, who cite these events as part of the worldwide oppression of Christians by Islam, they cling to dissident views, which regard these eruptions as socio-political clashes that are devoid of any religious connotations. Even the severe cases of church burning in Ambon in the Moluccas in the 2000s—which were sometimes interpreted against the background of the East Timor's war of independence against Indonesia[24]—were dismissed by theses dissident voices as problems of social struggles between rival classes. However, these novel interpretations seem to be contradicted by the acts of terror against Christian tourists, which culminated in Bali, where two hundred foreign tourists, half of them Australian, were slain by Muslim extremists, who were later put to trial and convicted. But it is also understandable that some observers may comment on those violent horrors as mere manifestations of xenophobia, or demonstrations against the laxity in the conduct of these visitors, who just happen to be mostly Christian, something similar to developments in Tunisia in the aftermath of the Arab Spring, as regards attacks against European tourists by radical Islamic groups.

In 1998–2007 violent riots occurred in Sulawesi, which were given an Islamic-Christian interpretation, and which—in view of the shifting demographic imbalance between the majority of Muslims in the south and in the archipelago as a whole, and the quickly dwindling Christian predominance in the north of the island—ended in the defeat of the much weaker Christians. These were termed Christian-Muslim clashes, which may be regarded by many as religious conflicts, resulting in the Christian minority retreating from the center of the Island into the highlands, and triggering a long

21. Sura 4:34.

22. "Misunderstanders of Islam admit to Beheading Christian Schoolgirls," 11 May 2006. www.jihawatch.org/archives/011382.php

23. I am indebted for this passage to my colleagues, Ran Shauli and Giora Eliraz, at the Truman Institute, who analyze the occasional eruptions against Christians as ethnic and socio-political clashes between them and the Muslim majority, not as Christianophobia.

24. For the chain of event surrounding those clashes, see Ricklefs, *A History of Modern Indonesia*, especially chapter VI.

process of attacks and retaliations. The intervention of other Islamic groups from Java in the clashes has lent to them an interfaith nature, until they began to recede in 2002. Thus, even though the ethnic interpretation of the antagonism remained prevalent, when Muslims attack Christians and vice-versa, and churches are burned down, no one can blame the followers of those faiths-in-conflict, and especially the observers of both creeds abroad, for regarding them as one more illustration of similar clashes going on in the rest of the world. In Egypt and Iraq, for example, the oppression of the Copts and the Assyrians is viewed as an interfaith conflict, most of all by both sides of the warring militias, and certainly by Christians and Muslims worldwide, although a strong ethnic element is identifiable in both cases too.

According to one of the foremost authorities on modern Indonesia, Merle Ricklefs cited above, there were shades of religious wars, or at least religiously motivated confrontations following the axial year of 1965, when violent and brutal "anti-Communist" eruptions resulted in the slaughter of hundreds of thousands. For after 1965, Islam's increased assertiveness was evident in the role of Islamic activists in the 1965–66 killings, in the call to prayer being broadcast at full volume over public address systems, and in repeated admonitions to believers to perfect their faith. Very many Muslims responded to this atmosphere of heightened religious awareness, claims Ricklefs, but some Indonesians found this assertive Islam to be unattractive and they therefore converted to other faiths, one of them Christianity, probably aided by the intensive work of missionaries. But such conversions to Christianity and other faiths were only partly for religious reasons, and partly for political reasons, because after 1965 everyone had to be registered as an adherent of a specific faith, lest one be accused of atheism (i.e., "Communist"). Some Indonesians who were loath to call themselves Muslims, therefore proclaimed themselves Christians, sometimes even when they had not encountered Christian preachers. Such proselytization practices, in some churches, especially of the Jehovah Witnesses and Seventh Day Adventists, attracted much criticism from Muslims. Thus, while in 1933 only less than 3 percent of the population was Christians, that figure grew to 7.5 percent in 1971. Although still small percentages, Christians were more visible because of the presence of Christian schools and the heavier conversions in urban areas, which in Central Java approached the 15 percent mark.[25] Ricklefs drew the consequences of these developments:

> Indonesia had always been a multireligious society, but in the past, different religious communities had for the most part been

25. Ibid., 354–55.

> based in different geographical areas or ethnic groups. Now, adherents of different religions lived in proximity of each other, indeed were often from the same ethnic groups or even families. In the wake of the period of extraordinary political conflict and violence, it is not surprising that Indonesia's transition to this new form of multireligiosity was not entirely smooth. In April 1967 a series of violent incidents began when Muslims attacked churches in Aceh. In October very serious anti-Christian riots broke out in Makasar, and religious violence was reported from Java and Sumatra. . . . The government convened an inter-religious dialogue in Jakarta where Christian and Islamic leaders came to the conclusion that there was no basis for compromise. Since both Islam and Christianity are missionary religions, anxious to bring their universal message to all people, to expect either to restrain its mission work, is to ask it to be untrue to itself. . . . Yet, religious violence did decline after 1967, not least because the military made clear that it was prepared to stop it.[26]

We may, then conclude that since Indonesia is probably the only Muslim-majority country where Islam is not proclaimed as the state religion, and other faiths are recognized as equally valid, it is also the place in all Islamdom where the rulers are not committed to please the mobs of believers, and they act to quell any inter-religious trouble. It is also equally true, that though religion had been identified as identical to a certain ethnic group or geographical area, there were no opportunities for clashes to erupt. But since the ethnic and geographic mix between various groups took place, especially in the post-1965 period, high visibility, hyper-activism, day-to-day frictions, and instant reports from other lands of Islam about constant clashes between Islam and its minorities, have no doubt exacerbated the situation in Indonesia too. But a difference remained nonetheless: while in other lands the state often overlooks cases of oppression and discrimination of Christians, and sometimes even actively condones them and participates in them, in Indonesia, the state actively *prohibits and prevents* them, although they remain the domain of radical groups, from one party or another, who triggers eruptions like the Ambon, Aceh, or other attacks. From among the many clashes between the many religious groups in Indonesia, those against Christians are particularly heightened by the Western media and singled out as Christianophobia, hence the world resonance they have.

All this having been said, one has to realize that occasionally, though not in any sense with the same frequency and exposure as in Iraq, Egypt, or Nigeria, reports continue to come out from this largest of Islamic countries

26. Ibid., 355.

about Muslim-Christian clashes, though it is not official policy. For example, in May 2012, the story filtered out of gunmen who opened fire on the GKI Yasmin Church—which had been sealed off by the authorities since 1988 due to Muslim demands—causing much damage to that structure. The report said that Christians have tried to hold services in front of the sealed building, but have been met by violent opposition from Muslims. Previously, Muslims had made death threats, played loudly, and even rode a motorcycle through the congregation. A church spokesman said: "We are constantly having to change our location because our existence appears to be unwanted, and we have to hide so that we are not intimidated by intolerant groups.... We had hoped for aid from the police, but after many attacks on the members of the congregation, we see that the police is also involved in this."[27]

Indonesian Islam was also tested in colonized Papua (Irian Jaya), the Melanesian and predominantly Protestant Christian tribal nation, which since 1963 was under Indonesian rule. There, the Indonesian military were involved in human rights abuses against the Papuans, where Islamic radicals and pro-Indonesian militias have converged since East Timor became independent. In 2001, the Jakarta government announced "autonomy" for Papua, but later reneged and divided the vast land into three separate districts governed directly by Jakarta, against the will of the indigenous Papuans. Due to the mass migration of many Javanese into Papua over the past decades, a remarkable transformation of the demographic make-up is noticeable, thus turning two of the three provinces into Muslim-majority. The feared militia leader, Eurico Guterres, established a local force, the *Laskar Merah Putih* (the Red and White Warriors). He had been sentenced to ten years jail in 1999 for his role in the referendum massacres in East Timor, but was later released. What is worse was the nomination of Timbul Silaen, the previous chief of police in East Timor under Indonesian occupation, to head the police of Papua, knowing that he had been implicated in the attack on Bishop Belo's compound, as well as the Liquica Church massacre, although he was acquitted of any wrongdoing by an Indonesian court in 2002. Therefore, Papuan church leaders fear that the combination of those two powerful chiefs might step-up the Islamization of Papua, thus causing the military to close it off to the outside world, and an ethnic cleansing and Jihad could then be unleashed, which could ultimately bring about the genocide of the Christians. All remembered that when, in 1963, Indonesia took control the territory, it was renamed West Irian and then Irian Jaya. In 1969, Indonesia, under the 1962 New York Agreement, organized a referendum named the

---

27. Ibrahim, "Muslim Persecution of Christians," *Gatestone Institute*, May 8, 2012.

Act of Free Choice, in which Papuan tribal elders reached a consensus to continue the union with Indonesia. Simultaneously, there was resistance to Indonesian integration, where some 100,000 Papuans were dead. In 2000, Irian Jaya was formally renamed "The Province of Papua" and a Law on Special Autonomy was passed in 2001. The Law established a Papuan People's Assembly (MRP) with representatives of the different indigenous cultures of Papua. Although President Megawati Sukarnoputri was able to create a separate West Papua province in 2003 as a *fait accompli*, plans for a third province on Western New Guinea were blocked by the courts, once it became clear that the "special autonomy" scheme had failed.[28]

A poignant report by noted Islamologue Robert Spencer, sums up the situation.[29] He says that the Militant Islamists in Indonesia, meaning that there are some, in spite of the many denials of other Islamic experts of that area, do target the Christian minority in Indonesia, as expressed by an Indonesian Muslim attack on the Catholic church in Jakarta, the capital. The Muslim-Christian relations are strained in Indonesia, and the Muslim-Christian dialogue was unable to reconcile between these two big religious groups of the Indonesian Archipelago.

An incident occurred in the parish of the Sacred Heart in Pugeran, in the south of Yogyakarta, when three groups of unknown assailants riding motorcycles attacked the church during the Mass in early morning, with their faces hidden under black masks and they were dressed in black. They broke through the Catholic church's gates shouting "Allahu Akbar." This incident coincided with the start of the Ramadan, the Islamic holy fasting month. According to the reports to the press of Father Pariya of the Catholic church in Jakarta, these unknown assailants targeted the posters and the objects that were exhibited by the members of the local Roman Catholic church, while the reasons behind this attack were unknown, and the Indonesian authorities tightened the control on the Christian holy places in Jakarta and Indonesia in the face of the Islamic resurging attacks on the Christian Indonesian minority and in the fear of more attacks in the future. In the month of May 2014, there was another attack on the Catholic church in Jakarta that was led by Islamic extremist militias, which targeted Catholic Indonesian prayers in church and beat the officiating priest. The Evangelical Protestant community in Jakarta also sensed the danger of attack by Muslim assailants when Pastor Niko was accused of presiding over an "illegal" house

---

28. "A Christian People Seriously at Risk," FreedomNews.com, 3 December 2003.

29. Spencer. "Indonesia: Muslims Screaming 'Allahu akbar' attack Roman Catholic Church during Sunday Mass." *Jihad Watch*, 20 June 2015.

of worship for the Lord Jesus Christ and for the Evangelical Protestant Church, without permission from the Indonesian authorities.

In neighboring Malaysia, where Islam's majority is less decisive than in Indonesia, the anxiety of the ruling Muslims to remain predominant, together with the democratic pretensions of the state, keep that society in a permanent state of tension between the Muslim majority and the local minorities. In 2009, a landmark ruling of the High Court in Kuala Lumpur shook the country and the world when it declared that the word Allah was not exclusive to Islam and allowed *The Herald*, a Catholic newsletter, to use it in its publication to refer to God.[30] (In other parts of the world, where Christianity feels more comfortable with its domination of the scene, it usually insists on the reverse: that Allah is the God of the Muslims, who has nothing to do with the Christian God, specifically since the angry, vengeful, and cruel Allah stands in total opposition to the forgiving, loving, and graceful Christian and biblical God. Non-Muslims might also claim that since Allah was a pre-Islamic God, the knowledge and use of the name has remained unique to the Muslims, who inherited him from the Arabian pagans; Christians might counter that precisely because Allah was specific to Arabia, and his name was used by pre-Islamic Arabs, he could not be the same as the biblical God that Christ believed in and then all Christians.)

High Court Judge Datuk Lau Bee Lan also declared that the order by the Home Minister banning the use of the word Allah by non-Muslims was illegal, null, and void, and that the *Herald* had the constitutional right to use the word Allah in the magazine to propagate the Christian religion. She determined that while it was an offence for non-Muslims to use the word Allah *to Muslims* to propagate the faith, it was not an offence for non-Muslims to use the word to other non-Muslims for the purpose of religion. Using the word was permitted in the exercise of the freedom speech and expression, she said. She also said that the Home Minister failed to adduce evidence that the use of the word would threaten national security and create misunderstanding and confusion among Muslims.

As would be expected, the Catholic Archbishop, Tam Sri Pakiam, the publisher of the magazine, lauded the court decision. *The Herald* is read by the 850,000 Catholics of Malaysia, and therefore it was necessary to settle this controversy rapidly, since in many of its articles it uses Allah to refer to the Christian God. Supposedly, no Muslim would have taken the term seriously if it did not refer to the only terminology Muslims knew, heeded, and recognized. The fact is that indigenous Malaysian Christians do use

---

30.. Ganesh Sahathevan, "Court: Allah Not Exclusive to Islam," 1 January 2020. Article cited by Time Leonard and Joseph Masilamany, 31 December 2009, www.thesundaily.com/artiocle.cfm?id=41857.

the name Allah in their prayers, influenced by their predominant Islamic neighborhood.[31] On the other hand, immediately following that liberal verdict, the Inspector General of Police, Tan Sri Musa Hassan, informed the churches that they had to tighten their security at their premises, because "there were not enough policemen to guard everyone of them," but he did not explain why in a Muslim country with such a liberal constitution and judiciary Christians needed to be protected at all, while Muslims did not.[32]

There are hundreds of churches in Malaysia. So, while the Chief of Police said that mosques and other places of worship too would have to be "covered," he acknowledged the potential of inter-communal violence over religious issues. He disclosed that since he gave his cell-phone number to the public, he received hundreds of calls and SMSs, among them those from Christians who asked police to step up security in their premises, while others called to thank police for its efforts. While all those communications and precautions came in the wake of a major arson of a church, which was also visited by the Prime Minister Abdul Hadi, the Chief of Police asked his callers to stop speculating about who the perpetrators might have been. In Port Klang, there was a report about a stone that was pelted into a Muslim place of worship and shattered a glass, but no elaboration on the incident was given. What is certain, judging from the explosions of rage in certain quarters, is that many Muslims were not receptive to the court verdict, and they may have been retaliating with violence, not understanding why Christians needed to use the name Allah—which the critics felt "belonged to Muslims"—to refer to their God. In fact, days after the court judgment, masked men were seen riding motorcycles firebombing three churches in Kuala Lumpur, gutting the ground floor of the Metro Tabernacle Church. The attack was condemned by government and opposition alike. Muslims who counter-demonstrated in their mosques, quite peacefully, held placards that read: "Leave Islam alone! "Treat us as you would treat yourself!" and "Don't test our patience!," amidst the cries of "Allah Akbar!" that are heard throughout the Muslim world.[33]

---

31. Ibid. See also Debra Chong, "Court says Yes to Allah for Christians," 31 December 2009, www.themalaysianinsider.co/index.php/malaysia/48112-headline-court-says-yes-to-allah-for-christians; and Shazwan Mustafa Kamal, "Cautious Celebrations over 'Allah' Judgment," 31 December 2009, www.thelemalaysuaninsider.com/index.php/malaysia/48133-cautious-celabrations-over-allh-judgment.

32. Ganesh et al., "Tighten Security at Premises, IGP Advises Churches," ganesh.sahathevanmail.com, 10 January, 2010.

33. Kuppusamy, "Can Christians say Allah in Malaysia? Muslims say No!" *Ganesh*, 26 January 2010,

To many Malay Muslims, the Court judgment crossed the delicate line between the two systems of law: one for the 60 percent majority-Muslims, the other for everyone else, including the Christians, the authorities regarding that compartmentalization as essential to social stability. In fact, prominent Muslim clerics, lawmakers, and government ministers have questioned the soundness of that judgment, and a coalition of twenty-seven Muslim NGOs wrote to the nine Malay sultans, who are each head of Islam in their respective states, to intervene and help overturn the verdict. A Facebook campaign also started on 2nd January 2010, which attracted many thousands of supporters, including some Islamic celebrities, claiming that a court of law is not the proper place to decide on religious affairs, while the few Muslims who did support the court decision, were shouted down as "traitors." Non-Muslim Malays worry lest the vehement Muslim opposition to the use of Allah reflects a growing trend of Islamization of their society.

In October 2009, a Muslim *Shari'a* court sentenced a Muslim woman who drank beer to be caned in public, while in another case Muslims were enraged over the construction of a Hindu temple near their home, and they demonstrated their wrath with a severed cow's head, knowing that cows were holy to the Hindus, who watched the demonstration helplessly. All were agreed that in order to avoid escalation, Christians and Muslims had to meet and try to cool the tempers.[34]

To seal the debate, the editorial of *The Herald* replicated a pastoral letter dated 1st April 2011, from the Archbishop of Kuala Lumpur, Murphy Pakiam, under the title: "Protect and Defend Christians' Right to use *Al-Kitab*" (i.e., the Scripture, namely the Bible). The letter defended the right of Christians to use any language they chose for their worship, and rejected the criticism against them for using their Holy Book. It also protested the progressive pushing back of the public space to express the faith, and defended their right to wear and display crosses and other religious symbols, using religious words, or constructing places of worship. It lamented the fact that shipments of the Bible, which were labeled as a "Christian publication," had been subjected to arbitrary conditions for release, and demanded that there be no impediment to the publication, importation, distribution, and use of the Bible, including the revocation of the orders that had considered the Bible a "threat to national security." The text also reiterated the position that the Home Ministry's stamping of the Bibles amounted to defacement, disrespect, and treating with disdain the Holy Book of Christians. The document concluded by stressing that

---

34. Ibid. See also Kok Leong, "Muslim NGOs Protest Use of Allah by other Religious groups," *Ganesh*, 9 January 2010.

Given the unfortunate experience of the Home Ministry of taking arbitrary action without consulting affected parties or respecting the religious sensitivities of the Christian community, any decision to collect copies of the Bible which have been stamped and serialized, would be with a view to prevent the possibility of further arbitrary desecration, disrespect or destruction being committed against the Holy Scripture of the Christians by the Ministry and its officers. . . . We remain committed to uphold the freedom of religion, which includes the free availability without hindrance or obstacle of the Bible and all sacred scriptures in Malaysia . . . .[35]

Nonetheless, one has to face the reality that Christians are leaving Malaysia, and people do not just leave when they feel that their safety, rights, and creed are respected. As recently as 2015, a report by Yoder[36] indeed contended that the imposition of *Shari'a* laws on the Malaysian Christian minority was considered a real threat to the Christian presence under Malaysian rule. For many Malaysian laws were enacted according to the *Shari'a* Islamic laws that may include: beating the wives, chopping the hand as a punishment for theft, and killing apostates from Islam to Christianity or to atheism. These laws are considered to represent the Islamization of Malaysia, which may affect nature of Malaysia, from an officially secular and liberal country to a more Islamic, conservative, and backward Muslim country, looking more like other Muslim countries in the Middle East and North Africa. As a result of the growing Islamization of Malaysia, and the decline of liberalism, reformism, and secularism, the Christian minority[37] is beginning to think about emigration to the Western World—Europe, America, and Australia, in view of the religious tensions with the Muslim authorities, and the resulting Christian persecution. Malaysian Christians are worried about their religious freedom because under *Shari'a* law they were not allowed to say the word "Allah" when referring to the God of Christianity, they are not allowed to build and renovate the churches, nor to preach the gospel. This could lead to more anti-Christian sentiments and Christianophobia in Malaysia in the coming years which may cause the Malaysian Christian to emigrate out of Malaysia, seeking better life in the West.

35. "Church in Malaysia Protests Loss of Freedoms, Classification of Gospels as Threat to National Security," Editorial in *The Herald*, 1 April 2011.

36. G. Yoder, "Malaysian Christians Leaving Malaysia?" *News around the World*, 13 April 2015.

37. It is important to note that the vast majority of Malaysian Christians are Chinese, Tamil, Indians, and other groups, who have mixed among themselves in Malaysia. They collaborate in their Christian front against Islamization.

Malaysian Christians have already left the country to USA and Australia in search of religious freedom, democracy, and a better future outside of the Muslim World.

CHAPTER FOUR

Christian Minorities in the Holy Land

The small territory of the Holy Land, which comprises Israel, the Palestinian territories, and Jordan to an extent, for Jordan had been part of the definition of Palestine until World War I, deserves a separate treatment because that was the original land where Christianity was born, and thereafter the Christian communities were divided between those three separate entities. While in Israel and Jordan, the Christian congregations are well protected by the authorities, in spite of sporadic acts of hatred against them by fanatic individuals, the Palestinian Authority has seen many traditional Christian locations, most important of all—Bethlehem, losing their Christian identity once they were taken over by radical Muslim majorities. Indeed, in the decade between 2002 and 2014, twenty-five cases of Christianophobia were registered in the A area, which is under full Palestinian domination, according to the Oslo II Accords, and noticeably less in areas B and C, where Israel still wields some power. That is the reason why the Palestinian Authority scores 25th place in the World Watch List, with a ranking of 58/100, while Jordan is 30th, with a ranking of 56/100. Israel not even on that list, due to its respect for Christian rights. In 1999, a Palestinian-appointed commission of inquiry established that Jerusalem was a Muslim city with some Christian enclaves. Bethlehem, which remained Christian in its inner city around the Church of Nativity, has been encircled by the surrounding Palestinian Muslim refugee camps, like the *favelas* in south America, which are hugely disturbing the total population balance to the Christians' disadvantage.

Historically, the territory of Palestine had become important in Islamic history well before there was any mention of the Palestinian people. The Prophet Mohammad, in the years of his religious and political activity in Medina (AD 622–32) had attempted to lure the Jews of the city to his faith, *inter alia* by declaring Jerusalem, which was beyond his purview, as the *Qibla* (direction of prayer), and indeed the first Muslims were turning north during the prayers led by the Prophet. After Muhammad broke away from the Jews, when they rejected him and his message, and after he turned the ancient pagan shrine of the *ka'ba* in Mecca into a Muslim one, by claiming that it had been founded by no other than Abraham, the first Patriarch, he declared Mecca as the new *qibla*, to which all Muslims of the world turn during their prayers. But the place of Jerusalem as the First Qibla (*ula al-qiblatain*), remained firmly established, and that is the way the Muslim believers refer to Jerusalem to this day. Additionally, when the Umayyad King abdul-Malik built the Aqsa Mosque and the Dome of the Rock in the eighth century, as a competing avenue to Mecca, those great structures were retroactively associated with the "farthest mosque" (*al masjid al-Aqsa*) that was mentioned in the Qur'an as the destination of the Prophet in his mysterious nightly journey on the back of his winged horse al-Burak. As the Qur'an said that Muhammad landed in al-Aqsa, and as a majestic structure was in place in the eighth century that was crowned by that name, this became incontrovertible "evidence" that the two were identical. Since then, even though Jerusalem became a neglected backwater when ruled by Islam after its occupation from the Byzantine Christians, and was never made a capital or even a regional main city under Muslim rule (except during the Crusader inter-regnum of the twelfth century, when it was the hub of the Kingdom of Jerusalem), it remained recognized as the first direction of prayer and as the third holiest city in Islam, after Mecca and Medina. It was modern Israel that declared it as its capital city, going back to its ancient status as the capital of Kings David and Solomon.

Because it was the closest geographically, Palestine was the first Western non-Arab area invaded in the imperialist expansion of Islam, though today, by relating Palestinian identity to the Canaanites of antiquity, and baptizing Jesus Christ as a Palestinian, they have constructed an imaginary history where the Arab conquerors of the land, where they later wiped out Judaism and Christianity, had preceded both Judaism and Christianity. In this fashion, they have taken over the PC historical debate by claiming that no one could have preceded or contended with the Palestinian identity of the land. Because the Muslim conquest swiftly took the land over from the Eastern Church of the Byzantine Empire based in Constantinople, Muslims described it as "peaceful" and "bloodless." The few Jews of Palestine welcomed the Muslims as liberators, due to the harsh persecutions of non-Christian religions by the ruling Byzantine church. Jerusalem fell to the Muslims in 638, following a five-months siege, after which the Christians and Jews were made to pay the *jizya*, although large-scale massacres of infidel believers were avoided by the Muslim conquerors. Instead, the Caliphate in Baghdad used the conquered people to provide an unceasing stream of slaves, whose men were made eunuchs to serve the Caliph's court. It is estimated, nonetheless, that in their conquering sweep of the Middle East and North Africa, Muslims killed more Christians (their main opponents) than the Christians killed Muslims during all the Crusades combined. For about a century, Jerusalem prospered under the Umayyads (661–750), but under the following Abbasids it declined at a period when converting Jews and Christians to Islam became a policy, and the language of government became Arabic. Under the following Fatimids, churches were destroyed by Muslim mobs in Palestine, while thousands of Christians were making the pilgrimage from Europe to the Holy Land, and were taken care of by their many churches and monasteries, which were prosperous. But then the Crusades took place, which aggravated the relations between the Muslims and the Christians and set the patterns of hatred, violence, and accusations that last to this day and in which none of the parties emerges as a saint.[1]

Nonetheless, Arab scholars, and certain Western historians, using the academic sponsorship of politically correct Western institutions, have made great efforts to encrust in Western consciousness the argument that under Islam the Holy land in general and Jerusalem in particular had reached the pinnacle of its development, tolerance, and multiculturalism. While this may be true, it is *only* so when compared with the extreme fanaticism, bigotry, and xenophobia of the Crusaders. The comparative humanity of the Muslim rule could stand only when Jews and Christians submitted to the Muslim conquest, recognized its superiority, and accepted their second-rate status by paying the *jizya*.

In September 1999, the London School of Oriental and African Studies (SOAS) convened the "Third International Academic Conference on Muslim Jerusalem."[2] As if there were no Jews and no Jewish holy places in Jerusalem, let alone Jewish historical links to the place, the Conference was sub-titled: "Muslim-Christian relations in Jerusalem—Past, Present and Future," though it was supposed to discuss the status of non-Muslim minorities in general in an Islamic state, following the conquest of the Holy land

---

1. See Csaplar, "1400 years of Islamic Aggression: an Analysis," CBN.com Commentary, 3 December 2002.

2. *Al-Hayat al-Jadidah,* 10 September 1999. Reported by MEMRI, Special Dispatch No. 50, 15 October 1999.

in AD 638 under the Caliph Umar. The Arab saying that "the content of the text is evident from its title" is evidently applicable here, in view of the total detachment of the biased deliberations, reflected in the list of the exclusively Arab panelists, which obviously used the docile and PC British cover for a purely Arab propaganda conference. One of the Muslim participants, Zaki Badawi, indeed lamented the absence of Jewish scholars from the panel. The declaration of Jerusalem as a Muslim-conquered territory, as if it were a divine act and not the result of brutal force, together with the total denial of its Jewish historical roots, in themselves provide ample evidence of the political and biased purpose of this so-called "academic" conference. Genuine academic conferences have no need to declare themselves as such, just as truly democratic countries have no need to declare themselves the "Democratic Republic of Romania/ Congo" and such.

One speaker, Said Ramadan al-Buti, claimed, contrary to historical and archaeological evidence, that non-Muslims are not viewed by Muslim rulers as a burden, as long as they remain submissive, just like the Muslims, to the Islamic regime. He also said that the first Islamic state of the Prophet in Medina included both Muslims and Jews. He neglected to mention that soon the Jews were accused of "betraying the Prophet," and therefore he either forced them to convert, or else slaughtered them or expelled them, so that to this day, 1400 years later, Arabia remains *Judenfrei, or Judenrein*, as one prefers.

Shafiq Mahmud saw in the permitted intermarriage of Muslims with Christians, a proof of the favorable approach to Christians, bringing as an example one of the Fatimid Caliphs, who took two Christian women as wives. But he "forgot" to mention that this "tolerance" was only towards non-Muslim *women*, who by marrying Muslim men were considered Muslim converts, and their children as always following the faith of their Muslim fathers; but if, Allah forbid, a Muslim woman should marry a non-Muslim man, that was considered an act of treason and punished accordingly. Freis Khuri, a third Arab participant in the panel, who as a Christian conserved his dhimmi spirit, praised the Muslim conquerors of the land and qualified them as "liberators"! He recognized, though, the harsh treatment of the Christians, who were humiliated and segregated from the Muslim community, forcing them to wear special clothing, forbidding them from riding horses, and imposing *jizya* over them, and even stated that the Caliph's mistreatment of Christians contradicted the teachings of Islam. He meant that in spite of the submissive conduct of the Christians and the disbursing of the humiliating *jizya*, they were still discriminated against and oppressed. One wonders how could they have felt "liberated."[3]

The expansion of Muslim "holy places" in Palestine, in place where they had never existed before, apart from in the fabricated history of the Aqsa mosque, came only in recent times as part of the self-assertion of Islam as a world religion that needed to show that it deserved a place under the sun, together with, and ultimately instead of, the other prevailing monotheistic religions of Christianity and Judaism. Three cases in point, in addition to Jerusalem, depict that long, insistent, and determined process: the turning of the Rachel Tomb in the outskirts of Jerusalem and the Tomb of the Patriarchs in Hebron from millennial Jewish sites into "Muslim shrines"; and the explosion of radical Muslims in Nazareth in the 1990s, aimed at erasing the long-hailed Christian history of the Basilica of Annunciation, and imposing instead the conversion of the city into Islam, by attempting to erect a dominant mosque that was planned to dwarf the Basilica in size and importance. In the first instance, it is in such UN bodies as UNESCO and the Human Rights Commission/Council, which are supposed to eliminate calumniations and discrimination and to cultivate *entente* and harmony among nations, that the worst acts of racism and violations of human rights are perpetrated. These acts are presided over by the worst violators of human rights, like the Iranians and their allies, who constantly try to co-opt the role of those organizations into their own essentially anti-Jewish and anti-Israeli operations, as prescribed by their Islamic radicalism. If it were not for the US, who out of a sense of decency, almost single-handedly, and sometimes aided by Canada and Australia, prevents those UN institutions from completely inveighing against Israel and Judaism; and for some Western-Christian nations, who at least keep neutral out of their respect for their American ally (though they at other times abandon their own Christian tradition in order to align with the Muslim united front of hatred against Israel), then Israel, one of the great bastions of Jewish and Christian rights, would by now have been turned into a total outcast.

Indeed, in the beginning of November 2010, UNESCO in Paris, charged with the task of cultivating and preserving sites of cultural heritage, decided that two millennial Jewish holy sites—the Tomb of Rachel near Bethlehem and the Tomb of the Patriarchs in Hebron—were "Muslim mosques and Palestinian sites, which had to be evacuated by Israel." Never before had UNESCO been charged with the task of determining the outcome of conflicts between nations, and never was it authorized to act as arbiter between different national or cultural claims. Every member of

3. Ibid.

UNESCO knows that the Jewish claim antedated the Islamic one by many centuries, and that today it was up to the negotiating parties to come to a consensus on how to use the site; but it was certainly not up to the UNESCO Council, which knows nothing beyond its own politics, to determine political rights of access and spiritual claims of culture and religion. Nonetheless, not only the Muslim state members of the Council, who felt self-assured of the automatic vote in their favor no matter what they demanded, but Christian representatives, who should have an appreciation of the Old Testament they share with Jews, also voted for the absurd resolution to call the Hebron Tomb of the Patriarchs the *Ibrahimi Mosque* (the Abrahamic Mosque) and Rachel's Tomb the *Bilal Ibn Rabah Mosque*. Quite incredibly, they delivered a self-destructive blow to their own heritage under pressure from resurging Islam, when demanding that those two historical shrines be removed from the inventory of Jewish heritage places, which were part of the Judeo-Christian tradition. UNESCOs resolution redefined them as "mosques," as if they had been Muslim from time immemorial.

That resolution sought to detach seminal biblical place names from any Jewish connections, as part of the attempts of newly assertive Islam to delegitimize and deny any Jewish attachment to its historical roots in the land of their ancestors, thereby paving the way to Palestinian monopoly and Muslim rule on what they claim as their exclusive land. No wonder then that Muslims, supported by Christian nations, felt that their rights in the Holy Land are internationally recognized and that as a result, they could insist also that Christian sites are also Islamic. That permitted Yasser Arafat, the Palestinian leader, to decide that Jesus—a first-century Jewish man—was Palestinian, and therefore the holy sites of Palestinians were both Christian and Islamic, and he consecrated his declaration by marrying a Palestinian Christian—who had, of course, to convert to Islam. Since then, when any Palestinian leader spoke of Holy Places in Palestine/Israel, they were either Christian or Muslim, *never* Jewish, and in any case their Palestinian identity hovered over them. In other words, when the Palestinians celebrate today the part of Muslim history that described the submission of the Byzantine Patriarch of Jerusalem, Sophronius, to the conquering Caliph Umar, by handing him symbolically the key of the city, they confirm their belief that Palestine had become sacred Muslim turf, a *Waqf* (holy endowment) that was inherited by Muslims for all generations to come. That meant that when Christians ruled the land, as under the Crusaders, they *had* to be fought and extirpated from it (unless they submitted as *dhimmis*); and now that the land is ruled by Jews, then one is advised to ally with the Palestinian Christians, who should have been Muslims in the first place, with the backing of their coreligionists in the West, in order to overrule the Jews, defeat them, and expel them once and for all. As the *Jerusalem Post* argued, politically incorrect as it may be in our postmodern and multicultural existence, Europe's and America's democracies, which are still constructed on Christian foundations, by submitting to Muslim deconstructionist diktats, they not only injured the Jews, but undermined their own legacy and the longterm existence of Christians in Islamdom. The *Jerusalem Post* explained:

> Consequently, Christianity could expend so much effort on cleansing the historic Jesus of his Jewishness. But telltale vestiges remain in the New Testament attesting to the truth which volumes of convoluted rationalizations and distortions could not quite erase. Just turn to Mark 12:28-30, where Jesus is asked which is the most important commandment of all. He replies without equivocation: "Hear, O Israel, the Lord our God is one; and you shall love the Lord your God with all your heart, with all your soul and your mind." Any Jew would instantaneously recognize this as the primary article of Jewish faith, a direct quotation from Deuteronomy 6:4-9. For observant Jews it is an obligatory prayer each morning and evening. It is the Jewish bedtime prayer. It is the prayer inscribed within the *mezuzah* on every Jewish doorpost. It is the final prayer uttered by the faithful before death. It is the prayer with which Jewish martyrs perished at the hand of their blood libel executioners, whether from the ranks of the Catholic Inquisition, Muslim Jihadists, or Hitler's henchmen. It was what Jesus valued most. He surely would unreservedly identify Hebron and Bethlehem as incontestably Jewish and the tombs therein as unquestionably sacred to Jews like him. Thus, when Christians voted as they did [in UNESCO] to call the Cave of the Patriarchs the *Ibrahimi Mosque,* and Rachel's Tomb the *Bilal ibn Rabah Mosque* [after an obscure companion of the Prophet, who existed and died a millennium or more after Rachel was buried there], they thereby also belied and betrayed Christianity. Their narrative cannot stand apart from Jewish history.
>
> Since Islam's debut, however, Muslims have made it their routine custom to expropriate the holy sites of others. When Muslim conquistadors first invaded Jerusalem, they called it *Bayt al-Maqdis*, their adaptation of the Hebrew *Beit Hamiqdash* (the Holy Temple*). Al-Quds*, the contemporary Arabic contraction for this original appellation, daily highlights the very Jewish heritage which the Arabs now take inordinate pains to obliterate. Their latest claim is that the very inclusion of the

Hebron and Bethlehem tombs among Jewish heritage sites will somehow compromise Muslim freedom of worship . . . .[4]

What is one to conclude from this fanatic behavior, which did not recognize the rights and feelings of others, and was afraid to share what they felt was exclusively theirs, even though they should have known better that Jewish attachment to this place pre-dated theirs by more than one millennium? That they were scared to expose their creed to others means that they are perhaps uncertain of its validity. Secondly, while they had accepted in wonderment the Jewish attitude of sharing since Israel took control of the Cave of the Patriarchs (1967), belligerent Islam suddenly remembered that Islamic sites were to be *monopolized*, instead of being open to apply the same concept of sharing in other places too, like Temple Mount in Jerusalem. Therefore, taking advantage of their leverage by their sheer numbers (fifty-seven of their countries are members of the Muslim bloc at the UN), of the terrorizing effects of their threats, and of the unexplained submissiveness of most of the Western countries, they were able to extract from UN organizations the resolutions about Hebron and Bethlehem. Someone had joked that even if they tabled a resolution that the world were flat it would be passed by that automatic vote, exactly as they got to appoint to the Human Rights Council such liberal champions as Iran, Saudi Arabia, and Sudan; and to appoint Saddam Hussein's Iraq to the Commission on Disarmament! Successive Secretary Generals of the UN, instead of interfering to correct the travesty, kept quiet hoping for a second term in their lucrative office.

The Palestinian Authority, far from recognizing its bigotry towards its preceding rival faiths (Judaism and Christianity), on the contrary takes the liberty to accuse them of "having forsaken the teachings of Jesus and Moses," as if the modern Muslim Arabs of Palestine had become the guardians of true and original monotheism. On its official television it taught the world its own gospel:

> 700 years had passed since the birth of Jesus the Christian, during which the Christians had distanced themselves from the teachings of love. The Jews have forsaken the commandments of Moses and returned to worshipping gold. . . . In one of the crude tents an orphan child was born, who will in the future become responsible for the quenching the world's desire for justice, love, freedom and truth. . . . While far from Mecca, the city of Yathrib (later Medina) became full of Jews who escaped from the Byzantines, and they landed like wolves on the most fertile lands and the most important commodities, and established their villages

---

4. Sarah Honig, *Jerusalem Post*, 11 November 2010.

by taking advantage of the loose Arab presence and their internal disputes. The Jewish scholars would make business of the Torah. They hid pages of it, falsified other pages and went on to become rich. And while the Jews were worshipping the gold, frantically engaging in trade, specializing in scheming, the Arabs worshipped the stones, dedicated themselves to warfare and specialized in composing poetry . . . .[5]

The more specifically Christian problem of the Basilica of Annunciation in Nazareth unfolded in the 1990s, but since it was a domestic Israeli issue and not UN-dependent, it was resolved by Israel without much foreign interference. Since the Crusade era, Nazareth was considered as a Christian city with a clear Christian majority. But during the 1948 War, many Muslim refugees from the adjoining villages sought refuge in the course of the war in Nazareth, altering forever the demographic balance and turning it over the subsequent years into a Muslim-majority city. With the rise of the world stature of Islam after the Iranian Revolution, and the concomitant capitulation of Western powers to Islam, the Muslims of Israel also came to the fore with a novel self-assurance that enabled them to lay new claims that had never occurred to them before. The new moves were mainly motivated as part of the surge of militant Islam worldwide, especially after the victory of Islam in Iran, Afghanistan, and the Sudan, and its significant inroads in other Muslim countries such as Algeria, Lebanon, Jordan, Egypt, and Pakistan, all either under the umbrella of the Muslim Brothers, or movements affiliated with them, which resulted in the identification of militant Islam in terms of religio-nationalism.[6]

Thus, many Arab Muslims in Israel and Palestine have come to cling to their Islamic identity more markedly than to their Arab or Palestinian stock, as a divide separating them from non-Muslims and as a common denominator attaching them to other Muslims worldwide. Thus, while many of the differences between the Jewish majority and the Arab minority in Israel (both Muslim and Christian), are often bridgeable by common language, economic interest and neighborly relations, the Muslim radicals, who have injected massive doses of Islamic symbolism into the Arab-Israeli dispute, have often lent to it a religio-cultural veneer, thus turning it into *a qualitatively insoluble rift*. In turn, Muslim radicals in Israel, who would perhaps accept their minority status and adjust to the vagaries of life under a Jewish authority, side by side with their Christian compatriots, once imbued with

---

5. Itamar Marcus and Barbara Cook, "PA TV: Christians and Jews have forsaken the teachings of Jesus and Moses," *Palestinian Media Watch*, 1 May 2005.

6. See Israeli, "Muslim Fundamentalists as Social Revolutionaries," 462–65.

the general mode of thinking of other Muslim radicals, tend also to increase their anti-Israeli and anti-Christian rhetoric and attitudes. Their anti-Jewish posture has impelled them to rebel, more or less overtly against the Jewish state, and their historical anti-Christian bitterness has pushed them to eliminate the remaining rule of Christians over Muslim communities, such as in heavily Islamized Nazareth. In the 2010s, this trend has intensified as many Christian Arabs, who used to form a unified national front with the Israeli Muslim Arabs against the Israeli establishment, notably within the now defunct Communist Party, have decided to tilt towards the Jewish-Zionist state and they even offered to serve in the Israeli defense forces as a token of their new-found sentiment of loyalty and duty towards Israel.

The Muslims of Israel, even more than other Muslims worldwide, feel resentment and frustration at their inability to regain domination over their holy land and holy places. For they experience in an immediate fashion the humiliation of being ruled by an erstwhile *dhimmi* people which had itself, for long centuries, submitted to Islamic rule, and which had been depicted in the Islamic tradition as having a questionable reputation. The pious among them cannot overlook the vehement anti-Jewish and anti-Israeli arguments advanced by the masters of radical Islam all around them.[7] Add to that the general sense of discrimination among these Muslims in their uphill battle to gain equal treatment in the rights and services extended to them by the state, and the impossible emotional gap that they sense between their country of citizenship and their coreligionists in the Arab and Islamic camps, and you have a recipe for contradictions, soul-searching, radicalism, and upheaval. Some of these tensions are tapped by radical Muslim leaders among Israeli Arabs and directed towards the revival and self-assertion of the Islamic community, which are also directed against the minorities who collaborate with the Jewish majority, like the Druze and the Christians. Indeed, more mosques have been built in Israel during the past few decades than ever before, and more expressions of Islamic radicalism in politics, in social organizations, and in local government have come to the fore than at any time before. Islamic associations, which had previously watched over local *Waqf* affairs, or dealt with social welfare, suddenly took to election campaigns and became involved in local and national politics. Like the Muslim Brothers of Egypt, they have accumulated large enough pools of goodwill among their population—by their caring leadership, devoted work for the community, and networks of charity and educational and health services—to be able to expect political support from their constituencies

---

7. See for example, Sayyid Qu'tb, *Our War Against the Jews,* often quoted by Muslim radicals everywhere

Against this background it is understandable that the Muslims of Nazareth, who in the 1990s achieved the majority of the population in Nazareth and won a majority of the seats in the City Council, became determined to impose on the Christian Mayor, who had been voted in due to his popularity, the Islamization of the city. The head of the local *Waqf* Association, seconded by the Muslim opposition in the city, suggested the construction of a mosque on the plaza next to the Basilica of Annunciation, and taller than the Basilica, so as to dwarf it and demonstrate the changed nature of the city. To back their case, the Muslims claimed that the nearby Shihab a-Din tomb, of the alleged nephew of Saladin, which until then did not attract much attention, was a holy place and therefore deserving of the erection of a mosque nearby, just like the conversion of the Rachel tomb to the Bilal Tomb by the decree of UNESCO in latter days. The mosque was not allowed by the authorities, and by decree of two Israeli courts of law, the temporary mosque-tent that had been built in place by the Muslim populace, was dismantled, but the new "holy place" was approved by the Muslim hierarchy and included within the jurisdiction of the *Waqf* Association of the city.[8] Thus, the register of Muslim "holy places" kept growing under the impact of the increasing religiosity as a political tool of struggle in the Holy Land, as elsewhere around the world, and as a manifestation of the general ambience of Islamic assertiveness launched and maintained by the successes of Muslims in the international arena.

The bottom line is that while with the Ottoman takeover in the fifteenth century the majority of land was still Christian, and Palestine was still officially a Christian country under the British Mandate (1919–48), today, except for Israel, where Christianity continues to thrive, Christians are rapidly disappearing from the Middle Eastern scene. In Bethlehem, for example, the 90 percent Christians have become 10 percent of the population, and among the three million Palestinians of the West Bank and Gaza, only fifty thousand Christians remain. Under the title "the Exodus of Christians," Ayelet Kedem of the *Makor Rishon* Weekly,[9] wrote at the height of the Al-Aqsa Intifada (2000–2003), about the saga of the flight of the Christian Arabs of the Holy Land from their mixed Arab villages in the Galilee, where their separate Christian identity had been oppressed by their Muslim neighbors over the past few decades. They ran away into Israeli Jewish cities like Upper Nazareth, or mixed cities, like Haifa and Acre, where their minority status can be diluted within the general plurality of denomina-

---

8. For the entire story, see Israeli, *Green Crescent over Nazareth: The Displacement of Christians by Muslims in the Holy Land*.

9. Ayelet Kedem, *Makor Rishon*, 14 June 2002, 8–11.

tions. As a matter of fact, she wrote, one millennium after the Crusaders had been repulsed from the land, their descendants have been now forced to migrate, under threats and violence, seeking protection either from the Jewish authorities of Israel, or seeking asylum in Western countries like the US, South America, Australia, and Canada. Kedem counts among the main reasons for this increased pace of migration the two successive Intifadas of the Palestinians (1987–92 and 2000–2003), which have seeped into the Arab population of Israel, the rise of the Islamic radicals in the country, the rapid rate of population growth among the Muslims, the problem of the Basilica in Nazareth (see above), which has generated rioting against Christians and looting of Christian stores in Nazareth, and the short-sighted unwillingness of the Israeli labor government of Ehud Barak to take a firm position in defense of the Christians. It was not until the takeover by Ariel Sharon of the newly elected government in 2004, that Israeli policy began to shift and the Basilica issue, together with the Shihab-a-Din crisis, were finally put to rest.

So much more so in Beit Jallah and Bethlehem, which had been Christian cities for centuries, when Muslim terrorists took over the Church of Nativity and other churches too. The fear of the persecuted Christians to speak up, lest their Muslim-majority oppressors step-up persecution against them, does not even permit us to get precise data on the rates of Christian migrations, internal and international. Western Christianity and the Vatican have done so little to interfere on behalf of their coreligionists, either for fear of worsening their situation or for carelessness and greed. It appears that they which always lent priority to political, economic, and diplomatic considerations over the fate of so many oppressed people. This oversight has added to the Christian plight, and to the attempts of fleeing refugees to find other lands to shelter them, an experience that had been lived for two millennia by world Jewry, until the US on the one hand, and the State of Israel on the other, opened new avenues of peaceful existence for them. The latest attempt by a group of Israeli Christians to throw their lot with Israel in order to enjoy its protection, like the recognized Druze minority which also serves in the IDF, has been the new conclusion they have finally come to, hoping that integrating into Israeli society, and fulfilling their duties to it, also legitimize their demands for equal rights, and their expectations for protection and security.

In a very thorough though unpublished M.A. thesis by Tsahi Katz, submitted to Bar Ilan University in Israel,[10] the author examined the history of Christian presence in the Holy land, focusing on the Bethlehem case study. He argued that the Christian presence in Bethlehem, which is consid-

---

10. Katz, *Why Bethlehem Isn't a Christian Town Anymore*, 18–27.

ered the birthplace of Jesus, and is one of the holiest places for Christianity on earth, has lost its majority due to Christian emigration from the city of Bethlehem as well as from the rest of the West Bank, Jerusalem, Israel, and the Gaza Strip. During the British Mandate and in the wake of 1948 war, Bethlehem had a Christian Majority of about 70 percent, but during Jordanian rule between the years of 1948–67, deteriorating economic and living conditions had led many Christians to seek better living opportunities abroad, especially in Western Europe and the Americas. The second turning point extended from the Six-Day war of 1967 until the First Intifada in 1987, when Israel's rule over the West Bank and Gaza affected Muslim-Christian relations, especially since the rise of Islamic radicalism against Israel. For after 1967 there were several Muslim families who came to settle in Bethlehem from the neighboring cities and villages, and that affected the growth of the Muslim Arab population, which turned to a majority for the first time in the 1990s and remains so to this day. Moreover, the first Intifada (1987–93) caused a dramatic effect on the Christian population in Bethlehem, who chose to flee to the West due to Muslim terrorism, political instability, and bad economic conditions. At that time, the Bethlehem Christian community relied for living on souvenir shops and tourism, which were badly harmed by violent events of the Hamas and the Islamic Jihad movements, that gained popularity in the West Bank due to the Palestinian Islamic struggle against Israel and the Jews. Furthermore, there are other factors that contributed to the Christian emigration from Bethlehem and the Holy Land: low birthrates in comparison with the Muslim Arabs; the educational base of the Christian population, which is generally wider than that of Muslim Arabs; the knowledge of foreign languages, which helped them to emigrate and to find suitable jobs commensurate with their abilities and their education; and the better-connections, through the churches, with the Western World.

The *Sinnara* (fishhook) report[11] about the ISIS pamphlet that was distributed to the Muslim community in Jerusalem, argues that the Muslim residents of Jerusalem were asked to report to ISIS and to other Islamic militants on the Christian homes and neighborhoods, in order to allow their religious cleansing and their slaughter on the eve of *Al-Fitr* (August 2015), the Holiday that ended Ramadan. This ISIS pamphlet dubbed the Christian community in Jerusalem as "infidels" who should leave Jerusalem before the *Al-Fitr* Holiday, failing which they would be slaughtered by Muslims like ISIS. In fact, the Christians are considered *dhimmis* and infidels in the eyes of the radical Muslims, who wish to strain the Muslim-Christian relations

---

11. *Al-Sinnara*, 3 July 2015.

and produce more tensions and severe persecution, which would prompt the Christians to emigrate from the land. In short, the Christians in Jerusalem, Israel, and the Palestinian Authority and Gaza strip, are constantly under threat from the Muslim sheikhs and imams, who incite against them (and Jews). In the sanctuary of Al-Aqsa Mosque, Muslims are urged to fight the Christians, to persecute them until they pay the *jizya*, or convert to Islam, or depart from Jerusalem and the Palestinian Territories and immigrate to the West. The deteriorating Muslim-Christian relations are expressed by the attack on churches in the West Bank and on the Christian villages, and on the churches in Ramallah and Bethlehem. In response to the ISIS pamphlet of Jerusalem, Bishop Atallah Hanna tried to calm the tempers and allay the fears, by assuring his communities that they ought not to panic, since Christians have always found their place in the Holy Land. But many Palestinian Christians are nonetheless leaving the country for a better future and life opportunities in the Western World.

In general, the Arab media do not report much about the tensions and violence between Muslims and Christians under Arab and Muslim rule. But during the Nazareth crisis over the Basilica, when the Catholic Patriarch of Jerusalem and the Vatican Custodian in Jerusalem threatened to close all the churches in the Holy Land in protest of the Muslim seizure of Christian land, the Arab media could not avoid jumping into the fray and candidly, if reluctantly, reporting about the controversy. For example, when Sheikh Yussef Salameh, the under-secretary of *Awqaf* (holy endowments) of the Palestinian Authority, participated in the Intercultural Conference in Tehran in May 1999, he praised the seventh-century system of dhimmitude under which monotheistic non-Muslims are inferior to Muslims, as the proper paradigm for relations between Muslims and Christians today. He also said in the same breath, that "Islam [always] respected people of other religions and did not hurt them."[12]

But the Palestinian Christians do contribute to the debate, when outrageous statements are heard regarding their status. For example, they reject the Muslim notion of dhimmitute, arguing that they are not guests of the Muslim host culture, but they had been invaded and taken over in their own lands where they should remain free. In June 1999, a symposium was held in Ramallah on Islamic-Christian relations in Palestine, where Father Marun Lahham said explicitly that "contemporary Palestinian Christians reject the dhimmitude system, and also the frequent Muslim declarations that Palestine is a Muslim *Waqf*, or that Jerusalem is an Islamic city."[13]

---

12. *Al-Hayat al Jadida*, 12 May 1999.
13. *Al-Quds*, 18 June 1999.

In the same month of June, 1999, when the Basilica of Nazareth crisis was still brewing, a reconciliation (*sul'ha*) ceremony was held in the Arab village of Tur'an in the Galilee, between Christian and Muslim families who had been engaged in a violent feud for two years. But soon, due to the high tempers, the reconciliation grew into a dispute. For there and then the Vice-Chief of the Islamic Movement in Israel, Sheikh Kamal Khatib, found it necessary to recall the encounter between the Prophet Muhammad and the Christian Kingdom of Najran [in northern Yemen in pre-Islamic Arabian Paninsula], where Muhammad had called for tolerance, friendship, and mutual respect. He cited a Muslim tradition, often repeated to these days, like in Boston after the September 11 tragedy,[14] that when the Prophet quoted to his Christian guests, in his mosque, verses from the Qur'an, "they were deeply moved and burst into tears." But in the context where it was said, this citation angered the Catholic bishop of the Galilee, Butrus Mu'alem, because he knew that the Christians of Najran had been subjugated and bound by the second-rate dhimmi status. Thereupon, the bishop rejected Khatib's reference to the status of the Christians in the seventh-century under Islam, and stressed the deep Christian roots in the Holy Land, which did not make them "residues, foreigners or beggars of mercy."

One week after that *sul'ha*, which ended in frustration, Sheikh Khatib insisted on responding to the bishop's reluctance to recollect on the Najran episode, or on the Ethiopian King, Najashi, who had allegedly converted from Christianity to Islam, or on the Byzantine Patriarch, Sophronius, who had submitted Jerusalem to the Caliph Umar, events that the bishop had referred to as "fossilized notions" that ought not to be quoted today. Khatib reminded his rival that they were there in order to "reconcile," not to create a new antagonism. To the bishop's contention that Christian Arabs were in the Holy Land before the emergence of Islam, Khatib said that it sounded like claiming that Islam was a foreign phenomenon to the land, while for Muslims their faith was not only the religion of Muhammad, but also of Moses, Jesus, and Abraham the Patriarch. He also stressed that the Arabs of the Holy Land had joined Islam willingly, and were not forced into it. The bishop also thought that the Christians were too forgiving towards Muslims, only since Jesus had demanded from them to forgive their enemies and to bless those who cursed them. A week later, the weekly of the Islamic Movement continued to roll the snowball of that unpleasant debate, protesting against the bishop's statements. In the communiqué the Islamic Movement released, a long litany of anti-Christian grievances was listed:

---

14. Israeli, *Islamikaze: Manifestations of Islamic Martyrology*, 387.

> Muslims conquered Egypt and Greater Syria, where Christians lived. To this day, they enjoy freedom of faith and religious practice. History does not recall even one case where Islam forced a non-Muslim to convert to Islam. This is why the majority in India are still non-Muslim, though Muslims ruled India for generations.... On the other hand, Islam suffered abominable crimes in the Crusades, in the time of the missionary onslaughts, the deportation of Muslims from Spain, ... and Western Imperialism and Communism. Such terrible things were not committed by Islam, because the Qur'an says: "there is no compulsion in religion." ... Muslim tradition says that Allah forbade us entering the house of the People of the Book without permission, and he forbade Muslims to beat Scriptuary women, or eating their cows, if only they paid the *jizya* set for them. Their homes, properties, money and the honor of their women are protected, and the Muslim is not allowed to harm them.... This means that the honor of any man is protected as long as he fills his duties. . . . Therefore, Christian clergymen must refrain from statements that do not help to restore unity to the Palestinian people in the Holy Land, and the good relations that it took Islam 14 centuries to build.[15]

Khatib's and his Islamic Movement version of history, which cleanses Islam from any wrongdoing, and expects Christians (and Jews) to submit to Islam and pay their poll-tax without protest, even when their houses and houses of prayer are burned, entire communities are forced to convert, as happened to Christians in the Holy Land, Egypt, Syria, and elsewhere; and to Jews in North Africa and under the Almoravids and Almohads, while their Muslim oppressors were hiding behind their Qur'anic verses, are indications of their biased narrative and of the blinders they put on their eyes when they sermonize to others about the tolerance that, in fact, they have never known. Nor do they mention the *Shari'a* books that give details of how the Scriptuaries who did not submit to the rule of Islam should be treated and their children and women taken in slavery. Yes, the Crusaders had indeed committed abominable crimes against Muslims (and Jews), but the Kingdom of Jerusalem they came to build was erected on the Christian land they had been forced to leave by the Muslim conquerors, not an innate Muslim territory.

While in Israel proper Christians can still feel protected by Israeli rule, as it was manifested during the Nazareth crisis, under the essentially Muslim government of the Palestinian Authority in the Palestinian territories,

---

15. *Sawt al-Haqq wal-Huriyya*, 18 June 1999, and 25 June 1999; Sura 2:56.

hostile developments seem slightly more complicated to control. It is estimated that some thirty-five thousand Christians live in the West Bank and three thousand more in the Gaza Strip, not counting the thirteen thousand Christians who live in East Jerusalem, which has been under Israeli rule since 1967. Not only has the Palestinian Authority adopted Islam as its official religion, but the strong factions of Hamas and Islamic Jihad, which probably comprise at least half the Palestinian population, make sure that Islamic influence has been preponderant in Palestinian society. Officially, the Palestinian Authority treats the Christians equally, and tries to display this policy in public. For example, Christmas is recognized as a Palestinian official holiday, and the Chairman of the Palestinian Authority, since the time of Arafat, attends the Mass and holds an official reception of that day. Jesus Christ has been adopted as a "Palestinian," and Arafat has stated that his mission was to protect the Muslim and Christian holy places in Palestine, and he nominated prominent Christians, like Hanan Ashrawi to important positions in the Palestinian Authority.[16] Nonetheless, contrary messages by leaders, especially among the Islamic opposition, as well as popular anti-Christian outbursts, occasionally darken the scene. For example, in a Friday sermon broadcast live on Palestinian TV from a Gaza mosque, Dr Ahmed abu Halabiya stated:[17] "Allah the almighty has called upon you not to ally with the Jews or the Christians, not to like them, not to become their partners, not to support them and not to sign agreements with them."

As has been the wont in other Muslim countries, no law protects religious freedom, and certainly not that of non-Palestinians. For example, one day in January 2001, at the height of the Al-Aqsa Intifadah (2000–2003), the Israeli press carried the picture of a procession in Ramallah, which paraded a donkey wearing a Jewish prayer shawl and sporting on its forehead a Star of David in the shape of a swastika, with Palestinian police standing by and applauding the parade. The Israeli public was shaken, regarding this act of profanation and abuse as a continuation of the torching of the Jewish synagogue in Jericho and Joseph's tomb in Nablus, which had been conceded to Palestinian protection under the Israel-Palestinian Oslo II Agreement, during the initial stages of that upheaval. In all those cases, what transpired was a Palestinian determination, born out of frustration and hatred, and made explicit in violent acts, to express their hostility to Jewish religious symbols, knowing full well the hurt and anguish they would cause among the Israeli public. Conversely, the angered Israeli readership of the papers was reminded that when in 1997 a young Jewish settler in Hebron had held up a

---

16. Tsimhoni, "The Christians in Israel, the West Bank and the Gaza Strip."
17. MEMRI Special Dispatch, No 138, 13 October 2000.

poster in public, in which the Prophet Muhammad was reviled by the drawing of a pig in his proximity, she was duly arrested by the Israeli police, tried for religious incitement, and incarcerated for three years. Her outrageous deed, which rightly provoked Muslim rage, was duly condemned across the board by Israeli politicians and clerics, who understood the sensitivity of such provocations. The Israelis had expected, in vain, to see a similar reaction by the Palestinian authorities and clerical hierarchy. Moreover, the Israelis had expected the Palestinians to protect their Jewish sites, as they had undertaken in their Oslo II engagement, under which Israel had withdrawn from those places. Those desecrations, which were committed while the Palestinian police were watching idly, helped remove Israeli readiness to evacuate more territories or to put faith in Palestinian commitments.[18]

Since then the Palestinians have tried to delegitimize Israel by denying the historical attachment of the Jews to Palestine, and inventing a new "history" that crowned the Palestinians as the original inhabitants of the land. Thus, when history is fabricated at will, popular hatred is indoctrinated by the official media, and commitments are broken at the whim of leaders or at the pace of a violent populace, how can one have faith in rights, guarantees, or the recognition of others, unless they are the rights of Muslim or Palestinians? Indeed, while asserting that the Palestinians' "liberty and freedom to worship and practice their religious beliefs are protected," the Palestinian Authority Minister of Information—a job peculiar to totalitarian regimes—has also declared:

> The Palestinian people are also governed by Shari'a Law . . . with regard to matters pertaining to religious issues. . . . According to Shari'a Law, applicable throughout the Islamic world, any Muslim who converts or declares becoming an unbeliever, is committing a major sin punishable by capital punishment. The PA cannot take a different position on this matter. . . .[19]

Other signals of the Palestinian "tolerance" towards their Christian minority were not far behind. Consider the following: In August 1997, Palestinian policemen in Beit Sahur opened fire on a crowd of Christian Arabs, wounding six. The Palestinian Authority tried to cover up the event and warned against publicizing the story, by having the local police commander instructing journalists not to report the incident. In late 1997 a Palestinian convert to Christianity in the northern West Bank was arrested by agents of the Palestinian Authority, since he was regularly attending church and

---

18. See the entire story in Israeli, *The Oslo Idea: The Euphoria of Failure*.

19. Palestinian Authority Ministry of Information, December 1997. www.lawsociety.org/Reports/reports/1998/crz4.html

prayer meetings and was distributing Bibles, and a pastor in Ramallah was warned by Palestinian Authority agents that they were monitoring his evangelistic activities, and invited him for questioning for "spreading Christianity." Other incidents of this sort occurred also in other parts of the West Bank, often using Muslim preachers to try to convince Christian converts to renege and return to Islam, under the threat that if they refused they would be prosecuted for "insulting a Muslim cleric." In another case, a Christian preacher was threatened with being accused of "spying for Israel"—an accusation that could have serious repercussions—unless he relented from his evangelistic activity. It was repeatedly confirmed in those years, both from Israeli intelligence and public sources, that Arafat and his Fat'h party and secret services were intimidating and maltreating the Christian population of Bethlehem, extorting money from them, confiscating their land and property, and leaving them to the mercy of street gangs and radical Muslim activists, affording them no protection, which often left them no choice but exile.[20] Similar findings were reported by the *Washington Post* when in March 2002 Muslim militants in Bethlehem took over the Church of Nativity, triggering a thirty-nine-day siege by Israel, which ended with the deportation of thirteen of them to Cyprus and twenty-six others to Gaza, much to the relief of the Christians following two years of rape, murders, and extortion by those Muslim radicals who were dubbed by their Christian neighbors as a "criminal gang which demanded protection money from Christians." Their sigh of relief could be heard far and wide, and was expressed by Miss Helen, fifty, a Christian and mother of four, who said: "We are so delighted that these criminals, who have intimidated us for so long, are now going away." When a Christian seventeen-year-old boy, Johnny Talgieh, was shot down in October 2001, a small stone monument was erected in his memory in Bethlehem's Manger Square where he died. But for Muslim radicals, he did not deserve to be a "martyr," therefore his monument was destroyed and spat at by the Muslim gang members.[21]

The oppression of Christianity was so harsh that the three mayors of the Christian cities: Bethlehem, Beit Jallah, and Beit Sahur, were known to have begged Israel to annex their municipalities to the territory under Israeli jurisdiction before they were submitted to Palestinian Authority rule in the wake of Oslo. One can understand their reluctance to remain under Muslim domination, as expressed in their massive emigration when Israel

---

20. Dani Naveh, "The Involvement of Arafat, PA Senior Officials and Apparatuses in Terrorism against Israel, Corruption and Crime, 2002," www.mfa.gov.il/mfa/go.asp?MFAHOlomO.

21. Anwar, "Exiled Palestinian Militants ran two-years of terror," *The Washington Times*, 13 May 2002.

foolishly submitted that Christian enclave to Arafat's government. Even the Christian holy sites, which had been a major reason for the Christian attachment to the Holy Land, were being desecrated by Muslims, and the Christians felt helpless to redress their grievances, for lack of support from either the Vatican or other Christian countries, who chose their immediate diplomatic and economic considerations over extending a rescuing hand to their heavily repressed coreligionists in Palestine. For example, without prior consent of the church, Arafat decided to turn the Greek Orthodox monastery near the Church of Nativity in Bethlehem into his domicile during his visits to the city. On 5th July 1997 the PLO seized Abraham Oak Russian Holy Trinity Monastery in Hebron, violently evicting monks and nuns from there. During the Aqsa intifada (2000–2003), the Palestinian Authority chose the Christian city of Beit Jala to shoot at Jewish Jerusalem, and it specifically positioned its weapons in or near Christian homes, hotels, churches, and the Greek Orthodox Club, to deter Israelis from returning the fire that could harm Christian institutions. In short, they preferred to make Israel look bad over respecting the sanctity of Christian sites. The most glaring example of Palestinian disregard for Christian sites was the March 2002 invasion of the Church of Nativity by Palestinian Authority forces, taking as hostages forty Christian clergy and nuns. A PLO commander, Abdallah abu-Hadid (Iron-man) later revealed that:

> The idea was to enter the Church in order to create international pressure on Israel. . . . We knew beforehand that there was there two years' worth of food for 50 monks . . . [an indication to the lack of safety the monks felt in that environment]: oil, beans, rice, olives, good bathrooms, and the largest water wells. You did not need electricity because there were candles. In the yard they planted vegetables. Everything was there . . . .[22]

Three Armenian monks, who had been held hostage by the Palestinian gunmen inside the church, managed to flee through a back door, and they immediately thanked the Israeli soldiers for rescuing them. They told Israeli officers that gunmen had stolen gold and other property, including crucifixes and prayer books, and had caused damage to the church. One of the monks, Narkiss Korasian, later told reporters: "they stole everything, they opened the doors . . . one by one and stole everything. They stole prayers books and four crosses. They stole prayers books and four crosses, they did not leave anything. . . . Thanks you for your help, we will never forget it."

22. Yoram Ettinger, "The Islamization of Bethlehem by Arafat," in *Jerusalem Cloakroom, 117*, Ariel Center for Policy Research, 25 December 2001; and *Yedioth Aharonot*, 24 May 2002.

After the gunmen left, the church was in a terrible condition: they seized church stockpiles of food and "ate like greedy monsters," one eyewitness commented that they depleted the food reserves while the 150 civilians who were inside went hungry; they guzzled beer and Johnny Walker scotch [as devout Muslims] that they found in priests' quarters. That indulgence lasted for two weeks into the thirty-nine-day siege, until the food and drink ran out. One of the Greek Orthodox hostages insisted that "they acted like animals and like greedy monsters." They left behind them empty bottles of beer and hundreds of cigarette butts strewn on the floor of that holy site. They took computers apart and dismantled a television set for use as a hiding place for their weapons. Archbishop Ironius, who showed reporters into the main reception hall of the Greek Orthodox monastery, told them: "you can see the repayment we got for hosting these so-called guests." Catholic priests said that some Bibles were torn up for toilet paper, and many valuable sacramental objects were removed. They took candelabra, icons and anything that looked like gold, said the Mexican Franciscan Reverend Nicholas Marquez.[23]

In those days, a wave of illegal land seizures by Muslims exemplified Palestinian lawlessness. Tony Sabella, a tour guide, found three men squatting on the 600squ/m plot of Bethlehem farmland that his family had owned for twenty-five years. The squatters proffered documents that Sabella insisted were forged, as was another alleged bill of sale under which another multi-million dollar property owned by Samir Asfour, a wealthy Bethlehem doctor, was "sold." The people who seized the land presented their "ownership" document from 1970, bearing a Jordanian seal, though since 1967 that territory was ruled by Israel. All in all, thirty-four cases of Christian land seizure in Beit Sahur occurred during two months, and no other reason was given than the determination of the Palestinian Authority to Islamize the Bethlehem area, according to Father Peter Marcos, an official of the Latin Patriarch, and a teacher at Bethlehem University. Marcos also claimed that local Muslims were seeking to change the name of the famous Manger Square to Umar Plaza, to commemorate the second Caliph who took over Jerusalem from the Byzantines in 638 CE. The inhabitants of adjoining Beit Jallah began to advocate a radical step of asking that their village be annexed to Israel, and the security fence be extended around its borders to keep the Muslims out, a plan that the Israelis were not eager to fulfill due to their

---

23. "Greedy Monsters Ruled Church," *The Washington Times*, 15 May 2002; Margot Dudkevitch, "Gunmen Stole Gold, Crucifixes, Escaped Monk's Report," *Jerusalem Post*, 24 April 2002.

shortsightedness and the illusory hopes that they still attributed to the Oslo Accords of a decade earlier.[24]

The Christian holy places in Jerusalem have similarly been encroached upon by Muslims, though the city has not been under their rule since 1967. For, as they deny the existence of the Jewish Temple in history, they also reject, by inference, the New Testament description of Jesus Christ's visit to the Temple; hence Father Marun Lahham's worry that "frequent Muslim declarations that Jerusalem is Muslim troubles Christians."[25] The Palestinian Authority has tried to interfere with the Christian holy places in Jerusalem by breaking into the Church of the Holy Sepulcher from the adjacent Hanaqa Mosque, which leans on the wall of the Sepulcher, in an attempt to add construction to the courtyard of the mosque. Israel intervened to calm down the conflict by ordering the stoppage of the work. The Israeli District Archaeologist wrote to the *Waqf* director in Jerusalem, pointing out the damage the new construction was causing to the antique holy site, but only following threats of a legal procedure and international pressure, did the work cease. Temple Mount also, though principally holy to Jews, due to the location of the two successive Temples, became also sacred to Christians, due to its linkage to Jesus Christ, as attested by the Templars order that linked its very name to that holy site, which served their aim of protecting the pilgrims to the Holy land during the Crusades and the routes leading thereto. The heads of the Islamic authorities among both the Palestinians and the Israeli Arabs, announced that the entire area of Temple Mount (the *Haram al-Al-Sharif*, in Islamic parlance) was an inseparable and integral part of the Aqsa Mosque![26]

On another level, the Palestinians accelerated the Islamization of Bethlehem and its satellite Christian towns of Beit Jallah and Beit Sahur, since they took control of them in 1995, by annexing 30,000 Muslim inhabitants of the adjacent refugee camps (Dahaisha, al-'Aidah and Al-Azeh) and Bedouins of the Ta'amrah tribe to the city boundaries, thus tipping the demographic balance to the Muslim favor, in addition to encouraging immigration to Bethlehem of Muslims from Hebron. Thus, the area's twenty-three thousand Christians were reduced from a 60 percent majority on the eve of the Palestinian takeover (1995) to a minority in 2001, which continues to shrink ever since, mainly by emigration. To affirm the change institutionally,

---

24. Joshua Hammer, "Dark Days in Bethlehem: Under Siege from all Sides, Christians in the Holy Land Have Never Been So Beset," *Newsweek*, 19 September 2003.

25. *Al-Quds*, 18 June 1999, as reported by MEMRI, Special Dispatch 41, 2 August 1999.

26. Nadav Shragai, "Islamic Movement Planning Forth Mosque for Temple Mount," *Ha'aretz* 18 June 2000.

Arafat had appointed a Muslim from Hebron, as governor of Bethlehem, Muhammad al-Ja'bari, dissolving the city council, which consisted of nine Christians and two Muslims, reflecting the demographic reality, and replacing it with a 50:50 appointed council. At the outset, just as in Nazareth, the Mayor remained a Christian, but all levels of the bureaucracy, security, and politics were gradually drained of Christians. Nationally too, while six seats (out of eighty-eight) in the Palestinian Legislative Council were reserved for Christians, namely a higher rate than their proportion in the general population, in effect that body has no power, and the government, which does exercise executive authority, does not comprise any Christians. The obvious reason is that for many Muslims Christians are some sort of fifth column collaborating with Israel, therefore they were consistently persecuted both in the West Bank and Gaza.[27]

Palestinian Muslims find a myriad ways to intimidate their Christian minority: from graffiti, proclaiming: "first the Saturday people [Jews], then the Sunday people [Christians]," to desecrating Christian cemeteries, to threatening Christian women for wearing Western dress, to adducting and raping Christian women, to breaking into convents. In July 1994, the *Wall Street Journal* reported Muslim refusal to sell land to Christians, and Muslim attacks on Christian clubs and other facilities. Not only were Christian crosses, graves, and statues desecrated, but individual Christians were beaten and suffered Molotov cocktail attacks. Loud Muslim sermons have been aired during Christian services, including during the Pope's address in Nazareth in April 2000, which had to be halted until the loud Muslim call for prayer was completed. The *Boston Globe* reported:

> The rampage began after Hanna Salameh, a member of a wealthy Christian family, allegedly killed Jibril 'Id, a Muslim construction contractor from the Qalandia refugee camp [in northern Jerusalem], after the two men argued at the Israeli Army's Qalandia checkpoint. Salameh also allegedly assaulted 'Id's brother and a policeman, then fled the scene and turned himself in to police in Ramallah. A few hours later, hundreds of men poured out of the refugee camp and went to Ramallah where they burned Salameh's house and store. They then burned his brother's store, damaged several businesses owned by Christians not related to the Salamehs, and torched the exercise room and terrorized more than 100 children at Sariya, a scouting and youth center....

---

27. See Ettinger "The Islamization of Bethlehem by Arafat"; Tsimhoni, "The Christians in Israel, the West Bank and the Gaza Strip"; Dudkevitch, "Church Denies Christians Fleeing PA Areas."

Palestinian police did nothing to stop this destruction, according to numerous witnesses, but drew the line as the mob moved toward Christian churches, whose leaders the Palestinian leadership is cultivating for international support in the struggle with Israel. . . . While Officials of the PA and of Fat'h insisted that the incident was simply about revenge and anger, many in Ramallah said otherwise. The truth is that this is a problem between Christians and Muslims [said a Christian businessman]. There is no security for us. Everyone is taking the law into his own hands. . . . They burned this accused man's brother's house, his shops, his cars, and the police of Ramallah stood by and watched. This is the democracy of Palestine. . . . Some witnesses said that some members of the security services participated in the mob action. . . . The chief of security at Qalandia was in charge of this rampage [said a Muslim shopkeeper]. The Mayor of Ramallah came, saw what was happening, and withdrew. [He only reportedly said]: "I am a Muslim but I condemn this. These are savage people."[28]

On another occasion, a Muslim "peeping Tom" who photographed a Christian woman in the changing room of a clothes shop, sparked a riot in Beit Sahur. At the height of the disturbances, hundreds of Muslims and Christians fought each other with metal rods and stones in the streets of Beit Sahur. "It was like a war," commented a local resident. The explosion was triggered when a Muslim sneaked a camera and snapped several pictures of a Christian woman dressing. The intruder, from a nearby Muslim town, raced in a taxi with the shop owner in hot pursuit. But he was forced to flee to a mosque when dozens of Beit Sahur residents arrived and began smashing the taxi, which they later set in fire. By then both sides had called reinforcements, and the Muslims demanded that the police free the man, who was badly beaten during the melee, but the suspect was arrested and taken to jail. Then the fight started, with rocks and sticks, and police reinforcement was summoned from Bethlehem and Ramallah. Police tried to quell the melee by firing volleys in the air with automatic weapons, and violence died down only when the district governor of Bethlehem imposed curfew. Two injured people were taken to hospital, and many others were bruised and cut, leaving the streets littered with stones.[29] This incident attracted the attention of the media, not for its inherent severity, but for the

28. Charles Radin, "Mob Fears Grow in the West Bank," *Boston Globe*, 6 February 2002.

29. Magnus Johansson, "Peeping Tom Sparks Muslim-Christian Riot in West Bank," *Reuters*, 14 July 2004.

extreme sensitivity in this society about the need to protect women's honor, failing which the entire community's reputation is stained. "Peeping Toms" exist in other countries too, but nowhere would this incident be taken beyond a regular event of indiscretion and violation of privacy, certainly not a *casus belli* of such a scope and violence.

Faced with this outrageous conduct, and with more murderous attacks on their facilities and youth,[30] Palestinian Christians, instead of submitting to Palestinian Authority jurisdiction and asking for its protection, have been fleeing for safety. Indeed, from the twenty-eight thousand Christians that were accounted for in Bethlehem by the last British census in 1947, only eleven thousand were left by the 1967 War, meaning that their majority had left during the nineteen-year Jordanian rule. This outflow has increased under Palestinian Authority rule. Between the Oslo Accords (1993) and the transfer of Bethlehem to the Palestinian Authority (1995) the late Christian Mayor of Bethlehem, Elias Freij, sensing what was coming, lobbied Israel against the transfer, arguing that Bethlehem would become a city of churches but without Christians to worship in them. He asked that Bethlehem remain within the boundaries of greater Jerusalem, as had been the case under Jordan, but short-sighted Israeli governments, lured by the elusive prospect of peace with the Palestinians, and under Western pressure, submitted that city and its satellites to the Palestinian Authority jurisdiction. Even the *The Times* of London, no great supporter of the Israeli cause, wrote in those days:

> Life in PA-ruled Bethlehem has become insufferable for many members of the dwindling Christian minorities. Increasing Muslim-Christian tensions have left some Christians reluctant to celebrate Christmas in the city, at the heart of the story of Christ's birth. The situation has become so desperate for the Christians that during his visit to Bethlehem Pope John Paul II had felt it necessary to urge Palestinian Christians, already in 2000, not to be afraid to preserve their Christian heritage and Christian presence in Bethlehem.[31]

In the developed Christian community of Ramallah, north of Jerusalem, where the Palestinian Authority has advisedly established its HQ, as the Muslim seat in Gaza, initially chosen by Arafat, proved unsettling, anti-Christian provocations are also rife. The reactions of the Christians to this

---

30. Bill Hutman, "Concern over Muslim Attacks on Christians in the Old City," *Jerusalem Post*, 18 July 1994.

31. Cited by Jonathan Adelman and Aggie Kuperman, *Rockie Mountain News*, 22 December 2001.

onslaught on their identity, existence, and pattern of settlement in the Holy Land, have found various, sometimes even polar, ways of expression: from the classic *dhimmi*, who the more beaten and humiliated, the more tends to identify with his tormentors, to Christians who call upon their oppressors to join hands in their common struggle against Israel, to Eastern Christian leaders who have disclosed their loathing to Western Christianity. Some of the Christians of the Holy Land have, on the contrary, become Israel's best friends, following their evangelical coreligionists in America, as narrated by Don Feder:[32]

> At the dawn of the 21st Century, when one thinks of Israel's most prominent defenders, the names that spring to mind are Robertson, Bauer and Falwell. . . . The God of Abraham, David and Isaiah, is also the God of Matthew, Mark and Luke. Christians view the Jewish Scriptures as a prologue to the New Testament. Moses was a Jew, not an Arab Sheikh. Jesus came from the House of David, not a Bedouin tribe. . . . Christian affinity to the parent faith is understandable. . . . When God tells the Children of Israel that he will bless those who blessed them and curse those who curse them, Christians note that this is a covenant binding for all time. Similarly, when God gave the land between the Jordan and the sea to Abraham's descendants, that precluded a future claim to any of the territory . . . .
>
> As to non-Biblical considerations, since the fall of Communism, Islam has become Christianity's main adversary, as it had been during the last 14 hundred years. . . . Wherever Christianity is persecuted in the Third World, Islam is the force responsible for their plight. Gunmen murder women and children at Church services in Pakistan, Coptic Christian villages are burned to the ground in Egypt; in Indonesia, Christians are forcibly converted to Islam, Sudanese Christians are enslaved, Nigerian Christians have Islamic law forced on them. In Saudi Arabia, the most Muslim nation, conversion to Christianity is a capital offense, church services are forbidden (even in private homes), Bibles are confiscated as contraband, and during the Gulf War US military personnel were told not to wear crosses lest they offend the sensibilities of their hosts. Saudi schools teach unvarnished hatred of Christians and Jews. . . .
>
> Under the Palestinian Authority, Bethlehem Christian population has been reduced from a clear majority to a minority of 20%. The London *Times* reported that life in Bethlehem

---

32. Don Feder "Why Christians Have Become Israel's Best Friends," *National Religious Broadcasters Journal*, February-March 2003.

has become insufferable for many members of the dwindling Christian minority. Muslim-Christian tensions have left some Christians reluctant to celebrate Christmas in the town at the heart of the story of Christ's birth. All of this has increased feelings of solidarity with Islam's Jewish victims. Many Christians understand that should the PLO banners fly over the Old City of Jerusalem, the city most holy to their faith would be lost to them as well as to the Jews. . . . Israel speaks to the essence of what it means to be a Christian, . . . it is the validation of the Bible's promises. Thus, it evokes the hopes as well as the deepest longing of Christians everywhere. After two millennia, Christians and Jews find themselves on the same side of the barricades, confronting the forces of darkness. Perhaps it was always intended to be so.

The plight of the Christians in Bethlehem reflects a microcosm, that is better known and more closely studied due to its limited territory, and its proximity to Israel, of the trauma that most Christians of the Middle East are experiencing, accompanied by a sense of an epoch-making era comparable perhaps to the year of 1453, when Mehmet II and his Turkish Muslim fighters scaled the unassailable walls of mighty Constantinople, bringing to its end the millennial Christian Byzantine Empire, and ushering in the still mightier Muslim Ottoman Empire, that launched its dominance for the next half millennium, until it faltered and fell in World War I. Bethlehem, the town where Christianity was born, is being depleted of its Christians, after years of violence and an economic free-fall. Most of all, however, the Muslim harassment, which has occasioned the erection of the separation barrier by Israel to combat Palestinian terrorism from the outside, has not affected the domestic Islamic threat from within for the remaining Christians. Their only outlet is emigration. The *New York Times* made the skewed contention that Christians were leaving Bethlehem due to the hardships imposed by the security fence. However, if that were true, Muslims too should have left, and they do not; their numbers, on the contrary, keep increasing as their Christian neighbors depart. Besides, the Christian exodus had begun well before the fence was constructed, and it had begun simultaneously in other parts of the world where there were no separation fences, indicating that there must have been other reasons for this mass departure, and the reasons lay principally with the Muslim aggressive takeover, which the PC Western press is reluctant to mention, as in other parts of the Muslim world.[33]

---

33. Joseph Farah, "Why Christians Leave the Middle East," *WorldNetDaily*, 3 January 2005.

An illustration of the transformation of Bethlehem is provided by the pace of Islamization of the city. This city had been 90 percent Christian until the middle of the twentieth century. But during the 1948 War, which was launched by the Arabs when Israel was founded, the influx of Muslim refugees into the city effected the demographic shift that had caused a permanent trickle of Christian emigration, which remained steady until the 2000s, when the Al-Aqsa Intifada and the increasing Islamic harassment of the Christians turned it into a gushing current and then into a flood, which turned the Christians into only one third of the city population. In the early days of that uprising, Muslim gunmen in the Bethlehem area took hilltop positions in neighboring Beit Jallah, a predominantly Christian town, which afforded them a clear firing line at the southern part of Israeli Jerusalem. When the Israeli military responded, the Beit Jallah residents, who were not a party to the Palestinian attacks on the Israeli neighborhood of Gilo, found themselves on the frontlines of the conflict, and occasionally among its fatalities too. The Muslim terrorists who initiated the battle had intentionally placed Christians in the crossfire between them and Israel. That became evident when they seized the Church of Nativity, nearly destroying it, defecating in its hallways and smashing its statues and stealing precious objects, as ISIS is now doing in Christian and historical sites in Mosul and Palmyra. The Israelis negotiated an end to the standoff, rather than destroy the church that is so central to Christians around the world. But when they withdrew from Bethlehem after that crisis was resolved, and from the rest of Palestinian territories in the West Bank and Gaza, the Palestinian Authority has waged a war against the remaining Christian minority, causing the rape of Christian women, the extorting of businessmen and the lynching of "collaborators" with the Israelis and the seizing of their homes. Those were good enough reasons for the Christians to leave when the direct protection by Israel was sacrificed to the Palestinian Authority assurances that law and order would be guaranteed after Israel withdrew from parts of the West Bank and Gaza under the aborted Oslo Accords of 1993.[34]

In 2006, Hasan al-Masalmeh, a member of the Bethlehem City Council, publicly advocated implementing the *jizya* discriminatory tax. He said very openly that: "we in the Hamas intend to implement this tax sometime in the future, and we welcome everyone in Palestine, but only if they agree to live under our rules." In late 2007, an evangelical pastor was forced to leave Ramallah under threats from PLO gunmen, soon after his congregation dissolved, instead of making a great effort to use his media connections

---

34. Ibid. For the Bethlehem area, see also Khaled Abu Toameh, "Bethlehem Christians Claim Persecution," *Jeruslaem Post*, 25 January 2007.

to gain protection by publicizing his community's plight. For that reason, tens of thousands of Palestinian Christians have left their ancestral homes and have emigrated to the Americas, to Europe, or to Australia. In fact, they flee to any country that will issue them a visa, in addition to those Christians among the streams of undocumented refugees who take the risks of crossing seas and continents in order to seek shelter from the misfortunes of war and persecution in their Muslim countries of origin.

The Christian city of Ramallah, north of Jerusalem, which Abu Mazen has chosen as the HQ of the Palestinian Authority, unlike Arafat who shuttled between it and Gaza, has also known its anti-Christian pogroms, in spite of its being the show window of Palestinian prosperity and relative peace and order, compared to the prevailing overall chaos and misery of the West Bank and Gaza. In September 2005 a two-day (Saturday and Sunday) rampage on a Christian village near Ramallah left many houses and vehicles torched, before the PA forces interfered to put an end to the pogrom. As a result many houses were looted in Taiba, and helpless families were compelled to leave the city and its environment. The village of 1,500 was attacked after a Muslim thirty-year-old woman from the nearby village of Deir Jarir was murdered by members of her family for having had a romance with a Christian man from Taiba. When her family discovered that she had been involved in a forbidden relationship with a Christian man, they apparently forced her to drink poison, then they buried her without reporting her death to the authorities. So, when the Palestinian Authority security forces decided to launch an investigation, her family protested for fear that her forbidden (and shamefully dishonoring) relationship would be exposed, especially that her body was to undergo autopsy. But despite the severity of the rampage, it was not made a priority and it took police many hours to reach Taiba, and naturally, Israel, which is in charge of the overall security in the area, was also accused of the inappropriately slow reaction to the events.[35]

As described by a Christian Taiba resident, more than five hundred Muslims, chanting the familiar "Allahu Akbar!" war cry, attacked their victims at night, they poured kerosene on many buildings and set them on fire, then broke into houses and robbed furniture, jewelry, and electric appliances. This event not only brought to bear the latent anti-Christian hatred that is part of the supremacist Muslim culture, but especially illustrated in the open the inherent intolerance towards the "treason" of any Muslim woman who lets herself be tempted into a relationship with a non-Muslim

---

35. Khaled Abu Toameh, *Jerusalem Post*, 5 September 2005. See also Daniel Pipes, *New York Sun*, 13 September 2005.

man, while the reverse, namely cases of Muslim men taking in non-Muslim women, are viewed as natural and feasible. Worse, the notion of "collective punishment," which Muslims everywhere complain against as "anti-democratic," has exploded in their face in this unfortunate incident, in which an entire Christian community was rampaged, to retaliate for the "misdeed" of one individual Christian who had dared to "desecrate" the honor of one Muslim woman. The day after the events, the streets of Taiba remained deserted, with only police forces patrolling them and the Christians hiding indoors, while the torched houses and cars and the destroyed statue of the Virgin Mary littered the streets of the entire disaster area. Unaware that the man from the Khoury family who was accused of the romance had fled the village for his life, the rampaging crowds first looked for him or his family for retaliation, and they first broke into their houses and destroyed them and then invaded the beer factory, that had been established by the Khoury family in that unique village of the West Bank, which is completely Christian. It is believed that it was Saladin who gave that name to Taiba (the good one), due to the good conduct of the villagers, after they had carried for centuries the name of Ephraim, based on a story about Christ (John 11:54).[36]

The fate of the tiny Christian community has been even worse in the Gaza Strip due to the rule of the Hamas there, which is doctrinally committed to act against Christians. The occasion for the eruption against them unfolded in 2006, during the Danish Cartoon crisis, which acquired world proportions when throughout the Muslim world Muslims demonstrated, often violently, against what they regarded as the "insult" to their Prophet in cartoons that depicted critically the founder of Islam. Although this eruption in Gaza took place prior to the takeover of the Strip by Hamas in 2007, the situation had been explosive enough to be expected to blow up at any moment. Exactly as Muslims everywhere attacked foreign embassies and Christian institutions, causing the death of many Muslim and Christian individuals, and the destruction of many structures, signaling to the world that the "honor" of their Prophet was more important than property or even human life, the Gaza Strip played its part too. Palestinians threatened to blow up a Christian Center in Gaza, the Palestinian Bible Society was accused of missionary work, and handed an ultimatum to leave Gaza within a week. In early February 2006 the only church in the Gaza Strip was vandalized and clerics were threatened, despite the fact that Palestinian Christian clerics condemned the cartoons, but Palestinian anger was diverted to the Christian Center, where the Bible Society employed eleven people in its computer room, library, and multi-purpose hall. Christians

36. Ibid

believe that those threats were orchestrated by the Fatah faction, headed by Mahmud Abbas, who was trying then to block Hamas from taking over, and could not afford to be seen by the Palestinian audience as too lenient towards the Christians.

Rami Khader Ayyad lived in the city of Gaza with his wife and two children, while his spouse was pregnant with her third child. His Teachers Bookstore sold Bibles and Christian literature, and he was personally associated with the Palestinian Bible Society, which promotes Christian presence in Muslim areas. In April 2007 his store was firebombed by a Muslim "vice squad" that was attacking targets they connected with Western influence. According to Ayyad's family and acquaintances, he had regularly received anonymous death threats from people angered by his missionary work. He was abducted the night of 6th October 2007, after closing his store, and he simply called his family to announce that he would return home late. His body was found early next morning with signs of torture, including a gunshot in the head and numerous stab wounds. Witnesses said that they had watched three armed men, two of them masked, beat Ayyad repeatedly with clubs and the butts of their guns while accusing him of spreading Christianity in Gaza. The witnesses said that after beating him, all three assassins shot him in the head. It was Sheikh Abu Saqr himself, the Head of the Salafi program in Gaza, who, while denying that his group had any hand in the murder, confirmed that "Christians engaging in missionary activity in Gaza would be dealt with harshly."[37]

Other stories of Christianophobia continued to pour out of Gaza in spite of the insignificant size of the tiny community remaining there. Constantine Dabbagh, the Secretary of the Near East Council of Churches, complained that three masked men broke into his house in Gaza, and beat him and his wife before stealing money and jewelry. The assailants told their victims that they came to search for wireless devices of communications.[38] In December 2007, after the Hamas took over the reins of government, Christmas celebrations were canceled and display of crucifixes became taboo. When the Latin Patriarch came to Gaza's Holy Family Church to celebrate Christmas, he instructed the full house of Catholic and Orthodox families to pray for reconciliation. For, due to the conflict between Hamas and the PLO, fewer than 1,400 Christians remained in the Strip and they too were preparing to leave; the hope was that reconciliation between the

---

37. "Palestinian Christian Activist Killed in Gaza," *Kuwait Times*, 8 October 2007; and Eric Young, "Witnesses: Slain Palestinian was Tortured for Spreading Christianity," *Christian Post*, 11 October 2007.

38. Khaled Abu Toameh, "Church Official, Wife Beaten and Robbed in Gaza," *Jerusalem Post*, 23 July 2009.

warring parties would stop them going. There had not been a Christmas tree in Gaza's main square since Hamas took over in 2007, and Christmas is no longer a public holiday, as it is in Bethlehem. In fact, if it were not for the special Israeli permission to Gaza Christians to visit the West Bank to celebrate there, they would have had no Christmas festivities at all.[39] One of the young Christians in town described how he was stopped by a Hamas official who ordered him to remove the wooden cross he was carrying, and when he refused he was threatened with arrest.[40] According to Rev. Al-Shafie, President of One Free World International (OWFI), Hamas digs up the bodies of the dead from Christian burial sites in the Gaza Strip, claiming that "they pollute the earth." He also said, when heading a delegation visiting Israel from Canada, that among the three-hundred million Christians being persecuted in the world, 80 percent lived in Muslim countries. Al-Shafie himself is an Egyptian Muslim originally, who converted to Christianity, an offense that cost him a death sentence, but he managed to escape to Canada where his organization operates from.[41] More recently, in 2012, Christians in Gaza staged a sit-in protest, after the family of a young man was being forced to convert to Islam by an armed group.[42]

After the Hamas takeover, things worsened. The drama of the kidnapping of Sana al-Sayegh, a Ramallah-originating Christian Professor, who teaches at the Palestine University in Gaza and was forced to convert to Islam, has brought the matter of Christianophobia in Gaza to a boiling point, especially that her abduction by Hamas terrorists was rumored to have been assisted by the President of the University, Dr. Zaher Khail, her boss, who was supposed to protect her. Her forced conversion was sponsored and encouraged by officials from Prime Minister Isma'il Haniyeh' office.[43] The saga of the abduction and forced conversion of the professor had started two weeks earlier, when she was held by her abductors and not allowed to contact her family, in spite of her position as the Dean of Science and Technology Faculty at the Palestine University. In her role, she had represented her institution in various conferences around the world, and was

39. "Israel Lets 557 Christians out of Gaza for Holidays," IMRA@netvision.net.il 21 December 2012.

40. "Gaza Christians Long for Days Before Hamas Canceled Xmas," *The Guardian*, 23 December 2011.

41. Matthew Wagner, "Human Rights Group: Hamas Disinters Christians in Gaza," *Jerusalem Post*, 12 December 2009.

42. "Gaza Christians Protest Kidnapping and Forced Conversion of Young Man," IMRA@netvision.net.il, 17 July 2012.

43. Khaled Abu Toameh, "Hamas Forced Christian Professor to Convert to Islam," *Jerusalem Post*, 5 August 2007.

highly regarded in her professional field. After she disappeared and her family became concerned for her fate, they turned for help to Prime Minister Hanieh's office. Two weeks later, her family was summoned to a meeting with Haniyeh's aides who were accompanied by the detained professor. The meeting took place at the home of Hamas official, Rafik Makki, where the family was told that she had converted to Islam and married a Muslim man. When queried by her mother whether that was true, she nodded and murmured: "Yes, Allah has guided me through the right path," while Hamas gunmen were present in the room, which gave the impression of a "forced acquiescence," in spite of the document her abductors produced that was signed by her and attested that she had converted and married a Muslim man. But the family also claimed that they talked to the man who claimed to have never married her, and that their request to meet her and Mr. Hanieh had been repeatedly turned down. The remaining three-thousand-member Christian community in Gaza intervened and asked for a meeting with the Prime Minister, but they were also turned down. Her university confirmed that she had converted, and refused to comment under the pretext that it was a "private matter." A female activist for human rights in Gaza met with the professor and confirmed that she had indeed converted and married her colleague, and that he had become a truly devoted and veiled Muslim women, out of her own volition.[44] However, taking into account the syndrome of victims who end up identifying with their abductors, or prisoners with their captors, it is doubtful that this announced "happy end" can be independently confirmed.

In another documented event,[45] unidentified gunmen blew up the YMCA library in Gaza, two guards were kidnapped while the offices were looted, a vehicle stolen, and eight thousand books destroyed. The Fatah faction blamed the Hamas for the attack, but the latter never shouldered the responsibility for it. Some non-identifiable sources told the *Jerusalem Post* that the onslaught was a retaliation for the reprinting in Danish newspapers of the Prophet's denigrating cartoons. For the three thousand Christian Greek Orthodox believers surviving in Gaza, the fact that this event did not make any big headlines anywhere was a sign that all attacks by al-Qa'ida types in Gaza and elsewhere, intended to drive the remaining Christians out, did not raise much interest in the world any longer. It is noteworthy, that the YMCA was not an exclusively Christian club anymore, and was open to Muslims too, including its school, sports club, and community activities, and that anti-Christian mobs are always ready to flare up, even when unrelated events

44. Ibid.
45. Father Raymond De Souza, *National Post*, 19 February 2008.

in remote Denmark provided the pretext. It is well known that Christian Palestinians who have been subject to firebombings, seizures of homes and businesses, assaults and death threats, still tell foreign visitors that they have excellent relations with their Muslim neighbors. Because when the visitors go, the Christians have to remain, and they are loath to give any reasons for Jihadi fanatics to think that they are stirring trouble.[46]

The tempers are so hot regarding the plight of the Christian minority that absurdities occur in the propaganda struggle between the parties. So, while some Christians in Israel cry out that they are neither Arab nor wish to be, anti-Israeli Christian groups in the West, who are bent on demonizing Israel, accuse *Israel* of the persecution of Christians in Islamdom. For instance, Diarmaid MacCulloch, a fellow of the St. Cross College, who wrote against the American support for Israel, the consequences of which "have been particularly dire for the traditional Christianities of the Middle East."[47] MacCullouch describes Islam as "tolerant," in total disregard to Indonesia's closing down churches and forcing Christians to celebrate Christmas in the streets, or Boko Haram, which was murdering thousands of Christians and destroying dozens of churches, or Hamas in Gaza, which abducted Christians and forced them to convert to Islam.

By contrast, the advent of an independent and free Christian voice in Israel was celebrated in a conference in Jerusalem, starring its Greek Orthodox priest, Rev. Gabriel Naddaf of Nazareth, who heads the Israeli-Christian Recruitment Forum, when he declared: "I am here to open the public's eyes. If we want to refrain from lying to our own souls, we must say clearly and unwaveringly: enough!!" He assured that the Christian public wanted to integrate into Israeli society, against the wishes of its old leadership, which had been pushing the Christians to the margins, keeping them the victims of a nationalism that is not theirs. He confirmed that Christianity came out of the Jewish faith and its biblical roots, and articulated his realization that Israel was the only country in the region that protected Christians, with the consequence that the Christian minority of Israel wished to repay by contributing to the State of Israel. He also stressed that Christian children in Israel should not be raised on the history of the *Nakba* and on the hatred of Jews instead of being taught their history.[48]

---

46. Weiner, "Palestinian Crimes against Christian Arabs and their Manipulation against Israel."

47. Ibrahim, "Exploiting Christian Persecution to Demonize Israel."

48. "We are not Arabs, we are Christians who speak Arabic," *Israel Hayom Newsletter*, 4 October 2013.

CHAPTER FIVE

Muslim Minorities under Western Christianity

It turns out, however, that the worldwide Muslim onslaught on Christians (and Jews) is not limited to the Middle East, or to the fifty-seven Muslim-majority countries, populated by 1.5 billion believers, which also host more or less vital Christian communities that have their roots in their lands prior to the Muslim occupation, but have been dwindling under fear and threat, in the past few decades. That attack has been taken to the core of the Christian West, in the recent attempt of self-confident and aggressive Islam to flood it with new immigrants. Judging from the continuous stream of homegrown European Muslim youth to swell the ranks of the Jihadi movements like al-Qa'ida, IS, *Jabhat al-Nusra*, and others, one would think that the Muslim immigrant population of Europe, which has been established there for the third generation now since the 1950s, has become part and parcel of the Islamic upheaval in the Middle East, that has been threatening both the West and the Arab conservative regimes to such an extent, as to occasion their clustering together to fight Islamic terrorism both domestically and internationally. In addition to the dichotomy in which they had lived in their countries of origin, between universal Islam and local nationalism, Muslim minorities in the West are now caught in another contradiction between the House of Islam, where believers are urged to dwell, and the Abode of War where they now live in practice. In the West, where they already constitute sizeable populations (thirty million in Europe, not including Russia, and a few millions in the Americas), they already experience an emotional hardship to identify as French or Swedish, for they lack cultural and religious roots in their chosen countries of asylum. Hence, apart from those Muslim immigrants who have nearly totally integrated, or were born in place (for the third generation now), many others still live divided in their hearts as to their identities, to the point that we see some of them, or their descendants, mounting acts of terrorism against their host countries (e.g., Spain 2004, London 2005, Paris 2015).

A striking example became *cause celebre* when some young Frenchmen of Algerian origin—"homegrown," as the British like to dub their Pakistani-originating Muslim youth—refused to sing the *Marseillaise* with the rest of their compatriots, and even booed those who sang, during an international soccer game between their new adoptive country and their original one. In some cases, notably in the "big three"—France, Britain, and Germany—which have absorbed more than three or four million Muslims each, signs are evident of many independent Muslim educational systems that encourage separation and dissidence, rather than integration and assimilation in their chosen countries of shelter.[1] At any rate, the consistent flow of European Muslim volunteers to areas of Jihadi Islamic fighting in the Middle East, first in Afghanistan, then in Iraq, and now in Syria and Iraq, is evidence enough of the strong spiritual, emotional, and religious ties of young Muslims in their Western diasporas to the core areas of Islam and to their original culture and faith. Moreover, this growing appeal of the Muslim areas of conflict to a wave of Western converts into Islam, tends to show that many facets of the contemporary Muslim identity, as of old, are crystallizing around Jihad and the aura of romance, excitement, adventure, and fulfillment of religious duty that surrounds it.

Since September 11, mainly due to the extraordinary security measures adopted in the US, which were much maligned by the Europeans and by Muslims, whose acts of terror had caused the tightening of security in the first place, not one more significant terrorist event has occurred on US soil, at least for now. Conversely, European allies of the US, including some of those who had reneged on their alliance and elected to cut deals with the terrorists, and even more so Asian countries, many of them among the fifty-seven Islamic Cooperation member-states, who thought they were immune to such horrors, have become the immediate and frequent victims thereof. But we are not dealing in detail here with the already well-established and deeply entrenched Islam in the Big Three of Europe (Britain, France, and Germany) where its demographic impact amounting to millions (four, six, and four, respectively) has irretrievably altered the social and political make-up of those countries; nor with Islam in Europe in general, as it

---

1. For a fuller picture see Israeli, *Muslim Minorities in Modern States*.

concerns its participation in the global scheme to Islamize Europe in the long haul; but only with radical Muslim movements, which are actively seeking Islamic predominance in the world. Islam had penetrated Europe and the West since the early Middle Ages, first during the invasion by the Arabs in the seventh century from the south, when they conquered Spain, Portugal, and half France, before they were arrested by the Charles Martel victory in 732 near Poitiers. This was followed by eight centuries of Muslim rule in Andalusia that ended with their final withdrawal from Granada in 1492, under the relentless advance of the Spanish *reconquista*. The second invasion was launched at about the same time by the Ottomans from the South-East, which led to the fall of Constantinople into their hands, and went as far as the gates of Vienna, before it was arrested and thwarted in 1683, and ultimately led to the break up of the Ottoman Empire during World War I. The current third penetration is done by immigration, and the demographic flooding of Europe, together with a campaign of *da'wa* to propagate Islam, aided by a terrorist wave to intimidate the Christian West, which is lending itself to it.

Worldwide terrorism has not been limited to the confines of the Islamic struggle against the West in the international arena, but has expanded into the domestic scene of Islamic countries, where local radical oppositions aspire to seize power from current considered-illegitimate rulers, who are usually supported by the West. This is the genesis of the Bali, Casablanca, Istanbul, Sinai, Amman, Riyad, and Jedda acts of terror that were primarily directed against visiting aliens after September 11, in order to destroy the tourist source of income or the economic base of those hated regimes. More ominously, many a homegrown Islamic radical, who was allowed to sow lethal propaganda in Western democracies where he had initially sought asylum from oppression in his land of origin, has used his familiarity with his adoptive country to turn it into his target of terror. This is the background for September 11 and then the Madrid (March 2004) and London (July 2005) horrors.

For too long had the world accepted as a "natural" calamity the Palestinian hijackings of the 1970s and 1980s, which had inaugurated this era of international terrorism. Instead of fighting against them and uprooting them, Western governments and passengers accepted with staggering docility being stripped at airports and searched, to have their otherwise sacrosanct privacy encroached upon and trampled upon in public, to pay ever-increasing air-fares in order to cover security costs, and to repeat the mantra that a "solution of the Palestinian conflict will resolve the problem." America has reversed itself and resolved to fight, though only following the September 11 attacks on its soil, while Madrid has elected to yield to the terrorists' demands and change its government, and abandoned the American alliance which fought against terror in Afghanistan and Iraq. London on its part, "changed the rules" only after it was rocked by a series of attacks on its public transportation, and the rest of the Western countries slowly began to follow suit.

After the Van Gogh murder in the Netherlands in 2004, and then the anti-Denmark outburst of Muslim rage in the Cartoon Affair of early 2006, the public debate in Europe was turned on its head. Previously, far from recognizing that the fight against terrorism in Iraq, Afghanistan, and worldwide was launched by the US as a *defensive* measure, after it was attacked on its home territory, America's detractors in Europe and the Muslim world claimed, on the contrary, that it was American offensive moves in those countries that prompted terrorism, exactly as it was Israel's "injustices" towards the Palestinians that had triggered terrorism in the first place! *Cause and effect were reversed* in a Kafkaesque fashion. So, instead of joining the US in its universal struggle against terrorism, and thus also rid themselves of its menace, they blamed the violence on American and Israeli policies, thus unwittingly becoming its unwilling accomplices and its unsuspecting next victims.

But the Cartoon Affair of early 2006 has also dramatically demonstrated that the general Muslim wrath against the West and Israel had just been suppressed for years, due to the measures taken by Muslim governments who were afraid of American retribution. It is also likely that the wrath was suppressed until Muslims were confident that their presence in the West constituted a critical mass, large enough numerically to instill fear of potential civil disorder in the European governments. The fear from American retribution in Muslim countries, which was brought to bear in Afghanistan and Iraq, may have been somewhat mitigated by America's proven constraint to passively absorb atrocious behavior from Syria, Iran, or Egypt, or the havoc of the 1973 oil-price rise. In that regard one might say that the Arabs were constantly testing the limits of what America could tolerate, but they were also aware that America turns a blind eye to misdemeanors in order to secure uninterrupted oil flow from the Middle East. Thus America (and other Western countries for that matter) were seen to favor totalitarian rulers in the Middle East, fearful of the regimes that may replace them—the "better the devil they know" approach. No American President wished then to be responsible for creating another Iran, after the ignominious behavior of President Carter vis-a-vis the Shah. It was not until the 2010s that America, under Obama, became energetically independent and felt free to act (as in the case of IS) without being paralyzed by threats of energy upheavals.

The waves of recriminations of the Muslim world against the West and Israel have also been expressed by the rise of Muslim parties in Turkey, Egypt, Jordan, and the Palestinian Authority; by the unbridled desire of the Iranians to go nuclear, and by the thug-like rhetoric of successive Iranian leaders against Western values and the Jews in general. This went as far as Iran denying the *Sho'ah* in blatant terms, as a Western invention to placate the Jews and Israel! The zeal in the Islamic world was then directed not only against Israel and the West, but aimed primarily to sweep out of power their own Western-allied regimes in the Muslim countries, which were regarded as American stooges. As the major Egyptian paper *al-Ahram* put it, "religious identity has replaced nationalist ideology,"[2] and that applied not only to Muslim countries but also amidst Muslim minorities throughout their diasporas. This meant that Muslim terrorism would continue to rise in both Europe and the Muslim world.

One has to realize the distortions of the basic data of Islam, by both scholars and politicians, who wished to depict a more benign and less menacing picture of the radical Islamic rise than was the case. This was done through the distinction that has become conventional wisdom among both critics and proponents of Islam. Namely, the artificial bifurcation between the so-called "Islamists" or radicals, and the majority of Muslims, who are supposedly "peace-loving," shunning violence, and having no quarrel with West. It is clear that this "scientific" distinction, though pursued by some scholars of reputation, and may have some empirical merit to it, has much more to do with political correctness and with a degree of sheepish *dhimmi*-like submissiveness, or fear of being accused of racism, than with historical reality.

When one examines the spread of Islam into Europe one must take stock of all those considerations, and come to the conclusion that it is not enough to account for Muslim immigration into the Old Continent and its transformation as a consequence, but also go into the dialectic between European counter-measures after the major acts of terror that occurred there, and the Muslim worldview which regards those European defensive measures as acts of aggression, persecution, racism, and discrimination against the ever-docile and always "poor," helpless, innocent, and "victimized" Muslims, who had just come to seek work, not equipped with ill-intentions to cause any damage.

When Britain or Germany idolized multiculturalism as a way to "enrich" European culture, and celebrated the fake "difference" between moderate Islam of the mainstream and the violent few, the Muslims regarded

---

2. *Al-Ahram Weekly,* "Beyond the Vacuum," 13–16 April 2006.

that, by and large, as an attempt to dilute Islam in order to dominate and eliminate it. For them, only their unrestricted and violent activity in favor of recognition of their own mores and norms, such as wearing the veil, forcing marriage on their women, or pursuing "honor killings," would be acceptable as a fair and honorable behavior of the host countries towards them. In other words, not satisfied with full equality of opportunity, freedom of speech, and of religious cult, Muslims demand special privileges for themselves, like the prerogative to train terrorists or incite violence against other fellow-citizens, because in their skewed view of democratic society, only too much freedom and *laissez-faire*, even at the detriment of their host states and societies, is enough freedom for them. When they burn down a Jewish synagogue in Berlin or Paris, they expect their adopted countries to accept that as a matter of course, and they are often aided in that belief by the local extreme-left or extreme-right, or church organizations that boost Muslim demands in order to appear as "progressive" multiculturalists.

Europe had been stunned, like the rest of the world, by the horrors of September 11, and European delegations and leaders poured into Washington D.C. to present their condolences and sympathies to the US. But as soon as the US began to react to terrorism by fighting it actively, first in Afghanistan and then in Iraq, it would have found itself almost lonely on the scene if it were not for the devoted loyalty of Tony Blair, who harnessed the resources of his country to that battle. Moreover, many Europeans elected their bilateral deals with Saddam's Iraq over the eradication of its regime, and instead of instilling into their citizenry the need to stand up to the new barbarians, they behaved like the spoiled "soft" states who have lost the will to stand up for their values and future. One ought to remember that the rich and powerful Empires of Rome, Persia, Byzantium, and China, which had been dipped in their self-contentment, had much to lose because they had grown fat and lazy, and were unwilling to fight anymore, lost the battles to the Vandals, the Arabs, the Turks, and the Mongols (and then the Manchus), respectively, because the latter had nothing to lose, looked with contempt upon life, but coveted the wealth of their neighbors and concluded that it behoove them to inherit it, rather than abandon it in the hands of the declining and spoiled empires they attacked and destroyed.

In the 2000s terms, the Muslim world, which consists of some fifty-seven Muslim-majority countries spanning the two continents of Asia and Africa, comprises about 1.5 billion believers, making it after Christianity the second-largest faith. Islam spread since its inception, as did other faiths, by conquest, by missionary work, or by expanding trade from the core-areas of Islam in the Middle East to the Far-East and the Coasts of Africa. While it was extending its rule into others' territories, it necessarily came into armed conflict with the prevailing cultures, like the Zoroastrians of Iran, the Berbers in North Africa, the Christians of Europe, the Hindus of the Indian Subcontinent, or the Jews and the many Christian denominations of the Middle East. But since the arrest of the Muslim Ottomans at the gates of Vienna by the Europeans in the late seventeenth-century, and the defeat of the Muslim Moghuls in India by the British in the nineteenth century, a reversal in the fortunes of Islam has unfolded. Thenceforth, Islamic might would be in the descent and the European and Western power on the ascent. As Islamdom withdrew, independent Judeo-Christian and Hindu nations emerged in the Balkans, in India, and in the Levant, and the remaining Islamic world was colonized by Europe, until its re-emergence as independent nation-states after the world wars. The gap that continues to yawn between the medieval glorious days of supreme Islam and its fate of submission and backwardness in the modern world is the stuff that continually ignites the eruptions of Muslim frustrations against the West that had caused its demise.

Colonization of Islamdom by the West had its longterm mixed effects nonetheless, inasmuch as modernization, both in thought and in economic development, had set in and began gnawing at the monopoly of Islam in those societies. As a result, the elites of those emerging new nations had taken to Western culture and learned the languages, the mores, the civilizations, the institutions, and the thought of their occupiers, and remained tied to them long after their emancipation from Western rule. So, after attaining independence, many formerly colonized populations moved to the metropolis of their previous occupiers and established Muslim communities there. Some of the newcomers were more at home in the ambiance of their newly adopted cultures than in their original homes where they had become alienated. Others went in search of better economic opportunities, still others came for study periods or to seek political asylum, but then they were reluctant to relinquish the freedom, prosperity, and tranquility of the West and to return to the poverty, oppression, and turmoil of their own countries. Compared to the immense populations of their original homelands, these were tiny trickles of privileged individuals or families who were intent on adapting to their new environments, to adopt their new countries and cultures as their own, and to take the necessary steps to merge into the host-cultures of their choice. Their limited numbers on the one hand, and their dispersion among the alien general population on the other, was a built-in guarantee that in no time they would integrate into the mainstream and assimilate completely.

But the rapid economic growth of Europe in the aftermath of World War II, due to both the reconstruction of the ravages of the war and the economic and technological revolutions that those societies underwent, coupled with the very slow pace of reproduction of European populations, where both men and women were seeking careers rather than raising families, brought about an acute shortage of manpower. Previous colonies, where manpower was available, which required relatively limited cultural adaptation, became the never-drying-up sources for unqualified laborers, who little by little at first, and then in droves, would lavishly replenish the slacking pool of workers in Europe. Needless to say that vast countries like the US, Canada, and Australia, which had been founded as immigrant societies in the first place, would also absorb much of this massive immigration from Muslim countries to the West. This growing movement of populations now came to encompass not only adventurers and seekers of new economic opportunities, but also increasing numbers of "political refugees," some of whom were genuine asylum seekers from the oppressions of their regimes at home, but many of them learned to abuse the generosity, concern for human rights, and openness of the West, to run away from "justice" in their own countries, or to use their countries of asylum as launching pads for political struggle against their home regimes. Eventually, some of the latter would turn against their adoptive countries as well and launch terrorist campaigns against them.

These new immigrants, who for the most part gained local citizenship after the requisite period of residency, which varies from one country to another, no sooner had they raised their status from temporary immigrants to permanent residents or full-fledged citizens, than they began to increase their impact on their adoptive countries in different areas:

1. Under the humanitarian heading of "family reunion," they secured immigration rights for many of their relatives back home, thus markedly increasing their numbers; for many of the radical Muslims, this has become a sort of "soft Jihad" to encourage Muslim immigration into their new adoptive countries in order to increase their influence through sheer numbers;

2. Due to their social and religious needs, they constructed Muslim communities in certain localities throughout Europe, where their numbers created local majorities that no running candidate for elections could ignore; the growth of the communities required the construction of mosques and Muslim cultural centers, part of which were and remain innocent houses of prayer, but others grew into secret lodges of subversion and undercover nests for incitement and recruitment of radical youth;

3. Muslim communities, side-by-side with many of their irreproachable cultural activities, soon also engaged in illicit avenues of civil disobedience and criminal activities, and sometimes in radical incitement against the state; as a result, prisons in Europe are saturated with Muslim inmates out of proportion to their representation in the general population;

4. Muslim communities in the West have imported the Middle Eastern conflict into their host countries, with the attending acts of violence and an unbridled anti-Semitic campaign against local Jewish communities, which had otherwise lived peacefully for many centuries; many of the second and third generations of these Muslims (called *beur* in France), who were brought up in a Middle Eastern "environment" of conflict and war, find it easy and "natural" today to converge on the ISIS battlefield in Syria and Iraq.

5. Many Muslim individuals, and some of their leaders, make no secret of their intent to change Europe to dance to their tune, not to adapt to its. They demand, and in some cases achieve—in the name of democracy, multiethnicism, and multiculturalism—their own school systems, in their own native languages, financed by the host states of Christians in Europe, and in the long run to their own detriment.

6. European countries have adopted multiculturalism, and increasingly multi-lingualism, not as the implementation of the chosen social ideal of cross-fertilizing different cultural groups by allowing them to enrich each other, but as an imposed reality whereby they have abdicated their role to absorb the new comers and integrate them into the existing systems, and instead they let the immigrants dictate their own visions of "integration," which mean in effect separatism, secession, or an eventual takeover when demography had run its course.

The numbers of young Muslim volunteers from the West who flock to the Middle East as Jihadi fighters, have to be tackled together with the problems of the growing Muslim demography. For the inroads of the Muslim world into the Western societies of Europe, America, and Australia are a quite new phenomenon, and as their numbers increase incessantly—either via immigration (legal or illegal) or by high birthrates—their growing presence in the general population and their awakening to their Muslim identity discourage their integration, not only giving rise to the problems they encounter in their Western experience, but also augmenting the rate of their flow towards the battlefields of Islam, while at the same time they expect their host countries to accept their demands. There are already areas of France, Belgium, and the Netherlands, and also Germany and Britain, where Muslim children constitute the majority of the school population, a situation that is pregnant with disaffection and can potentially lead to unrest and terror. Those Islamized areas are also not only the potential pools of volunteer manpower of Jihadists, but also the grounds where Muslim Christianophobia will grow in the future, as these trends continue to advance.

While the demographic trends in Europe seem irreversible, in view of the European population's reluctance to perpetuate itself, on the one hand, and its pressing needs for manpower to replace its aging and retiring segments of society, on the other, it seems that a reassessment of the immigration policies is in the offing. For example, with regard to asylum seekers who do not necessarily respond to the labor needs of the host countries. Europe began rethinking its "safe haven" status also following Ayaan Hirsi Ali's departure from Dutch politics, which has played off fears about "bogus" asylum seekers. In Vienna, for example, tourists on the Ringstrasse were witnessing a "strange" and unusual sight—little girls veiled—and exclaimed: "Did you see that one girl—so young! And wearing a veil! They will form a separate culture." That sentiment is no longer isolated. Earlier in May 2006, Austria's Interior Minister Liese Prokop announced that 45 percent of Muslim immigrants were "unintegratable," and suggested that those people should "choose another country." This is another illustration of the changing mentality of initial welcoming to the Muslim immigrants in Europe, when Europeans suddenly wake up to the cultural incongruity between local cultures and the newcomers. And after the Muslim terrorist horrors of Paris (2015) and Brussels (2016), the security anxieties have been even surpassing the cultural ones.

Indeed, it was in the Netherlands that one of Europe's most integrated Somali refugees and a critic of radical Islam, Ayaan Hirsi Ali, resigned her seat in parliament in the wake of criticism that she had faked details on her asylum application to the Netherlands in 1992. And France's lower house of parliament passed a strict new immigration law. This came in the wake of recent rumblings from the top echelons of governments across Europe suggesting that the continent is rethinking its once-vaunted status as a haven for refugees, as it becomes more suspicious that many immigrants are coming to exploit its social benefits and democratic principles. "The trend today in Europe is more and more to try to control the immigration flow," said Philippe De Bruycker, founder of the Odysseus Network, an academic consortium on immigration and asylum in Europe. "At the same time we still say we want to respect the right of asylum and the possibility of applying for asylum. But of course, along the way, we create obstacles for asylum seekers," he acknowledged a day after Ms. Prokop made her controversial statement on 15th May 2006. Ms. Hirsi Ali, who was elected to parliament in The Hague in 2003, was informed by her own political party that her Dutch citizenship was in question. Immigration Minister Rita Verdonk, a former prison warden dubbed "Iron Rita," who has long promised a tough stance on immigration, said that "the preliminary assumption must be that—in line with case law of the Dutch Supreme Court—[Hirsi Ali] is considered not to have obtained Dutch nationality." At issue were inconsistencies in Hirsi Ali's application for asylum in 1992—giving a false name and age, and saying she was fleeing from Somalia's civil war, not from a forced marriage. Though she had publically admitted to the falsities in 2002, a TV documentary heightened public scrutiny of the controversial parliamentarian, who had been under twenty-four-hour protection from death threats since the murder of Theo Van Gogh, the director of a film she wrote. Hirsi Ali's case, heatedly debated across Europe in the days since Ms. Verdonk's announcement, was seen as particularly ironic. But it also highlights the dramatic change in Europe since the turn of this century.[3]

In the years following the World War II, a chagrined US and Europe vowed to follow the Geneva Conventions and create safe havens for refugees. Yet such lofty ideals were hard to uphold after massive influxes of workers in the 1960s and early 1970s were halted during an economic downturn. Those immigrant populations—often Muslims from North Africa and the Middle East—were swollen by family reunifications, yet often remained economically and socially distinct from the societies that they had adopted. The image of the immigrant began to change, and distinctions between those who came for work and those who came for safety began to blur. Now, said Jean-Pierre Cassarino, a researcher at the European-Mediterranean Consortium for Applied Research on International Migration in Florence, Italy, "asylum seekers are viewed as potential cheaters." Today, in once-homogenous Europe, tensions between immigrants and native Europeans appear to be increasing. The perception that an ever-increasing number of newcomers—who neither speak the language of their adopted country nor accept its cultural mores—are changing the culture, has increased support for ideas once only advanced by far-right political parties. "France, Austria, and the Netherlands [and we might add Germany], all have had very significant electoral success of the far-right parties," said Michael Collyer, a research fellow in European migration policy at the University of Sussex. Collyer had pointed to the success in France of a strict new immigration law

---

3. Sarah Wildman, *The Christian Science Monitor*, 24 May 2006. http://www.cs-monitor.com/2006/0524/p07s02-woeu.html.

proposed by Interior Minister Nicolas Sarkozy, who was in the meantime elected as France's President in May 2007.[4]

The basic datum when one considers demographic growth in the Islamic world is that, beyond its expansion into new areas, such as Western democracies, it has sustained a consistent internal growth of 3 percent for many years, that is a doubling of the total population every generation of twenty-five years. This means that with this breakneck pace of birthrate, which stems from traditional norms and is supported by prohibitions on birth control, it is difficult to break these trends. Moreover, a general trend exists in the developing world, where the poor are having more children and there is a decreasing mortality due to health improvement. Thus, the rapid population growth makes the pool of potential immigrants into Europe unlikely to recede. Indeed, in previous decades there seemed to be a virtual population explosion in the Islamic world. Countries like Iran, Turkey, Egypt, which boasted in the 1980s populations of thirty-five to forty million each, have *doubled it* since, not to speak of Indonesia, Pakistan, India, and Bangla-Desh, where the Muslim populations that were already high in the 1980s—attaining a hundred million in Indonesia and the seventy to eighty million mark for each or the rest—have also doubled since. Smaller-sized countries like Saudi Arabia, Syria, Morocco, and Algeria have similarly doubled their populations (from ten to fifteen million in to 1980s to twenty to thirty million today), and the Palestinians of the West Bank and Gaza (from 1.6 to 3.5 million). Some demographers believe that this trend is about to be reversed. However, even *if* that happens, it will take a long time to impact on the European Muslim population. But for now, the three-quarter billion Muslim population of the 1980s has soared during this period to one-and-a-half billion, that is about a quarter of the world population of an estimated seven billion. Moreover, since most of this population is young, the rapid demographic growth in those countries will continue apace as the innumerable populations of children come of age, and the wave of immigrants to the West, with the attending rise of Christianophobia, will grow in consequence.

Caution must be added nonetheless, insofar as demographic statistics in those countries are not always reliable, but there is little doubt that the *trends* are clear. Moreover, while European statistics on incoming Muslim legal immigrants can be counted on for accuracy, the countless illegal migrants tend to baffle the arithmetic and render much of the data on this massive human movement little more than educated guesswork. The lack of statistics in the Muslim countries of emigration, for either the legal or

4. Ibid.

the illegal migrants to the West, further complicates the calculations that demographers have attempted thus far. One thing is certain: immense surpluses of Muslim manpower, for the most part uneducated and unskilled, find their way to European shores. When this human wave does not find outlets into the rich Gulf States, which usually elect trained Arab workers in their education system and their bureaucracy, it sneaks its way into Western democracies, either as "political refugees," or as welcome manpower for manual jobs that Europeans are reluctant to do; or as illegal migrants who could quite easily slip through the porous European borders. When Europe changed the rules and began to tighten its control of the borders following the major terrorist attacks of Madrid and London in 2004–5, the large thirty-million-strong Muslim population of Europe was already difficult to supervise, due to the lax and liberal freedom of movement of Europeans across the entire expanse of the Union.

Another source of demographic growth of the Muslim population in the West is domestic proselytization, which though not massive at this point, produces some of the most devout and radical Muslims, like the Black Muslims of America, and potential recruits for terrorism, like Richard Reid in the UK. In France alone, it is estimated that in the decade between 1995 and 2005, some fifty thousand Christian French have converted into Islam.

These figures amount in their aggregate to a Muslim population of about 6 percent in the European Union today, with countries like France reaching the 10 percent mark (six million out of sixty million of the total), while in other countries something less than that (7 percent in the Netherlands and Belgium (one million out of fifteen million and 0.7 out of ten million, respectively), in Scandinavia 5 percent or less (in Sweden 0.5 million out of close to ten million; in Denmark 0.2 out of six million, and in Norway and Finland even less). In the large-population countries such as Germany, Britain, Italy, and Spain, though Muslims can be counted in the millions, they are diluted among the massive preponderant Christian environment and do not transcend a few percentage points for now. However, Muslim visibility and public prominence seem out of proportion to their real numbers for a number of reasons:

1. They are usually concentrated in the large cities and clustered together in certain neighborhoods, which in the eyes of the members of the host culture seem as having slipped out of their own jurisdiction. In many areas of Paris, Marseille, Malmo, Berlin, etc., local Europeans feel as strangers (in French "*depayses*") in their own countries;

2. Due to the background of the unskilled immigrants, who are usually uneducated, they feel alienated inasmuch as many of them preserve

their languages and mores, are different in dress, food, and way of life, and they build up a high degree of frustration, which occasionally explodes in violent demonstrations.

3. Alienation, poverty, and frustration often lead many of the youth among the immigrant Muslim population to crime. In all European countries that absorbed Muslim immigrants, statistics exist, which are not often publicized for fear of "bigotry" or "racism," telling the sad story of the disproportionately high number Muslim prison inmates. That often drives the host countries to frustration and self-pitying when they realize that their generosity and openness in welcoming the immigrants and supporting their training and welfare is often turned into a permanent burden on the state instead of a relief of its manpower shortage;

4. Muslim alienation has tended not only to lead them to build their own enclaves within their host societies, where even the forces of order sometimes think twice before entering, but it makes them insensitive to the general host population, something which in turn boosts the Europeans' reluctance to absorb them into their culture. For example, mosques that call for prayer at odd hours, when recurring and perennial, may turn the previously quite neighborhoods into areas of friction. Or when naturalized Muslims demand, in the name of their new citizenship, that the cross that garnishes the national flags of their host countries be eliminated because it hurts their feelings, their shelter societies are stunned by what seems to them as a presumptuous and arrogant demand.

5. The phenomenon of growing numbers of converts to Islam in major European countries such as France and Britain (fifty thousand in each in the past decade)—some of whom became famous (like the singer Cat Stevens, who became Yussuf Islam), or infamous (like Richard Reid)—though it contributes only marginally to demography, plays a growing role in the visibility and vocality of the Muslim community.

6. From time to time, scandals like forced marriages of young Muslim women in Europe, or their murder to protect the "honor" of the family, the Rushdie affair of the 1990s, acts of terror and violent demonstrations like in the Cartoon affair of 2005–6, all tend to raise the profile of Islam in Europe and make it seem particularly menacing.

On the other hand, several factors militate against an even faster rise of Muslim communitarian identity and demographic growth in Europe, as discussed in Amitai Etzioni's seminal work:[5]

1. The large numbers of Muslims who have assimilated over the past generation or two in their European environment, especially among the young who have been absorbed by the local educational systems, have grown ignorant of their original cultures and languages, and are more interested in developing peaceful and successful careers than in spreading Islam or responding to its call. Those Muslims, whose rate among their community is hard to ascertain, would not be likely to stand to be counted as Muslims, and may intermarry with the local people and ultimately assimilate.

2. Precisely due to the ascendance of militant Islam in Europe and the West in general, with the attending violence that sometimes accompanies its assertion of its identity and its manifestation of disaffection and discontent, the more assimilated and quietist Muslims who are reluctant to be identified with their radical kin, distance themselves from them and elect to melt unnoticed into the general population;

3. Unlike the radical militants who do not hide their intent to Islamize European societies—by peaceful means if possible, but also recruiting for terrorist operations if necessary—the nonobservant Muslims on the contrary seem to have reconciled to the idea of integrating into their adoptive societies and state their intentions to maintain peace and to mind their own business. While the radicals would rather establish their own Muslim political parties within their host political system, non-observant Muslims indicate their will to adapt via affiliation to the existing political system.

As long as Islam lived within the traditional boundaries of Islamdom, its tensions and frictions with the West remained outside the domain of the Western public's purview, except for politicians, diplomats, merchants, and military men who had to deal with it. Misunderstood, shunned, demonized as it may have been in the eyes of Europeans, it was remote and lay beyond the horizon. Similarly, when Muslim visitors arrived to the West since the turn of the twentieth century, for study or business, they were for the most part respectful, even admirers, of its culture and of modernity; they adopted the low-profile demeanor of a student who wished to learn, and a self-effacing attitude of awe towards everything Western, which was

---

5. Etzioni, *From Empire to Community*.

deemed superior. But with the rise of radical Islam in the past few decades, and the increase of Muslim immigration into the West, which brought it into permanent contact with Western societies, Muslims learned to face up to their host societies and even to confront them in debate. Their gathered self-confidence and self-assertion taught them that they could debate the West on a par, without being arrested, humiliated, or even imprisoned or executed, as in their home countries. For the Europeans, the clash of civilizations that had taken place from time immemorial on the borders of Christendom, had moved into their own heartland and they were unprepared to face it, on the psychological and the societal levels. Convinced that their open and democratic societies would prevail and entice the new immigrants to abandoning their roots and identity, they were shocked to discover that the gap between the two populations had grown over the years. For, far from bridging the differences that yawned between themselves and their un-integrated immigrants, the Europeans discovered that they had, on the contrary, widened, and the incompatibilities grew into clashes, the complaints into demands, the debates into explosions of violence. So much so, that once the Westerners realized that they were obliterating their traditionally homogeneous societies in favor of multicultural, multiethnic, multi-religious, and at times even multi-linguistic ones, the social contract that held together their respective homogeneous societies previously, began dissipating, much to the chagrin of local nationalist parties and to the frustration of the rest.

The explosion of the Cartoon Affair throughout the world in early 2006 did not make matters easier for the Europeans, who saw their goodwill and hospitality towards Muslims "rewarded" by violent demonstrations around the globe, as if cartoons of the Prophet, insensitive as they may have been, could be a real reason for this eruption of outrage against the West, and not a simple and direct occasion or pretext to air Muslim general anger and frustration with the West.

This will not facilitate the adherence of Turkey into the European Union either, primarily for demographic reasons. For, if the opponents of Turkey within the Union were thus far reluctant to let her in, due to the Islamic Party that has been at the helm of power there since 2002, now they realize that the so-called Islamic radicalism almost invariably translates into discord and trouble for Europe, and bringing Turkey in would mean not only freedom of movement of Turkish labor and nationals throughout Europe, but also spreading the message of Islam, and not necessarily only of the benevolent kind, into all corners of the continent. The numbers are staggering: with some 6–7 percent Muslims today (over thirty out of over four hundred million of the twenty-seven Union members), frictions are already difficult; how much more so when the nation of seventy-five million Turks would join, raising the rate of Muslims in the EU to 20 percent (one hundred million out of five hundred million). The rapid growth of the Muslim population on the one hand, and the shrinkage of the European family unit on the other, would mean that *in the next generation Europe may become half Muslim*. If that is the will of the Europeans, then there is no faster or more efficient way to achieve that goal than admitting Turkey into the EU; but if they are concerned to preserve their Christian heritage and European culture, their technological advancement and modern style of life, Islamization of their societies is not the most hopeful avenue to pursue. Already second thoughts about Turkey have begun to take root in the EU. Britain, the most ardent proponent of Turkish integration into the system, has itself agreed to suspend the talks between the parties, when it realized that Turkish oppression of the Kurds continues unabated; that women are still discriminated against in Turkish society; and that Turkish school textbooks, which are monitored by the Union, contain thousands of cases of racism and human rights abuses, notably negative portrayals of Greeks, Jews, Kurds, and Armenians.[6]

It turns out that even the US, which has seemed so far immune to the Islamic threat, due to both its security measures since 9/11 and to its distance from the pools of potential Muslim immigrants, has now started to beware the annual wave of one hundred thousand Muslim immigrants who add up to the four hundred thousand annual illegals who enter America from the its other porous borders. Matters have come to the boiling point, according to Leo Hohmann,[7] following the Chattanooga incident, where Yussuf Abdulazeez, who had arrived at age six with his parents from Kuwait in 1996, and was educated in the American school system, committed an act of terror, so it can be said that he has become a "homegrown" case of Muslim terrorism. At age twenty-three, indeed, he travelled to Jordan and Yemen, grew a beard on his return home, and started writing a Muslim blog in which he developed an anti-Western thinking. His father also had been arrested for a donation he made to an Islamic charity, but was released. Before Chattanooga, the Head of the FBI, James Comey, had warned the Congress that ISIS recruiters were hammering in their Guideline: "Come to the Caliphate, if you can't kill someone where you are." That was exactly what was done in Tennessee. With Obama's liberal immigration policy toward Muslims, which allows in eight hundred newcomers monthly from

---

6. Anthony Browne and Suna Erdem, "Education Clash Hold Up EU Talks," *The Times*, 8 April 2006.

7. Leo Hohmann, *World Net Daily (WND)*, 17 July 2015.

Somalia, one of the most Jihad-infested countries in the world, there is no telling how many Jihadists enter America every day and contribute to the radicalization of its Muslims. So much so as to alert the FBI to the impending dangers threatening America, to which Obama seems to turn a deaf ear. And these radicals get their instruction and guidance in Muslim-Brotherhood-dominated mosques, Islamic centers, and online indoctrination, which are rife across the American continent. But under the current federal policy, neither the FBI nor local law enforcement agency have the tools or the authority to identify and take measures against these brewing elements in American society.

One blatant example of the existing non-policy was blaringly pointed out by Milwaukee County Sheriff, David Clarke, who rightly argued that while he, a law enforcement officer, could not go through an airport without a meticulous scan, a person like terrorist-killer Abdulazeez could spend seven months traveling in the Middle East without any questioning. He also asserted that the perpetrator of the Boston bombing, had been traveling through Chechnya, a hotbed of terrorism, but no one paid attention to him until his bomb exploded. He expressly stated: "our immigration policy is a disaster. Multiculturalism is a disaster, and it failed miserably when European countries opened their borders, and now they are all tightening up. France demands assimilation now. So now, yes, we have to look at immigration as a national security threat." He also recognized that the American administration would do all it can to dissociate the Tennessee murder from Islam, as did the FBI, which scrubbed its training manuals of all references to Islam and terrorism, as part of National Security Adviser John Brennan's response to complaints by the CAIR (Council of American-Islamic Relations), which have evinced on many occasions their Muslim Brotherhood sympathies and orientation. Similarly, Senator Jeff Sessions has been warning against the liberal "rubber-stampings" of visa applications, which have allowed twenty-one cases of terrorist attacks and foiled attacks, involving immigrants into the US, from such Islamic countries as Somalia, Afghanistan, Morocco, Uzbekistan, and Yemen.[8]

Demography has a long-term effect on the chances of co-existence in countries where Muslims are now in the minority, because of the built-in contradiction between the requirement of Muslims to live under Islamic rule, since only there the Law of Allah can be brought to bear, and the grim necessity for many Muslims to escape from the persecutions of their Muslim regimes in order to seek refuge in the West. Believers who live in non-Muslim lands must either (a) regard their stay there as temporary, and in the

8. Ibid.

meantime do their best to live their Muslim life undisturbed, or (b) return to the Abode of Islam as soon as they can, or (c) try to turn their country of residence into a Muslim one by converting society into Islam, or seizing power in it. For this reason, the existence of Muslim minorities under non-Islamic rule has always alternately pursued these trajectories and driven the Muslim guest culture into a state of mind varying from a quietist acceptance of a permanent minority status to a violent rebellion against the majority. The response of the Muslim minority depends in no small measure on the perceived threat posed to it by the majority host culture. Whenever co-existence with it seems feasible, as was the case with Muslim minorities in the West before the rise of fundamentalism among them, they could always say that as long that they could perform the obligations of their faith without inhibition, they could consider themselves as living within enclaves of the Abode of Islam, a state of affairs they could bear indefinitely. But as soon as perceived oppression made their lives as Muslims untenable, and they diagnosed their position in consequence as dwellers of the Abode of War, they were set on a collision course with their hosts, and conflict ensued.

To this rather simplistic scheme one ought to introduce three more variables: first, the general Muslim environment, which when rising and embracing the road of militancy, can draw behind it Muslim minorities who are fascinated by its power, which compensates for their feelings of oppression, their under-privileged status, and the hopelessness in tackling the requirements of modern life. Then, the demographic data of the minority come into play, to wit, the larger the minority, to the point of constituting local majorities in certain areas, the more it feels self-confident to challenge the majority. Indeed, in areas where large concentrations of Muslims are clustered together, they feel strong enough to advance demands and to resort to violence, or to threaten the use of violence if their demands are not fulfilled. Thirdly, the nature of the regime under which they live plays its part too. Namely, if the regime is oppressive as in their own countries of origin, they would be less inclined to rebel, knowing what their punishment would entail; but, paradoxically, under the liberal democratic rule of the West it is easier for them to act to undermine it and seek its destruction, even though, or because, it gives them more leeway. This is the case with Muslims in the liberal democracies of the West in general.

Majority-minority relations in general are by nature dynamic and their fortunes usually hinge on the infringements upon the uneasy balance between the two parts of the equation. When the minority becomes or is perceived as a demographic, economic, or political menace to the majority, for example, fears and suspicions increase, followed by oppression on the part of the majority and self-imposed isolation by the minority, ultimately leading to alienation, conflict, separation, rebellion, and secession. All the while, both parties test the boundaries of co-habitation and co-existence and attempt to limit the autonomy of the minority on the one hand, or push it to its utmost on the other. The collision course is the result of the failure of the parties, or one of them, to stop on the verge of the precipice, and instead rush to trigger the violent explosion. These modalities come in cycles: material acculturation of the minority (in speech, dress, manners, mores, customs) goes a long way to condition it to become more sensitive to its environment and to the interests of the host culture. So next time it rebels it finds that it had accumulated more affinities with the majority than ever before, and that its rebellion, more than it states its disgust with the majority, proclaims its fear lest it be engulfed by it. Following periods of assimilation into the majority, voices of renewal are raised, warning the minority that unless it revives its roots it runs the imminent danger of total disappearance. Revival—religious, ethnic, cultural, linguistic, or otherwise—breeds opposition and rejection by the majority culture, sometimes leading to violent rebellions and attempts at secession by the minority, and its brutal repression, so as to remove the perceived threat that it poses to the majority, and back to square one. During this trajectory from quietism to violence, the minority people often embrace multi-identities, in periods of assimilation emphasizing the majority culture, in eras of conflict asserting their own ethno-cultural-religious-linguistic distinctiveness. Like the modalities of co-existence themselves, identities also vary, combining various components from the composite menu from which they are constantly called to choose.

These rules apply handily to Muslim minorities the world over, as their current predicament in non-Muslim lands readily illustrates. One more element is needed nonetheless to explain the mechanics of these dynamics, and that is charismatic leadership, without which the transition from quietism to rebellion is difficult, nay impossible. For if acculturation, assimilation, quietism, and a passive mood towards the majority require no leadership, just indifference and a societal *laissez*-faire, the traumatic cross-over to rebellion, violence, and upheaval which require risk-taking and a revolutionary spirit, depend much on a political or religious leader who commands authority and attracts followers. In the case of Muslim minorities, the actor is more likely to be religious or to combine religion and politics due to the inextricability of the sacred and the profane, the holy and the secular in Islamic political tradition. A distinction is called for nevertheless, between the activity of religious actors in Islamic-majority countries and Muslim-minority ones. If we take it for granted that a certain convergence of events is what provides the religious actor with the opportunity to act, it goes also without saying that in situations of Muslim-minority existence, the field of friction between the Muslim guest-culture and the majority host-culture is usually wider and more thorny than in homogeneous Muslim countries. For, granted that within Muslim entities too there are wide-open possibilities for conflict, as strife abounds on behalf of the Muslim majority towards non-Muslim minorities, notably Christians (Sudan, Iran, Egypt, Syria, etc.), or between different Muslim sects and factions (Afghanistan, Pakistan, the Gulf States, Iraq, and the like), the situation is different when Muslim minorities are concerned. The reason is that within Muslim-majority states it is the official government who conducts the repression against other factions or minorities; and while the oppressed (e.g., the *Gama'at* or the Muslim Brothers in Egypt, Syria, and Jordan, or the Copts in Egypt, or the Kurds in Turkey and Iran) usually produce charismatic leaders who lead the resistance as religious actors, they seldom challenge the state legitimacy. All they wish is to remove the regime, alter its policies, or gain a share of power within the state apparatus. However, since Muslims are required to live in Islamic lands, their presence under non-Islamic rule poses insoluble problems that end in crisis and unrest. Under such convergence of events, where the plight of the Muslim minority is identified as "religious," only recognized religious actors who arise to meet the challenge, are capable of dealing with it for the most part.

There was a time when Muslim minorities were quite limited in numbers and scope of dispersion throughout the West, usually as a result of the master-client interaction with the colonial powers, who encouraged a certain number of "natives" to tread the masters' cultural ways in their own metropolitan centers, and some of them intermarried and stayed. However, the large waves of Muslim immigrants since the mid-twentieth century to the Americas, Australia, and Europe, and more so the opening labor markets in the West to Muslim "guest-workers" (*Gastarbeiter*), coupled with important movements of conversion to Islam as a result of intense Muslim *da'wa* (mission), have dramatically increased the numbers of Muslims in those countries. Moreover, the "guests" have come to regard themselves as permanent residents with all attending privileges of citizenship and social benefits. In an interesting twist, not only don't they regard any longer their presence outside the realm of Islam as temporary, embarrassing, and requiring justification or rectification, but with the birth in place of the second and third generations, who grow to learn the languages, cultures, and ways of their new habitats, the process of their acculturation into their new homelands has accelerated. As long as their rate in the general populations of their new countries was negligible, and the socio-political environment was liberal (like in the US, Canada, Australia, Israel, and Europe), then social pluralism and individual freedom of worship were advocated by the Muslim minorities. Under oppressive regimes like the Soviet or the Chinese, the Muslims were quick to adopt material acculturation into their host society, with all the trappings of language, dress, education, and participation in the elites and social customs. The core of the faith was kept almost intact however, with the Muslim calendar, festivals, dietary laws, worship, and places of prayer preserved to the extent possible. This was easier in areas where Muslim minorities were more sizeable and commanded the critical mass necessary to entertain communal life, and much more difficult when the Muslim population was so sparse as to render any public display of Muslim identity impractical.

These situations of rebellious guest cultures, who no longer accept their minority status, can give rise to violence that is aimed either at secession or various forms of autonomy; or grows into an irredentist claim when the minority dwells in adjacent proximity/territorial continuity to their mother-country where the main bulk of their people is located (the Kurds in Turkey, Iran, Iraq, and Syria, the Hungarians of Transylvania and Voivodina, the Sudeten Germans prior to World War II, the Arabs of Israel, and the Turkic-Muslim population of Eastern Turkestan). Such claims, which may be bolstered especially when the minority becomes too sizeable to govern, or grows into a local majority in its area of residence, gain currency when the demographic growth of the minority is so much faster than that of the host culture, arousing hopes of a "democratic" takeover by the one-man one-vote device, the like of which had worked in Zimbabwe and South Africa. In other words, minorities of this sort, be they national or religious, do not seek to merge through integration, as in Brazil, and create a race-less society where no value is given to creed or original culture, but to dominate through victory for their group and governance of the others, when the numbers so allow. In these situations religious actors find a fertile ground to act, by advocating demographic growth in their communities, denigrating the majority culture so as to discourage acculturation into it, creating an atmosphere of separateness and strife, inventing irredentist claims, and mobilizing their community to obey them in the pursuance of those ambitions.

When Muslim minorities become frustrated by the unworkability of a pluralistic society (e.g., in Cyprus, the Philippines, Israel, China, and more and more within European countries), either because they believe they are discriminated against or their expectations are not met, they become antagonistic to their host society. So much more so when they perceive the majority as having transgressed the limits of previous coexistence and encroached upon their freedom of worship or conduct (like forbidding the veil, or not providing worship facilities, or restraining violent demonstrations in the public square, or prosecuting "honor killings"). In such cases, they use Western vocabulary (freedom, tolerance, democracy, human rights, etc.) to impress upon their hosts that while they wish to play by the rules of their adoptive countries, it is the latter that violate them.

In more extreme cases, like with some Muslim radical leaders (religious actors *par excellence*) in London and in other Muslim congregations in the West, they claim that they came to Europe in order to change it, not to be reshaped by it, or they reject Western attitudes lock, stock, and barrel (like the banning of the veil in French schools). This sets the Muslim minority, especially the radical elements in its midst, on the collision course with the host authorities. Militant elements among this disaffected minority may seek political or cultural autonomy (the London Muslim "Parliament," or various national or international Muslim Associations, or organizations of imams and mosque leaders, or the Heads of the Arab Local councils in Israel, or the demand for autonomy and for an "Arab" or "Muslim" university and other separate institutions).

In India Muslims had conquered the land and subjugated Hinduism, but when Muslim power was eroded by the British, Islam sought and achieved separation from the Hindus for the most part, rather than submit to the democratic rule of modern India that would have allowed the Hindus to exercise political domination over the Muslims. When the majority of Indian Muslims established their own state (Pakistan and then Bangladesh), their *'ulama* spoke of the reinstitution of the *Shari'a* as their state law. There was no alternative to this arrangement if one bears in mind the fact that Islam is incompatible with other political ideologies. Maulana Mawdoodi, the prominent Indian Muslim modernist has put it this way: "To be a Muslim and adopt a non-Muslim viewpoint is only meaningless. 'Muslim nationalist' and 'Muslim Communist' are contradictory terms as 'Communist Fascist' and 'chaste prostitute.'"[9] Thus, as orthodox Muslims see it, and much more so the radicals among them, Islam is ideally an either-or affair. Either Islamic law and institutions are given full expression and dominate state life or, failing that, if the state is non-Islamic, Muslims should try to reverse the situation or leave. In practice, however, things are not so clear-cut.

As long as an appearance of peace and accommodation can be maintained, the minority Muslim community, although entertaining a vague hope for the fulfillment of its political aspirations at some future time, can contain the discrepancy between dream and reality, and the tension between the two can go unresolved. But if persecution of the Muslim minority

9. Al-Mawdoodi, *Nationalism in India*, 5–11.

is intensified, for example in non-democratic countries, to the point where no real Muslim life can be ensured (like in China or Mianmar), and when a practical opportunity arises, the minority Muslims are likely to seize it and proclaim either a separate Muslim entity or a Muslim state, regardless of whether the Muslim population is a majority or a minority in the territory in question. For an Islamic state can encompass either. Muslims had experienced both a Muslim majority under non-Islamic rule, as in Christian Valencia where Muslims outnumbered the Christians four to one,[10] or the modern Muslim colonies under minority Christian rule; and a Muslim minority rule in Hindu-majority India, and the Umayyad Muslim rule over a Christian-majority state in the Iberian Peninsula. It is Muslim *rule*, then, that defines the borders of the Abode of Islam, *not* Muslim majorities or minorities.

In recent years the enhanced stature of Islam has led the Muslim center to take a keener and deeper interest in the minorities on its periphery. This renewed interest has been manifested in the resolutions of the Islamic Conferences which have been bringing under one roof delegates from some fifty-seven Muslim-majority countries representing some 1.5 billion believers.[11] More interest has been taken by remote Muslim communities in participating in the Pilgrimage to Mecca, where two million people from all nationalities share their fellowship with their brothers, and enhance thereby the identity of the universal *umma*. These are the building blocks of Muslim-minority discontent and rebellion, which in our days may lead to what is termed "terrorism."

Despite the initial naïve days of Muslim immigration into Europe, when it was a matter of course to assume that Muslim minorities would integrate painlessly into the much more prosperous nations where they made their new homes, difficulties began to emerge from the outset, which were dismissed as pangs of acculturation. But as the years elapsed, the Muslim communities grew, and their Muslim radicalism came to the surface, the illusion of integration began to fade, substituted by the illusory vision of multicultural societies, which made cultural concessions to the immigrants in order to accommodate them and make them partners of the system, not its clients. But that too, far from satisfying the Muslims of Europe, whose growing numbers gave them the necessary self-confidence to defy the system and even start acting against it, only further increased the sense of alienation in their midst from their host countries. The Europeans, in turn, sensing that

---

10. Burns, *The Crusader Kingdom of Valencia*, 303.

11. See Bat Ye'or, *Europe, Globalization and the Coming Universal Caliphate*, especially chap. 1.

their liberalism had turned against them, began to try to back-pedal, but it was too late, and the collision course became inevitable.

A survey done in Europe and published in April 2006 found that the degree of anti-Muslim bias was "dangerously high" among the Europeans, and "can lead to a vicious circle of isolation and radicalization of the immigrant youth." They were not willing to admit that they were already dragged into that vicious circle and that by abstaining from pronouncing the word "Muslim," substituting for it instead "immigrant youth," "suburb youth," "immigrant population," or "unemployed youth," they were simply hiding their heads in the sand. Beate Winkler, the Head of the European Monitoring Center on racism and Xenophobia, told a hundred European imams convened in Vienna to discuss integration of their communities into Europe, that European countries had enough laws to foster integration, but they were not well implemented, and real issues were often avoided. The Europeans attending the conference agreed that attitudes towards Islam had hardened since 9/11, and the subsequent Madrid, London, Paris, Amsterdam, and other attacks. Winkler suggested that Europe could help further by supporting mosque construction, providing time for Muslim religious broadcasts, and assuring proper education of imams and Islamic religious teachers. On the other hand, she demanded that work be actively conducted against Muslim extremism, honor killings, forced marriages, spousal abuse, and self-imposed isolation, in order to help solve issues raised by *halal* butchering or the wearing of headscarves.[12]

The mass migration of Muslims into Europe, only exacerbated by the unprecedented wave of the Summer of 2015, when hundreds of thousands of Muslim refugees from the Middle East and Africa knocked at the doors of Europe, compelling it to receive them and to devise a quota system that would distribute these masses among the twenty-eight members according to their population, economic development, and employment markets. This has already created a rift among the members, with East and Central Europeans, watching the problems and disturbances already caused in Western Europe, flatly refusing to allow the same breakdown of their own national homogeneous make-up by bringing in another cultural and ethnic variety that may disturb their own internal harmony. In addition, some of them brought up the tremendous security risk of absorbing in their midst latent agents of radical Islam, who were certainly dispatched among the crowds of refugees to act against their countries of refuge after they settle in and cease to raise suspicion.

---

12. *Reuters*, cited by *Haaretz*, 8 April 2006.

As an example of growing Islamic assertiveness following on from increasing numbers of Muslims, take, for example, the controversy about the Cordova mosque/cathedral. The Spanish Bishop of Cordoba, Demetrio Fernandez, has already been accused by Muslims of "trying to wipe out history," when he refused to call that structure a mosque. Originally that eighth-century mosque was built by the Muslim Caliphs in Cordoba, their capital of the Western Umayyads. The mosque became famous for its vast numbers of pillars and striped arches, painted in red and white, which to this day attracts millions of tourists.[13] It was subsequently converted into a church.

In the vast gamut of themes, occupying the Christian-Muslim field of historical debate, the conversion of houses of worship from one religion to the other (i.e., mosques into cathedrals and vice-versa), none of the parties can claim clean hands. In all Islamdom, at all times, churches and synagogues in conquered territory were converted into mosques, the most blatant and infamous case being the Hagia Sophia in Constantinople, which became a vast mosque in Istanbul, versus many mosques (and synagogues) in territories occupied by Christians, which were converted into churches. The mosque/cathedral in Cordoba, a UNESCO World Heritage site, has been at the center of a present-day clash between Spain's Catholic Church and the Muslim immigrants into the land, many of whom consider themselves the real owners of the country, who had been disinherited by the Christian *reconquista* of the fifteenth century. In those years the mosque been rebaptized as a cathedral by the Christians. Kamel Mekhelef, of the Muslim Association of Cordoba, complained that the bishop was trying to deny a part of the history of that national heritage site, but could not be made to consider the equivalent distortion made by the Muslim Turks concerning the equally famous Istanbul site. However, with the declining rate of church-going Spaniards, concomitantly with the rising numbers of mosque-going Muslims in Spanish cities, many Muslim radicals have been clamoring for the "return of al-Andalus" to Islamic rule, in the same breath as the lands of Kashmir and Palestine, which they also view as part of their holy heritage. In fact, eight Austrian Muslims, who entered the Cordova controversial building on a Good Friday, were charged in court as disturbing the peace, after they clashed with security guards when attempting to pray there.[14]

---

13. Graham Keeley, "Muslim-Christian Clash over Cathedral in Cordoba," *The Times*, 12 November 2010.

14. Ibid.

One example of the subtle, and sometimes blunt, Muslim impact on host countries in Europe to conform to Islamic customs is in the question of the *halal* dietary laws that the Muslim immigrants have forced onto the lands that have sheltered them in Europe.[15] Scandinavia may serve as an example.

To sum up, the legal situation in Scandinavia regarding *halal* slaughter in accordance with Muslim law is that it is permitted in the three countries of Scandinavia: Sweden, Denmark, and Norway, provided the animals are unconscious prior to slaughter. Many Muslims accept this method, while others do not. The Islamic Cultural Centre of Scandinavia, which aims at promoting charitable activities and good public relations, issues certificates to slaughterhouses in Sweden, and his verdicts are recognized by the UAE, Singapore, and Indonesia. The Swedish slaughterhouse Kronfågel, which specializes in poultry, does not slaughter in accordance with Muslim law. The poultry product *Ivars*, which is owned by Kronfågel, is *halal*, but the slaughter is carried out in Denmark. Two leading slaughter houses in Denmark, Danpo and Rose poultry, slaughter in accordance with *halal* requirements and their products are sold all over Sweden. Danpo and Rose poultry both explain that *halal* does not involve extra costs for the customer and that there is no real difference between *halal* and non-*halal*, apart from the fact that a Muslim is supervising the slaughter and that he recites "in the name of Allah . . . ." Rose poultry admits that all products at their plant are *halal*, since it is not clear from the start where the products will eventually be sold. According to The Swedish Board of Agriculture, the slaughter itself, not merely the supervision, is performed by a Muslim, and the animal is placed in the direction of Mecca. To some customers, who buy *halal* by mistake, this does not affect their choice of meat; to others it is an outrage and an imposition of someone else's religious obligations upon them.

There is reason to believe that not only Rose poultry's entire production is *halal*, but also the production of other slaughterhouses in Scandinavia. When these products are then marketed in Sweden, many supermarkets keep the *halal* meat in the same counters as non-*halal*, to the confusion and dismay of non-Muslim customers. The Swedish supermarket chain Co-op does not inform at all about *halal* on its official site, but customers have on several occasions found *halal* meat among the non-*halal*. The other large supermarket chain, Ica, informs its customers that *halal* is indeed permitted if the slaughter is carried out after the animal is unconscious. McDonald's in Sweden does not admit that its meat is *halal* and there is no information on

---

15. For this passage, I am indebted to Kathrin Dominique, from Malmo, Sweden, who has assisted me in researching this issue.

its official site. However, the fact that the food chain imports all its poultry from the Danish slaughterhouse Danpo indicates that all poultry sold by McDonald's is indeed *halal*.

The Swedish School Inspectorate claims that *halal* served to all students at the school system is not in fact a violation of the requirement that the schools be non-confessional, and there is reason to believe that non-Muslim students are indeed being served *halal* chicken on a regular basis. The fact that many Muslims do not accept meat from animals, which have been stunned prior to slaughter, raises the question what number of Muslim student in the Swedish school actually eat the *halal* meals served to all students. Or do observant Muslims know something that we do not regarding the issue of stunning? Whether customers buying *halal*, voluntarily or not, are in fact supporting Jihad is a question that must be left to individual Muslims, who are for the most part reluctant to reveal their private thinking.

There seems to be a certain reluctance to inform the public about the existence of *halal* products in supermarkets, for example in McDonald's. Whereas non-Muslim customers apparently are likely to purchase *halal* meat in stores around Sweden, this is not the case with imported *kosher* meat. In Malmo all *kosher* meat is sold in wholesale firm Martin Olsson. *Kosher* meat is kept in separate freezers in one section of the store. Some poultry products from Israel are kept in freezers together with non-*kosher* products, but the country of origin is printed on the food package for everyone to see. That way no customer will end up accidentally buying meat slaughtered in a way they do not support. The poultry products from Israel are imported to Sweden because of the quality, not because of kashrut, and are sold mainly to non-Jewish customers, mostly restaurants. The origin of *halal* meat in Scandinavia is, however, Denmark, Norway, or Sweden and if the customer is not observant of the *halal* certification on the food product, he or she will indeed buy *halal*. It is quite amazing that the Swedish School Inspectorate dismisses the opinion that *halal* is violating the idea of a non-confessional school. To Muslims *halal* is a religious requirement and the products are purchased by Malmö Skolrestauranger *precisely because* they are *halal*. The above information indicates that in terms of *halal* there seem to be a process of Islamization in Scandinavia. Some slaughterhouses, Rose poultry and most certainly others, have changed the entire procedure for all poultry in order to adjust to Muslim *halal* requirements. In other words, the non-Muslim majority is forced to adjust to the demands of the Muslim minority.

The Swedish council listed on this German site is Islamguiden (i.e. "The Islam Guide"). On this official site there is information about how to obtain certification of *halal*, and the council promises that by having such a certification, the food producer will reach four hundred thousand Muslims in Sweden and millions worldwide through export. Comparing this to the tiny Jewish community of some fifteen thousand individuals in Sweden, about six thousand in Denmark and fifteen hundred in Norway, it is easy to see the outcome of that comparison from a purely financial point of view.

Summary and Prospects

As we have noticed throughout, the onslaught of Islam on its minorities within Islamdom is clearly linked also to the attempt of Islam to overwhelm the West with a massive demographic wave of Muslims, as a means to flood it in the long run. As the waves of illegal migrants from mainly Muslim countries continue to wash the shores of Europe, at extraordinary risks to their lives, the plight of the Muslim communities in Europe is bound to augment, not to fade. For, as the minorities gain in numbers and feel stronger and more self-confident, their demands for accommodation by their hosts will keep increasing, and the frictions that they will necessarily experience with Europe will also peak to new heights. Muslims will not be grateful to their generous lands of shelter, but, on the contrary, bitter that more of their kin have not been absorbed or afforded an even easier settlement in their new homes. This will, in turn, create a dialectical relationship with the situation of the Christian minorities in Islamdom, for any difficulties or mishaps in the process of absorbing so many unexpected and uninvited waves of immigrants in the West, will necessarily pit the Muslim countries against their Christian minorities, by associating them with the Christian Europeans who will be accused of Islamophobia towards their immigrants. Moreover, the perceived "mistreatment" of Muslims by Europeans will invite more criticism against Western states that are already stretching their tolerance and generosity beyond the limits of their resources and capabilities. In other words, the more they take in Muslim refugees or asylum seekers, the more they will be jeopardizing not only their societal balance, but also the fate of the Christian minorities under Islam.

The French priest Jane Corbon,[1] who travelled to Syria and Iraq, asked on *BBC News* about the future of the Christian religion in Islamdom, reached the conclusion that Christianity today is being driven out of the

---

1. Jane Corbon. "Could Christianity Be Driven Out of the Middle East?" *BBC News*, 15 April 2015.

Middle East, the Arab World, and the Muslim World. She observed that the Christian exodus from the Middle East was intensified and escalated during and after the Arab Spring (2010–14), which was later sarcastically dubbed as the Islamic Autumn (or Winter),[2] and certainly not a Spring for the Christians in the Middle East, in the Arabic speaking and Muslim countries. Even though Christianity was born in the Middle East two thousand years ago, the Christians of Syria and Iraq are today in danger of annihilation as a result of their extreme persecution at the hands of such militant Islamic forces as ISIS, Jabhat Al-Nusra, Al-Qa'ida, and others. The Christians of Syria and Iraq are in fact fleeing away to the West, especially to European countries such as Sweden, Germany, France, and the UK. The USA, Canada, and Australia have also welcomed their Christian kin as asylum seekers and refugees, due to the death threat they have lived under from the Jihadist Islamic organizations.

The numbers of Middle Eastern Christians has been dwindling, and it is expected that they will become nearly extinct in the next few years in the Middle East and the Arab World, so that in the year of 2020, the number of Middle Eastern Christians will be down to an estimated six millions. They are fleeing in particular from Iraq, upon the capture of the Mosul in the summer of 2014 by ISIS, and the re-imposition of *jizya* on Christians of Syria and Iraq, which has accelerated their flight from those countries after the years of the Arab Spring. Furthermore, the Christians of the Middle East feel that they are under threat because they are considered "infidels" by the radical new rulers, who anchor their policy in the Qur'anic verses and in the Islamic *Shari'a* laws, that revive the old *dhimmi* rules which forbid the Christians (and Jews) to build new churches, to renovate their dilapidated houses of prayer, resulting in the demolition of many churches and monasteries, or in the conversion of some of them into mosques, or torture chambers, for the unfortunate Christians who were slow to escape the horror, or trapped in their inability to do so. That generally grim evaluation of the situation was generally backed, in its various aspects, by numerous Christian observers and writers who become cognizant of this tragic development.

Todd Beeman of the *New York Times*[3] wrote that the newly established Islamic State of Iraq and Syria, ISIS, in the year of 2014, has intended to displace the Christian minorities in Syria and Iraq and also was responsible for the vast Christian persecution and eradication of the Christian citizens of Syria and Iraq, because Christians are considered infidels, who

2. See, e.g., Israeli, *From Arab Spring to Islamic Winter*.
3. Todd Beaman, "Christians Facing Annihilation in the Middle East," *New York Times Newsmax*, the 22 July 2015.

have to pay the *jizya*, otherwise they will face the choice between the sword (literally) or to convert to Islam and become Muslims. These Christian communities face the danger of extinction in Iraq and Syria, and especially after the weakness and the demise of the Arab dictatorial regimes: in Iraq since 2003, when Saddam Hussein was dethroned, and now in the Syrian Civil war that started in 2011 and continues unabated to the present day (mid-2016). The reason is that ISIS is considered the renewal of the medieval Islamic Caliphate from the times of the *Rashidun*, the Abbasid and the Ottomans, who regarded their Christian subjects as second-class citizens (*dhimmis*) who lived under a regime of all kinds of discrimination in law, and had to pay the *jizya* if they wished to practice their religion freely. ISIS is committing atrocities also via its followers in Egypt and Libya against the Christian Copts, by running a campaign of intimidation by showing a video on how they behead Christian prisoners in front of the camera.

The rise of ISIS has also resulted in the rise of the numbers of Syrian and Iraqi Christian expatriates and immigrants to the West seeking a better future, better living condition, or simply living with their Christian brothers and sisters in the West, especially in the European countries that have offered them an asylum from the Islamic persecution, such as: Poland, Sweden, Germany, France, and the UK. The estimates are of sixty thousand Syrian Christians who have fled the country after ISIS and the Islamic militias launched their attacks on Christian villages, such as: Ma'aloula, and the Christian neighborhoods of the Syrian cities of Aleppo, Damascus, and other regions that were populated by Syrian Christians. Moreover, the Islamic resurgence that was a result of the Arab Spring, which turned an Islamic Autumn, didn't breed democracy, freedom, or human rights, but on the contrary ignited the Muslim militant organizations to suppress the Christians. The previous alternatives which could hold the Christians tightly within the prevailing national regimes like Pan-Arabism, or Arab Nationalism that were widely founded by the Arabic speaking Christians in the late nineteenth century and early twentieth century, have collapsed, and been replaced, for now, by mounting Islamic radicalism.

In *The Guardian*, William Dalrymple[4] argues that Christianity in the Middle East, in the Muslim and the Arab World, could came to an end, because of the rise of Islamic radicalism, for the Islamic terrorist organizations have targeted the Christian minorities in the Arabic speaking countries and the Muslim-dominated countries and regions. The Christian minorities are persecuted in all Middle Eastern countries, except Israel—the only democ-

---

4. William Dalrymple. "The End of Christianity in the Middle East Could Mean the Demise of Arab Secularism." *The Guardian*, 23 July 2014.

racy in the Middle East; in Egypt for example, the Copts face many anti-Copt riots, killings, kidnappings of girls, and church demolition, when they were bombed causing fatalities. As a result Coptic emigration increased, heading to the West—USA, Canada, and Europe. Christian persecution also occurs in Syria and Iraq, where the Arab Regimes, under the Ba'ath Party and the Pan-Arabism collapsed, which characterized both of those countries, and had been founded or supported by Christian intellectuals and politicians such as: Michel Aflaq, Faris Al-Khoury, Butrus Al-Bustani, Nasif Al-Yaziji, and George Antonius, to mention just a few. Therefore, when Saddam Hussein fell in 2003, after the American incursion into Iraq, many Assyrian Christians became the target of the Islamic terrorist militants, which increased the Christian emigration to the West. In Iraq, the Chaldean Christian minority too, and two thirds of all Iraqi Christians, have fled the country to the West, due to their inability to stand up to the chaos which afforded the Muslim radicals to opportunity to intimidate Christians and force them to run for their lives. Out of the million-and-a-half Christians in Iraq when Saddam was removed in 2002, maybe a third or less remain, in part while deploying efforts to get out.

There was a time in the Middle Ages when Christians from Europe wishing to rescue their land and their coreligionists from Muslims, sent Crusaders to do that on Muslim lands; now the trend was reversed, and the Christians in the West are doing their best to absorb their fleeing coreligionists into their lands, thus illustrating that it is Islam that is on the offensive, both expelling its Christians into Europe and migrating there itself to alter the nature of Europe; and, conversely, it is Christianity that is on the defensive, yielding to Muslim Christianophobic demands both in the Middle East and on its own turf. In Syria, the Syrian Civil War that begun in 2011 and is continuing relentlessly, has caused a rise of Islamic terrorism against the Christian minorities and subjects them in the areas that are controlled by ISIS to the *jizya*, for the first time since it was cancelled in the late nineteenth century, under the *Tanzimat* Reforms in the Ottoman Empire. Therefore, one may conclude that due to the Arab Spring, the Christians of the Arab World have no future in the Muslim populated regions in Jordan, the Palestinian territories, and Lebanon, because it is there that Christians face a real extinction and an imminent threat to their existence with the rise of Islamic radicalism which also generates terrorism.

Yusri Khezran[5] similarly argued that he Arab Spring that began in October 2010 in Tunisia and impacted the neighboring Arab countries such as

---

5. Yusri Khezran, "The Christians in Israel and the Arab Spring: From Arab Identity to Separatism?"

Iraq, Syria, and Egypt, and resulted in the rise of the Islamic terrorist organizations, after the fall of the Arab dictators. This was a surprise for many scholars, who were disappointed in their expectation of democratization and better life conditions as a result of the Spring. The Syrian Civil war, which was a direct result of the Syrian revolution in 2011, has caused the rise of the sectarian and religious war between Muslims and Christians insofar as the Christians were identified with the Pan-Arab regime of the Ba'ath Party of Syria, under the leadership of Bashar Al-Assad. Thus, this revolution has revealed the weakness of the Christian communities in the Arab World that heavily relied on Arab Nationalism, Arabism, and the centralized dictatorial regimes, and that helped them to combat the Salafi-Islamic radicalism which targeted them as a weak minority in the heart of the Muslim-Arab world. Furthermore, the fall of Mubarak in Egypt led to the rise of anti-Coptic riots, that led to attacks and massacres of Christian Copts, arson of Coptic churches, such as in Alexandria on New Year Eve of January 2011. The other Christians of the Middle East also became an easy prey, to attack and to annihilate, due to governmental anarchy, political instability and religious violence in Iraq, Syria, and Egypt.

These events have directly affected the Arabic-speaking Christian minority in Israel also but in a slightly different fashion. Father Gabriel Naddaf aided by Sergeant Shadi Khaloul, a Maronite Aramean in the IDF reserve forces, founded the Christian Recruitment Forum for the Israeli Arabic-Speaking Christians, indicating that at least parts of the Christian minority in Israel has decided to throw their lot with Israel's destiny as a Jewish-majority nation, and many Christians saw in their enlistment to the IDF a strengthening element of Israel's stand against annihilationist attitudes of the Islamic militant terrorism against their country. This has also prompted the rise of a specific Israeli Christian identity that tends to regard itself separated from the Muslim Arab majority and that will aim to get closer to the Jewish majority. In fact, the Christian Israeli minority proclaim their need for a central authority's protection, while the Christians of the Arab World are announcing their sense of alienation and exclusion, in view of their jeopardized existence and doubts about their survivability in the Muslim-Arab World. This new growth of Christian identity, in alliance with Israel, has expectedly raised protests and threats from the rest of the Arabic-speaking, Muslim-majority society in Israel, who particularly oppose any contribution of Israeli Arabs to Israel's security, and on the contrary who do their best to undermine it.

Walter Russel[6] of the *Wall Street Journal* embraces a more far-reaching view of the dwindling of Christianity in Islamdom. He argues that Christianity is on its natural turf in the Middle East, where it was born and proclaimed its creed to the world. And it was dispossessed by thirteen hundred years of Islamic invasion, colonization, and imperialism, which reduced it to near extinction, as its vestiges are fleeing to the West today. His examples are Syria and Iraq, which today are facing political turmoil, instability, civil war, and the rise of the Islamic radicalism that targeted the Christian minorities who had resided in these regions since the origins of Christianity, well before the advent of Islam. These most ancient Christian communities date back to the first century CE, with the apostles of Christ in the book of Acts. Assyrian, and Chaldean Christians in Iraq under Saddam Hussein, numbered some one-and-a-half million souls, but many Iraqi Christians fled the country after the US-led invasion to Iraq and the arrest of Saddam Hussein, the Ba'athist whose ideology stood for combating the Muslim-Christian frictions. In 2014, one-hundred-and-twenty-five thousand Iraqi Christians fled the country and three hundred thousand more Iraqi Christians may also leave in the coming years following the rise of ISIS and the Christian evacuation from the cities of Mosul, Baghdad, and others.

The Syrian Christians' situation is similar to their Iraqi brothers, for under Bashar Al-Assad's regime, until the year of 2011 when the revolution and chaos started, the Syrian Christians constituted 10 percent of the total Arabic-speaking population; but after 2011, the Syrian Christian exodus has accelerated and intensified, with thousands that flee Syria due to the rise of the Islamic militant terrorism, which rightly perceived the Syrian Christian minority as an ally of Assad, the Syrian dictator. Therefore, we can infer and conclude that the Christians today in the Middle East face a religious and ethnic cleansing process resulting in the Christian exodus from the Muslim world will be on the rise in the coming five years, culminating in the year of 2020, when the number of Middle Eastern Christians is expected to diminish down to six to four million (most of them the remaining Copts). Many historians and other scholars do compare between the Christian exodus from the Middle East and the Jewish exodus from the Muslim World in 1948 and in the 1950s, upon the establishment of the State of Israel. In so doing, they remember the famous threatening slogan: "After Saturday, comes Sunday."

---

6. Walter Russell Mean. "The Plight of Middle East's Christians." *The Wall Street Journal*, 15 March 2015.

A slight variation was offered by the Arab-Israeli *Sinnara (fishhook)* newspaper.[7] The Muslims in Iraq and Syria, where the Islamic State (ISIS) is in control, offered to the Christians the chance to leave their regions, but if they wanted to stay they would have pay the *jizya*, failing which they would face the sword, and would be killed. The paper expected the British Government to look after Christian refugees and give them the full priority to get asylum and protection in the United Kingdom. Moreover, Britain should not be indifferent to the Christian Assyrian persecution under Islamic State, and accord them shelter. Christian persecution in Syria and Iraq being considered severe and dangerous by the Open Doors-UK and by the Barnabas Fund, as well as the Anglican Church bishops, are called upon to rescue the Syrian and Iraqi churches from genocide, by helping them settle in Britain, to avoid a repetition, one century later, of the Armenian, Aramean, and the Assyrian genocide of 1915. It was noted that the British people and the British authorities were willing to help these Middle Eastern Christians to emigrate to Britain, and they lent them priority over the Muslim immigrants to the UK, who bring problems with them and demand the application of *Sharia* Law in Britain.

---

7. *Sinnara*, 3 July 2015

Bibliography

NEWSPAPERS/PERIODICALS, TELEVISION STATIONS/BROADCASTS, AND INTERNET SITES

Al-Ahram Weekly
Al-Arabiya News TV
Arab News (Saudi Arabia)
Asharq Al-Awsat (London)
Associated Press (AP)
'Ayn al-Yaqin
Barnabas Fund
BBC News
Battle Cry Magazine Bayan: Arabs in Israel
The Boston Globe
The Christian Post
The Christian Science Monitor
Cumhuriyet
Dagbladet (Norway)
The Dagen Daily Star
The Daily Telegraph
Dunya TV
The Economist
Egyptian Gazette
Al-Fajr
FrontPageMagazine
Gatestone Institute
The Globe and Mail
The Guardian
Ha'aretz
Al-Hayat al Jadida
The Herald (Malysia)
The Huffington Post
Human Events
The Iconoclast

Inquiry and Analysis
Israel Against Terror
Israel Hayom Newsletter
Al-Jazeera TV
Jerusalem Cloakroom
Jihad Watch
The Kurdistan Tribune
Kuwait Times
Journal of Terorism and Political Violence
Lapido Media
Le Monde
Libyan Herald
Makor Rishon
Al-Manar TV
MEMRI
MERIA Journal
Middle East Quarterly
Al Mushahid al-Siyassi, (BBC Arabic Weekly)
Muslim Persecution of Christians Nahdat Misr
National Catholic Reporter
National Post
National Religious Broadcasters Journal
National Review Online
The New Republic
The New York Sun
The New York Times
News around the World
Newsweek
Palestinian Media Watch
Palestinian TV
PJ Media
Qatar TV
Al Quds
Reuters
Research on Islam and Muslims in Africa
Rima Occasional Papers
Rockie Mountain News
Al-Safir
Sawt al-Haqq wal-Huriyya
Sinnara
Sverigedemokraterna
Sydsvenskan Think Israel
Al-Tarek TV
The Torch
U.S. News
Wall Street Journal
Washington Post
The Washington Times

Al-Watan
WorldNetDaily
Yedioth Aharonot

www.aawsat.net
http://www.christianfreedom.org
www.chroniclesmagazine.org
www.huffingtonpost.com
www.meforum.org
www.metransparent.com
www.raymondibrahim.com
http://thelede.blogs.nytimes.com

BOOKS

Bailey, Betty Jane, and Martin Bailey. *Who the Christians in the Middle East?* Grand Rapids: Eerdmans, 2003.
Barfield, Thomas. *Afghanistan: A Cultural and Political History.* Princeton: Princeton University Press, 2010.
Bat Ye'or. *The Decline of Eastern Christianity under Islam: From Jihad to Dhimmitude.* Madison, WI: Fairleigh Dickinson University Press, 1996.
———. *The Dhimmi': Jews and Christians under Islam.* Madison, WI: Fairleigh Dickinson University Press, 1985.
———. *Eurabia: The Euro-Arab Axis.* Madison, WI: Fairleigh Dickinson University Press, 2006.
———. *Europe, Globalization and the Coming Universal Caliphate.* Madison, WI: Fairleigh Dickinson University Press, 2011.
———. *Islam and Dhimmitude: Where Civilizations Collide.* Madison, WI: Fairleigh Dickinson University Press, 2000.
Bonner, Michael, ed. *Arab-Byzantine Relations in Early Islamic Times.* Burlington, VT: Ashgate, 2004.
Burns, Robert. *The Crusader Kingdom of Valencia.* Cambridge: Harvard University Press, 1967.
Coren, Michael. *Hatred: Islam's War on Christianity.* Toronto: McClleland, 2014.
Doyle, Tom, and Tom Parks. *Killing Christians: Living Faith Where It Is Not Safe to Believe.* Nashville: Thomas Nelson, 2015.
Durie, Mark. *The Third Choice.* Melbourne: Self-published, n.d.
El-Cheikh, Nadia Maria. *Byzantium Viewed by the Arab.* Cambridge: Harvard University Press, 2004.
Etzioni, Amitai. *From Empire to Community: A New Approach to International Relations.* New York: MacMillan, 2004.
Fernandez-Morera, Dario. *The Myth of the Andalusian Paradise: Muslims, Christians and Jews under Islamic Rule in Medieval Spain.* Wilmington, DE: Isis, 2016.
Hatina, Meir, and Uri Kupferschmidt, eds. *The Muslim Brothers: A Religious Vision in a Changing Reality* (in Hebrew). Tel-Aviv: Hakibbutz Hameuchad, 2012.
Ibrahim, Raymond, ed. *The Al Qaeda Reader.* Portland, OR: Broadway, 2007.

———. *Crucified Again: Exposing Islam's New War on Christians*. Washington, DC: Regnery, 2013.
Israeli, Raphael, *The Death Camps of Croatia*. Piscataway, NJ: Transaction, 2012.
———. *From Arab Spring to Islamic Winter*. Piscataway, NJ: Transaction, 2013.
———. *Green Crescent over Nazareth: The Displacement of Christians by Muslims in the Holy Land*. London: Cass, 2002
———. *The Islamic Challenge in Europe*. Piscataway, NJ: Transaction, 2008.
———. *Islam in China: Religion, Ethnicity, Culture, and Politics*. New York: Lexington, 2002.
———. *Islamikaze: Manifestations of Islamic Martyrology*. London: Cass, 2003.
———. *Man of Defiance: A Political Biography of Anwar Sadat*. London: Weidenfeld and Nicolson, 1985.
———. *Muslim Anti-Semitism in Christian Europe*. Piscataway, NJ: Transaction, 2010.
———. *Muslim Minorities in Modern States: The Challenge of Assimilation*. Piscataway, NJ: Transaction, 2009
———. *The Oslo Idea: The Euphoria of Failure*. Piscataway, NJ: Transaction, 2012.
Katz, Tsahi. "Why Bethlehem Isn't Christian Anymore?: The Reasons behind the Muslim Majority in Bethlehem since 1948 until Today (in Hebrew). MA thesis, Bar Ilan University, 2010.
Kobrin, Nancy. *The Banality of Suicide Terrorism: The Naked Truth about the Psychology of Islamic Suicide Bombing*. Lincoln, NE: Potomac, 2010.
Kuntzel, Matthias. *Jihad and Jew-hatred, Islamism, Nazism and the Roots of 9/11*. New York: Telos, 2007.
Levtzion, Nehemia, ed. *Conversion to Islam*. New York: Holmes and Meier, 1979.
Malik, Habib. *Islamism and the Future of Christians in the Middle East*. Stanford, CA: Hoover Institute, 2010.
Marlin, George. *Christian Persecution in the Middle East: A 21st Century Tragedy*. South Bend, IN: St Augustine, 2015.
Mawdoodi, Abu al-'Ala' al-. *Nationalism in India*. Malihabad, India: n.p., 1948.
Nissan, Mordechai. *Politics and War in Lebanon: Unraveling the Enigma*. Piscataway, NJ: Transaction, 2015.
Peroncel-Hugoz, Jean-Pierre. *Le Radeau de Mahomet*. Paris: Lieu Commun, 1983.
Qu'tb, Sayyid. *Our War against the Jews*.
Ricklefs, Merle. *A History of Modern Indonesia*. London: Palgrave, 2001.
Rowe, Paul, et al., eds. *Christians in the Middle East Conflict*. London: Routledge, 2014.
Sharh Kitab al-Tawhid (Explaining the Book of the Unity of Allah), for 8th Grade. Saudi Arabia: The Saudi Ministry of Education, 2001.
Shboul, Ahmed. "Byzantium and the Arabs: The Image of the Byzantines as Mirrored in Arabic Literature." In *Byzantine Papers: Proceedings of the First Australian Byzantine Studies Conference*, edited by Elizabeth and Michael Jeffreys, 43–68. Canberra: Australian Association for Byzantine Studies, 1978.
Weiner, Julius, *Human Rights of Christians in Palestinian Society*. Jerusalem: Jerusalem Center for Public Affairs, 2007.

ARTICLES

Abdelhadi, Magdi. "Saudis Lash US Christian Extremists." BBC News, 8 August 2002.

BIBLIOGRAPHY

Abu Toameh, Khaled. "Bethlehem Christians Claim Persecution." *Jerusalem Post*, 25 January 2007.
———. *Jerusalem Post*, 5 September 2005.
———. "Church Official, Wife Beaten and Robbed in Gaza." *Jerusalem Post*, 23 July 2009.
———. "Hamas Forced Christian Professor to Convert to Islam." *Jerusalem Post*, 5 August 2007.
Adelman, Jonathan. "The Christians of Israel: A Remarkable Group." August, 2015. Online: http://www.huffingtonpost.com/jonathan-adelman/the-israeli-arabs-trailbl_b_8010020.html.
Adelman, Jonathan, and Aggie Kuperman. *Rockie Mountain News*, 22 December 2001.
Ali Khan, Ghazanfar. "Products of Danish Dairy Company Return to Supermarkets Shelves." *Arab News* (Saudi Arabia) 4 April 2004.
Anwar, Sayyed. "Exiled Palestinian Militants Ran Two-years of Terror." *The Washington Times*, 13 May 2002.
Beeman, Todd. "Christians Facing Annihilation in the Middle East." *New York Times Newsmax*, 22 July 2015.
Bostom, Andrew. "Coptic Church Construction and Egyptian Muslim Emasculation." Online: www.americanthinker.com/blog/2011/10coptic.
Browne, Anthony, and Suna Erdem. "Education Clash Hold Up EU Talks." *The Times*, 8 April 2006.
Catan, George. www.metransparent.com/texts/george_catan_eclipse_of_christianism_in_orient.htm, 17 January 2006.
Chong, Debra. "Court Says Yes to Allah for Christians." 31 December 2009. Online: www.themalaysianinsider.co/index.php/malaysia/48112-headline-court-says-yes-to-allah-for-christians.
"Christian Persecution." *Al-Safir*, 23 December 2009; Reported by MEMRI, Special Dispatch No 2718, 29 December 2009
"Church in Malaysia Protests Loss of Freedoms, Classification of Gospels as Threat to National Security." Editorial in *The Herald*, 1 April 2011.
"A Christian People Seriously at Risk." FreedomNews2@aol.com, 3 December 2003.
Cohen, Ben, and Father Keith Roderick. "The Religious Silence on Christian Persecution." *The Wall Street Journal*, 30 July 2012.
"Copts in Egypt." *Al-Ahram Weekly*, Cited by MEMRI, Special Dispatch 3483, January 3, 2011.
Corbon, Jane. "Could Christianity Be Driven Out of the Middle East?" *BBC News*, 15 April 2015.
Csaplar, Richard. "1400 Years of Islamic Aggression: An Analysis." CBN.com Commentary, 3 December, 2002.
Dalrymple, William. "The End of Christianity in the Middle East Could Mean the Demise of Arab Secularism." *The Guardian*, 23 July 2014.
De Souza, Father Raymond. *National Post*, 19 February 2008.
Dudkevitch, Margot. "Church Denies Christians Fleeing PA Areas." *Jerusalem Post*, 26 October 2000.
———. "Gunmen Stole Gold, Crucifixes, Escaped Monk's Report." *Jerusalem Post*, 24 April 2002.
Durie, Mark. "Church Construction and the Dhimma Pact: The Case of the Diocese of Maghagha and Edwah." Markdurie.com, blog, 30 July 2010.

———. "Condolences for al Qiddisin Church in Alexandria and Copts Everywhere." Markdurie.com, blog, 3 January 2011.

———. "The Dhimma Time Warp Returns for the Copts of Egypt." Markdurie.com, blog, 11 April 2011.

———. "The Dhimma Returns to Syria." markdurie.com blog, 2 June 2013.

———. "The Mufti of Egypt Stands up for Christians—Or does He?" Markdurie.com, blog, 24 March 2011.

Eibner, John. "Turkey's Christians Under Siege." *Middle East Quarterly*, Spring 2011, 44–52.

Ettinger, Yoram. "The Islamization of Bethlehem by Arafat." In *Jerusalem Cloakroom, No 117, Ariel Center for Policy Research*, 25 December 2001; and *Yedioth Aharonot*, 24 May 2002.

Fadel, Leila, and Ali al-Qeisi. "Iraqi Christians Flee after Violence." *Wahsington Post*, 17 November 2010.

Fadlallah, Sheikh Hussein. "Interview." *Al Mushahid al-Siyassi, BBC Arabic Weekly*, 30 May 1999; cited by MEMRI, Special Dispatch No 35, 17 June 1999.

Farah, Joseph. "Why Christians Leave the Middle East." *WorldNetDaily*, 3 January 2005.

Feder, Don. "Why Christians Have Become Israel's Best Friends." *National Religious Broadcasters Journal*, February-March 2003.

"Friday Sermons in Saudi Mosques: Review and Analysis." MEMRI, Special Report. Online: www.memri.org/bin/articles.cgi?Page=archives&Area=sr&ID=SR01002

"Gaza Christians Long for Days Before Hamas Canceled Xmas." *The Guardian*, 23 December 2011.

"Gaza Christians Protest Kidnapping and Forced Conversion of Young Man." Online: IMRA@netvision.net.il, 17 July 2012.

German, Erik. "Morocco Orders Dozens of Christian Aid Workers in Five Cities to Be Deported." *The Christian Science Monitor*, 11 March 2010.

Gordon, Jerry. "Copts in Egypt." *The Iconoclast*, 27 September 2011.

"Greedy Monsters Ruled Church." *The Washington Times*, 15 May 2002.

Guindi, Adel. "Symbolic Victims in a Socially Regressing Egypt: The Declining Situation of the Copts." *MERIA Journal* 14.1 (2010)

Hammer, Joshua. "Dark Days in Bethlehem: Under Siege from all Sides, Christians in the Holy Land Have Never Been So Beset." *Newsweek*, 19 September 2003.

Herf, Jeffrey. "Foreword" to Matthias Kuntzel, *Jihad and Jew-hatred, Islamism, Nazism and the Roots of 9/11*. New York: Telos, 2007.

Hohmann, Leo. *World Net Daily*, 17 July 2015.

Honig, Sarah. *The Jerusalem Post*, 11 November 2010.

Hutman, Bill. "Concern over Muslim Attacks on Christians in the Old City." *Jerusalem Post*, 18 July 1994.

"Hundreds of Christians Die in Bloody Massacres in Kano." FreedomNowNews@aol.com, 14 May 2004.

Ibrahim, Raymond. "Exploiting Christian Persecution to Demonize Israel." *Human Events*, 5 November 2013.

———. "Islam's Christian Scapegoats." *FrontPageMagazine*, 29 April 2011.

———. "Islamist 'Justice': Slow Painful Death for Christian Mother in Pakistan." *Muslim Persecution of Christians*, 26 July 2015.

———. "Jihad on Egypt's Christian Children." Gatestone Institute, 3 June 2013.

———. "Mass Arrest and Torture of Christians in Libya." FrontPageMagazine.com, 1 March 2013.

———. "Muslim Persecution of Christians, April 2012." Gatestone Institute, 18 May 2012.

———. "Muslims' Inferiority Complex Kills Christians." *FrontPageMagazine*, 14 May 2011.

———. "Nigeria: Where Jihad and Christian Persecution Run Rampant." Online: www.meforum.org/3636/nigeria-christian-persecution 1 October 2013.

———. "Why the Media Do Not Cover Jihadist Attacks on Middle East Christians." *The Torch*, Winter 2014.

———. "Why Muslim Rapists Prefer Blondes: A History." *FrontPage Magazine*, 30 July 2015.

"Iraq Christians Killed, Christians are Fleeing." FreedomNews2@aol.com, 24 June 2004.

"Israel Lets 557 Christians out of Gaza for Holidays." IMRA@netvision.net.il, 21 December 2012.

Israeli, Raphael. "Established Islam and Marginal Islam in China." In *Islam in China: Religion, Ethnicity, Culture, and Politics*, by R. Israeli, 99–112. New York: Lexington, 2002.

———. "Muslim Fundamentalists as Social Revolutionaries." *Journal of Terrorism and Political Violence* 6.4 (1994) 462–75.

Janssen, Martin. "The Dhimma Returns to Syria." Translated by Rev. Mark Durie. markdurie.com, blog, 2 June 2013.

Johansson, Magnus. "Peeping Tom Sparks Muslim-Christian Riot in West Bank." *Reuters*, 14 July 2004.

Kamal, Shazwan Mustafa. "Cautious Celebrations over 'Allah' Judgment." 31 December 2009. Online: www.themalaysuaninsider.com/index.php/malaysia/48133-cautious-celabrations-over-allah-judgment.

Kaplan, Lawrence. "The Plight of Iraqi Christians." *The New Republic*, 3 April 2006.

Kashan, Hilal. "Arab Christians as Symbols." *Middle East Quarterly*, Winter 2001.

Kavi, Jose. "India's Minority Christians Struggle against Violence and Persecution." *National Catholic Reporter*, 29 May 2015.

Kedar, Mordechai "The Brothers and the Muslims." *Israel Against Terror*, 28 June 2012.

Kedem, Ayelet. *Makor Rishon*, 14 June 2002, 8–11.

Keeley, Graham. "Muslim-Christian Clash over Cathedral in Cordoba." *The Times*, 12 November, 2010.

Khalil, Magdi. "How the Mubarak Regime Enables the Persecution of Egypt's Copts." *Middle East Forum*, 4 March 2010.

Khezran, Yusri. "The Christians in Israel and the Arab Spring: From Arab Identity to Separatism?" *Bayan: Arabs in Israel* 1 (June 2014) 8–12.

Kirkpatrick, David. "Egypt's Christians Feel More Peril with Revolution." *New York Times*, 1 June 2011.

Kirckpatrick, David, and Karim Fahim. "Attack on Christians in Egypt Comes After a Pledge: Egyptian Violence Raises Anxiety over Islamists' Rhetoric about Minorities." *New York Times*, 10 April 2013.

Kuppusamy, Baradan. "Can Christians Say Allah in Malaysia? Muslims say No!" Ganesh Sahathevan blog. ganesh.sahathevan@gmail.com, 26 January 2010.

Leong, Chan Kok. "Muslim NGOs Protest Use of Allah by Other Religious Groups." Ganesh Sahathevan blog. ganesh.sahathevan@gmail.com, 9 January 2010.
Lewis, Jonathan. "Iraqi Assyrians: Barometer of Pluralism." *Middle East Quarterly*, Summer 2003.
MacFarquar, Neil. "Killing Underscores Enmity of Evangelists and Muslims." *New York Times*, 25 November 2002.
Mahjar-Barducci, Anna. "MNLA: The Fight for a Secular State of Azwad." Memri, Inquiry and Analysis, No 848, 19 June 2012.
Malek, Habib. "Arab Christians between Thoughts of Subjugation and Freedom." *The Daily Star,* 14 December 2004.
"Mali and al-Qaeda: Can the Jihadists be Stopped?" *The Economist*, 11 October 2012.
Mantzikos, Ioannis. "Boko Haram and ISIS: The Same Coin?" *Research on Islam and Muslims in Africa*, 3 November 2014.
Mandraud, Isabelle. "Meet Nina Wallet Intalou, Female 'Strongman' of the Tuareg Rebellion in Mali." www.Lemonde.Fr, 23 April 2012.
Marcus, Itamar, and Barbara Cook. "PA TV: Christians and Jews Have Forsaken the Teachings of Jesus and Moses." *Palestinian Media Watch*, 1 May 2005.
Mean, Walter Russell. "The Plight of Middle East's Christians." *The Wall Street Journal*, 15 March 2015.
Melnick, Edward. *Daily Telegraph*, 25 December 2012.
Merkeley, Paul. "Effects of the Arab Spring So Far on Christians in the Middle East." *Think Israel,* 4 January 2013.
"Misunderstanders of Islam Admit to Beheading Christian Schoolgirls." www.jihawatch.org, 11 May 2006.
Mudayris, Ibrahim. Friday Sermon. Palestinian TV, 13 May 2005.
Munadi. Sultan N. "Afghan Case against Christian Convert Falters." *The New York Times*, 26 March 2006.
"Muslim Countries Becoming Bolder in Persecuting Christians." *Battle Cry Magazine*, September/October 2001.
"Muslim Mobs, Seeking Vengeance, Attack Christians in Nigeria." *Associated Press*, 13 May 2004.
"Muslim Persecution of Christians." Gatestone Institute, 18 May 2012
Myers, Steven. "With New Violence, More Christians are Fleeing Iraq." *The New York Times,* 12 December 2010.
Naveh, Dan. "The Involvement of Arafat, PA Senior Officials and Apparatuses in Terrorism against Israel, Corruption and Crime, 2002." Online: www.mfa.gov.il/mfa/go.asp?MFAHOlomO.
"An Open Letter from the Afghan Christian Community: An Urgent Plea for Help." markdurie.com, blog, 17 June 2010.
Palestinian Authority Ministry of Information, December 1997. Online: www.lawsociety.org/Reports/reports/1998/crz4.html.
"Palestinian Christian Activist Killed in Gaza." *Kuwait Times*, 8 October, 2007.
Pipes, Daniel. *New York Sun*, 13 September 2005.
Qaradawi, Sheikh Yussuf. "Jews of Today Are Responsible for Their Forefathers' Crime against Jesus." Qatar TV, 26 August 2006.
Radin, Charles. "Mob Fears Grow in the West Bank." *Boston Globe*, 6 February 2002.
Raphaeli, Nimrod. "The Plight of Iraqi Christians." MEMRI, Inquiry and Analysis, No 213, 22 March 2005.

Sahathevan, Ganesh. "Court: Allah Not Exclusive to Islam." Blog. ganesh.sahathevan@gmail.com, 1 January 2010.

———. "Tighten Security at Premises, IGP Advises Churches." Blog. ganesh.sahathevanmail.com, 10 January 2010.

Sanders, Saul. "Time for a Christian Mobilization." *The American Center for Democracy, NY,* No 1052, 8 March 2015.

"Saudi, UAE.and Bahraini Envoys to Return to Qatar." *Al Arabiya News,* 17 November 2014

"Saudi Telethon Host Calls for Enslaving Jewish Women." *National Review Online,* 26 April 2002.

Shirbon, Estelle. *Reuters* AFP from Paris, 12 July 2006.

Shragai, Nadav. "Islamic Movement Planning Forth Mosque for Temple Mount." *Ha'aretz* 18 June 2000.

Shuli, Yussuf al-. "Interview with al-Mauritani." Al-Jazeera Television, also in *al-Sharq al-Awsat* (London) 27 September 2001.

Smith, Tanalee. "Violence Breaks Out across Sudan Capital." *Associated Press,* 2 August 2005.

Solomon, Hussein. "Boko Haram: Separating Fact from Fiction." *Rima Occasional Papers* 2.12, 2014.

———. "Death of a Somali Jihadi." RIMA occasional papers 2, 2014.

Spencer, Robert. "Indonesia: Muslims Screaming 'Allahu akbar' attack Roman Catholic Church during Sunday Mass." *Jihad Watch,* 20 June 2015.

Stack, Liam. "Egyptian Violence Raises Anxiety over Islamists' Rhetoric about Minorities." http://thelede.blogs.nytimes.com/2013/04/08/attack-at-coptic-funeral-increases-interfaith-tension-in-egypt. 8 April 2013.

Stalinsky, Steven. "Saudi Arabia's Educational System: Preliminary Overview." *MEMRI, Special Report,* No 12, 20 December 2002.

"Syrian Christians in Desperate Straits: Will the Churches Survive?" *Barnabas Fund,* 3 April 2012.

Tamimi, Aymen al. "Kurdish-Christian Rivalries." *The Kurdistan Tribune,* 25 September 2011.

———. "Middle East Christians and Anti-Semitism." Dunya TV, 24 July 2011, cited by *Jerusalem Post,* 2 August 2011.

Terdman, Moshe. *Islam in Africa Newsletter* 1, May 2006. The Project for the Research of Islamist Movements, Global Research of Islamic Movements (PRISM), Herzliya

Time, Leonard, and Joseph Masilamany. The Sun Daily. 31 December 2009.

Timmerman, Kenneth. "Iran's Christians Have a High Price to Pay." SliwaNews, 15 December 2005.

Trifkovic, Srdja. "The Disappearing Middle Eastern Christians." www.chroniclesmagazine.org. 4 September 2012.

Trifkovic, Srdja "A Grim Christmas." Trifkovic@netzero.com, 26 December 2011.

Tsimhoni, Daphne. "The Christians in Israel, the West Bank and the Gaza Strip." *The Middle East Quarterly,* Winter 2001.

Trofimov, Yaroslav. "As Islamists Flex Muscle, Egypt's Christians Despair." *Wall Street Journal,* 11 June 2011.

Valdmanis, Richard, and David Lewis. *The Globe and Mail,* 24 January 2013.

Wagner, Matthew. "Human Rights Group: Hamas Disinters Christians in Gaza." *Jerusalem Post,* 12 December, 2009.

Weiner, Justus. "Palestinian Crimes against Christian Arabs and their Manipulation against Israel." Interview, published by *Institute of Global Jewish Affairs*, No 72, 1 September 2008.

"We Are Not Arabs, We are Christians Who Speak Arabic." *Israel Hayom Newsletter*, 4 October 2013.

Wildman, Sarah. *The Christian Science Monitor*, 24 May 2006.

Yoder, G. "Malaysian Christians Leaving Malaysia?" *News around the World*, 13 April 2015.

Young, Eric. "Witnesses: Slain Palestinian Was Tortured for Spreading Christianity." *Christian Post*, 11 October 2007.

"Zanzibar: Church Attacked as Islamist Zeal and Anger Rises." FreedomNews2@aol.com, 26 March 2004.

Analytical Index

A

Abbasids, 18, 67, 105, 167, 230
Abdul Hadi, Prime Minister, 161
Abraham, the Patriarch, 166, 179, 190
Abu Bakr, Baghdadi, 127
Abu Dhabi, 8
Abu Mazen, 193
Afghanistan, 3, 12–13, 17, 30, 42, 56, 65, 91, 118, 130, 137ff, 147–48, 150, 202, 216
   "Afghani," 91, 138, 143
   Attorney General of, 144
   Kabul, 136, 138–39, 140
   Parliament of, 143–45
   Senate of, 145
   Tribes of, 138
Africa, 28ff, 117ff
   Black, ix, 17, 117
   East, 28, 91, 117–18, 122, 129, 132, 140
   Coast of, 204
   Horn of, 28, 91, 117
   North, ix, 1, 18, 28, 55, 59, 62, 119, 124, 153, 167, 180, 223
   South, 220
   Sub-Saharan, xi, 17, 65, 117
   West, 28, 117, 126
Ahl al-Kitab (Scriptuaries), 1–3, 60, 180
Ahmadinejad, President, 152
Alawites, 103
Al-Azhar, 84
Aleppo, 102, 109, 230
   Evangelical Church at, 102

Alexandria, 69–70, 81–82, 232
   Qiddisin Church at, 8
Al-Qa'ida, 38, 46, 49, 64–65, 91, 101, 104–5, 118–19, 126, 129–30, 134, 137, 154, 199, 229
   AQIM, 124, 126
   Jema'ah Islamiya, 154
America (see also USA), xi, 17, 113, 150, 163, 199
   South, 29, 35, 176
Anatolia, 18, 21, 23
Andalusia, 18, 201, 224
Anti-semitism, 38, 44, 60–62, 207
   Protocols of the Elders of Zion, 60, 62
Arab, xi, 9, 17
   Arabia, 1, 55, 58, 168
   Ba'ath Party, 60, 67, 99, 106, 231–32, 233
   Michel Aflaq, 60
   Christian, 55ff
   Dynasty, 18
   Pan-Arab, 68
   Revolt, 42–43
   /Islamic Spring, 3, 8, 37, 41, 43, 48, 51, 59, 64, 66, 69, 80–81, 88–89, 99, 117, 228–29, 231
Arafat, Yasser, 7, 29, 183–84, 187
Armenia, 109, 146, 184, 215
   genocide, 25, 234
Asia, 20–21, 28ff, 113, 136ff
   Central, ix, 17, 21, 65, 91, 137
   East, 17
   Far East, 204
   Southeast, 17, 28, 91, 152

Assad, President Bashar, 37, 51, 64, 66, 74, 102–3, 110, 232, 233
Assyrians and Chaldeans, 67, 99, 103, 105–6, 146, 156, 231, 233–34
  Democratic Movement, 104, 107
  genocide, 234
Atlantic Ocean, 18
Australia, xi, 34, 81, 104, 106, 113, 163–64, 169
Azarbaijan, 137
Azzam, Sheikh Abdallah, 130, 138

B

Baghdad, 18, 99, 105–6, 167, 233
  Cathedral, 105
Bahai, 63
Bahrain, 52
Balkans, ix, x, 91
Bangladesh, 17, 135, 136
Banna, Hassan, 37, 41–42, 46, 48, 51
Barak, Prime Minister, Ehud, 176
Bashir, President Omar, 91ff, 117, 140
Bat Ye'or, ix, 5, 84
Bwdouins, 45
Belgium, 208, 211
  Brussels, 208
Ben Gurion, Prime Minister David, 13
Berbers / Kabyles, 1, 18, 205
Bethlehem, 19–20, 29, 235, 61, 165, 171–72, 177–78, 183, 185–86, 189, 190–92
  Beit Jallah, 176, 183–86
  Beit Sahur, 182–83, 185–86, 188
  Church of Nativity, 61, 165, 183, 184, 192
  Mayor of, 189
  Rachel's Tomb, 169, 171, 175
Bible, 90, 93, 111, 146, 160, 162, 183, 185, 190–91, 198
  New Testament, 63, 146, 171, 186, 190
  Old Testament, 170–71
Bin Laden, Osama, 12–13, 70, 91, 112, 118, 130, 138–39, 140, 142Blair, Prime Minister Tony, 204
Bosnia, 42

Britain, xi, 5, 30, 33–34, 126, 130, 1`46–47, 189, 203, 208, 215, 229, 234
  London, 40, 63, 129, 200–201
  Olympic Park, 129–30
  School of Oriental and African Studies (SOAS), 167
  Mandate over Palestine, 175, 177
  Open Door-UK, 234
  Scotland, 7
  Secretary Hammond, 146Bush, President George, 118, 140, 142
Byzantine, 1, 4, 18, 21, 23, 30ff, 166–67
  Patriarch, 179

C

Caliph/ate, 4, 13–14, 21, 35, 37–38, 40, 86, 124, 127, 139, 167–68, 185, 230
Cameron, Prime Minister David, 39
Cana'anite, 166
Canada, 81, 91, 106, 169
Carter, President Jimmy, 202
Cartoon Affair, 8–9, 12–13, 17, 25, 50, 148, 194, 197, 202, 212–14
Catholics, 11, 23–24, 26, 57, 60–61, 63, 78, 106, 134, 151–52, 159–60, 178, 195
  Inquisition, 171
  Nostra Aetate, 63
Chechnya, 34, 91, 138, 216
China, 16, 28
  Eastern Turkestan, 220
  Muslims in, 16, 220, 222
  Tang Dynasty, 16
Christ, Jesus, 11–12, 19, 29, 53, 61, 63, 65, 102, 111, 160, 166, 171–72, 177, 179, 181, 186, 190–91, 194
Christian Solidarity Worlwide, 745
Clinton, President Bill, 129
Constantinople / Istanbul, 21, 23, 166, 201, 224
  Ecumenical Church, 26
  Hagia Sophia, 21–22–23, 224
Copts, 1, 44, 53, 55, 61–62, 69ff, 104, 156, 190, 216, 231–32

Crusades, 5, 12, 19, 29, 35, 71, 91, 118–19, 167, 173, 176, 180, 186

D

Damanhuri-Sheikh, 84
Dar-al-Harb, 2, 4, 31
Dar al-Islam, 2, 16, 35, 199, 217, 222
David and Salomon, Kings, 166, 190
Denmark (see also Cartoon Affair), 8–10, 13, 211
   Youth Council, 8
Dhimmi, 3–5, 10, 55, 69, 74, 80, 84, 104, 119, 147, 174, 177–79, 189, 229
Druze, 94, 174, 176

E

Egypt, ix, 11, 18, 28, 37, 42, 57, 138, 154, 156, 180, 190
   Cairo, 50, 70, 73
   Damshirieh Sanctuary, 72
   Gama'at, 219
   Hellenistic, 1, 69
   Officers Revolution, 48
   Parliament, 44
   Pharaonic, 69
   Sinai, 45, 56, 75
   St Mark Cathedral, 74, 83
   Union of, Human Rights Organization (UEHRO), 80
   1919, Revolution, 72
Erdogan, Prime Minister Tayyip, 21–24, 26, 27
Eritrea, 75, 119, 130
Ethiopia, 75, 119, 131
   King of, 179
Europe, x, xi, 7–8, 13, 17, 23, 113, 131, 163, 167, 199, 228
   Center of Monitoring Racism and Xenophobia, 223
   Central, 223
   East, 223
   -Mediterranean Consortium for Applied Research, 209
   Odysseus Network, 2078
      Union (EU), 10, 13, 21, 24, 81, 211, 214–15

Fatimids, 67, 167–68
Fernandez-Morera, Dario, 18–19
Finland, 211
France, xi, 5, 18, 147, 201, 208, 221, 229
   Charlie Hebdo, 148
   Marseillaise, 2000
   Paris, 200, 204, 208
   Poitiers, 18, 201,

G

Galilee, 19, 85, 179
Garang, John, 56, 92ff
Gaza, ix, 3, 17, 68, 183, 187, 189, 192, 195, 197, 210
   Holy Family Church, 195
   Strip, 177, 181, 194ff
   YMCA Library, 197
Geneva Conventions, 209
Germany, xi, 15, 38, 42, 200, 203, 208, 220, 229
   Berlin, 204
   Bishop of Cologne, 27
   Wehrmacht, 42
Ghali, Butrus, 73
Gom'a/ Jum'a , Sheikh Ali, 70, 80
Goodluck, President Jonathan, 124
Greece, 12
   Anti, 25, 215
Guantanamo, 12
Gul, President, 24
Gulf, (Arab/Persian)- donors, 52
   GCC Secretary, 52
   States, 20, 110, 112, 116ff, 211
   War, 103

H

Hamas, ix, 3, 35, 40, 46, 52, 66, 68, 86, 91, 177, 181, 192, 194–95, 197
Hanieh, Prime Minister, 197
Hassan, Muhammed Abdallah, 131–32
Hebron, 172, 181, 196,
   Tomb of Patriarchs, 169–72
Hezbullah, 19, 25, 35, 40, 57, 61, 66, 94, 98, 100, 147

Higazi, Sheikh Safwat, 49, 71, 86–87
Hirsi Ali, A'yaan, 208–9
Hitler, Adolf, 37–38, 43, 147, 171
   Mein Kampf, 39
Holocaust/ Sho'a, 44, 203
Holy Land, 1, 29ff, 57, 61, 165ff, 186
Holy Places, 21, 169
   Christian, 20, 22, 61, 72, 74, 82, 133, 156, 159, 184, 186, 188, 194, 232
   Jewish, 20, 181, 204
   Muslim, 20, 61, 169, 175
Hussein, King, 51
Hussein, Saddam, 19, 67, 99, 105, 107, 115, 172, 230, 231, 233
Husseini, Haj Amin, 41–42

I

Iberia, x, 18, 222
Ibn al-Kathir, 80ff
Ibrahim, Raymond, xi, 30ff, 53, 66, 74ff, 155
India, 5, 17, 57, 136, 150ff, 180
   Agra, 151
      St Mary's Church, 151
   Hindus, 4, 28, 134, 150–52, 205
   Maldives, 135–36
   New Delhi, 145, 151
      St Sebastian Church, 151
   n Ocean, 135
Indonesia, 17, 36, 65, 136, 152ff, 225
   Aceh, 153, 157
   Ahmadiyyah, 28, 36
   Ambon, 155, 157
   Bali, 28, 152, 154–55
   East Timor, 155, 157
   Jakarta, 50, 158
   Java, 153, 156–57
   Jehovah Witnesses Church, 156
   Moluccas, 155
   Muhammadiya, 36
   Seventh Day Adventist Church, 156
   Sulawesi, 154–55
   Sumatra, 153, 157,
Iran, 5, 7, 8, 19, 79, 100, 103, 136, 145ff, 169, 172
   Biblical Society, 146
   ian Revolution, 17, 137, 178
   Nuclear Program of, 203
   Sassanians, 1, 3
   Shah of, 202
   Tehran, 7, 57, 146
Iraq, ix, 3, 8, 12–13, 17, 30, 42, 56, 62, 99ff, 156, 202, 229
   Anbar Pprovince, 101, 130
   Baghdad Church, 60, 104
   Mesopotamia, 104
   Shi'ites in, ix, 107
ISIS, ix, x, 3, 14, 19, 38, 53, 56, 62, 67, 77, 79, 99, 100–101, 110–12, 105, 119, 124, 126–27, 143, 177–78, 199, 209, 229–31, 233–34
Iskanderun/Alexandretta, 23, 25–26
Israel, 6, 17, 19, 66, 68, 165ff, 220
   Anti, 60, 147, 169, 202
   Haifa, 63, 175
   IDF, 176, 232
   Knesset, 20, 35
   Muslims in, 179

J

Jerusalem/al Quds, 11, 19, 20, 29, 35, 49, 57, 86, 165, 171, 184, 186
   Al-Aqsa Mosque, 61, 166, 168, 178
   Dome of the Rock, 166
   East, 181
   Greater, 189
   Holy Sepulcher, 186
   Kingdom of, 180
   Latin Patriarch of, 35, 178
   Qibla, 166
   Rachel's Tomb (see also Bethlehem), 169
   Temple, 105, 171, 186
   Temple Mount, 172, 186, 191
   Via Dolorosa, 19, 63
Jews, 4–5, 8, 11, 14–15, 18–19, 25, 55, 62, 91, 113–14, 166–68, 169, 171–73, 215
   First Temple, 105
   Jewish National Home, 43
Jihad, 3–4, 23–24, 30, 34, 41, 46, 74, 94, 113, 122, 131, 133–34, 138–39, 154, 171, 199, 200, 208, 216
   Islamic, 68, 177, 181

Mujahideen, 91, 104, 113, 138, 171, 207
  Soft, 206
Jizya, 4, 64, 80, 109, 119, 127, 167–69, 178, 180, 192, 229–30, 231, 234
John, the Baptist, 22, 106
  Mandaeans, 106
John-Paul II, Pope, 189
Jordan, 51, 102, 108–10, 130, 138, 165ff, 177, 185, 215
  Amman, 91, 108
  King Abdallah of, 109
  Muslim Brothers in, 52

K

Kano, 120ff
  Churches, 128
Karzai, President Hamid, 140, 142, 144
Kashmir, 18, 91, 224
Kazakhstan, 21, 136
Kenya, 91, 117, 119, 129ff
  Nairobi, 129, 132–33
  Westgate Shopping, 132
Khamena'I, Ali, 147
Khomeini, Ayatullah, 8, 91
  Islamic Revolution, 137
Kirkuk, 99, 101, 104
Krekar, Mullah, 12–14
Kurds, 12, 27, 36, 103–4, 105, 215–16, 219
  Kurdistan, 103
  Kurdistan Regional Government (KRG), 103
Kuwait, 34, 52, 111, 115, 134

L

Lebanon, ix, 8, 17, 19, 57, 68, 94ff, 102
  Beirut, ix
  Maronite Patriarch, 37
Libya, 3, 19, 53, 56, 74
  Benghazi, 49, 88, 90
    American Consulate in, 88
  Copts in, 89ff
Lockerbie, 7
London (see also Britain), 129

Olympic Park, 129

M

Malaysia, 17, 28, 136, 152ff
  Hindus in, 162
  Kuala Lumpur, 160–62, 162
    Archbishop of, 162
  Metro Tabernacle Church, 161
Mali, 28, 56, 117, 119,
Martel, Charles, 18
Mauritania, 28
Mauritani, Abu Hifz, 118
Mawdoodi, Mawlana, 221
Mecca and Medina, 34, 111, 166, 172, 222, 225
  Ka'ba, 166
Mehmet II, Sultan (The Conqueror), 21, 191
Mianmar, 17, 29, 152, 222
Middle Ages, ix, x, 5, 21, 31, 117, 201, 205, 231
Middlle East, ix, 9, 17, 18ff, 28, 37, 55ff, 112, 119, 137, 147, 150, 153, 167, 191, 199, 199, 204, 216, 223, 228
  Christianities in, 187
  Near East Council of Churches, 195
Moghuls, x, 5
Morocco, 51, 55, 58ff, 65, 104, 216
  Almohads, 55, 180
  Almoravids, 55, 180
  Atlas Mountains, 1, 58
  Casablanca, 50
  Fez, 58
  Marrakesh, 59
  Muhammed Vi, King, vi, 59
  Rabat, 58, 59
  Tangier, 59
Moses, 172, 179, 190
Mosul, 101, 105–6, 107, 229, 233
  Nineveh, 105, 108
Mubarak, President Husni, 43–44, 45, 49–50, 69, 73, 77, 81, 83, 86, 232
Mudayris, Sheikh Ibrahim, 15
Mursi, President Muhammed, 43, 45, 49, 51, 69–70, 71, 73–74, 77, 80, 85–87

Muslim Brothers, ix, 11, 37ff, 55, 64–65, 69–70, 73, 77–78, 81, 83, 86–88, 173–74, 219
  Mustafa Mashhur, 46

N

Nablus
  Joseph Tomb, 181
Naddaf, Father Gabriel, 20, 197ff, 232
  Israel-Christian Recruitment Forum, 198, 232
NATO, 21–22, 91, 140, 142
Nazareth, 19, 29, 35, 169, 173–75, 176, 178, 189, 187, 198
  Church of Annunciation, 19, 57, 169, 173, 175–76, 178
  Shihab a-Din Tomb, 175–76
  Upper, 175
Nazis, 15, 37, 40, 42
Nepal, 17
Nestorians, 196
Netherlands, 202ff, 208, 211
  Immigration Minister Verdonk, 209
  Supreme Court, 209
  Van Gogh Murder, 202, 209
New York, 81–82, 140
  Agreement, 157
  Times, 142, 229
Nigeria, ix, 56, 117, 119ff
  Abuja, 124
  Boko Haram, ix, 28, 35, 119ff
  Christian Association of Nigeria -(CAN), 121
  Council of Ulama', 123
Nobel Prize for Peace, 12
Norway, 10, 12, 211

O

Obama, President Barack, 20, 24, 36–37, 44, 50 65, 69, 73, 202, 215
Obasanjo, President, 120
Okoh, Archbishop Nicholas, 117
Orthodox/Eastern Christians, 11, 21, 60, 62–63, 108, 184–85, 189, 195, 197
  Haki Theological Seminary, 26
  Orthodox Church of Annunciation, 102
  Patriarch, 22, 26
  Syriac Church, 101, 108
Oslo, 183
  Accords, 12, 35, 185, 189, 192
  II, 165, 181, 182
Ottomans, x, 5–6, 21, 23, 67, 78, 100, 175, 191, 201, 230, 231
  Tanzimat, 231

P

Padovese, Bishop Luigi, 23–24, 26–27
Pakiam, Archbishop Lamsri, 160, 162
Palestine, 15, 18, 29, 129, 131, 165ff, 210
  Authority (PA), 29, 35, 165, 172, 178, 180, 183, 188–89, 190, 192–93, 224
  Bible Society, 194–95
  Christians in, 35, 180ff
  Fat'h Party, 183, 188, 195
  Intifada, 7, 52, 61, 175, 177, 181, 184, 192
  Legislative Council, 187
  Nakba, 198
  PLO, 35, 184, 191, 192, 195
  TV, 15
  University (in Gaza), 196
Papua-New Guinea, 158–60
  Papua People Assembly, 159
Pattersen, Ambassador, 73
Philippines, 17, 28, 91, 153, 220
  Mindanao, 28, 153
Portugal, 201
Prokop,. Minister Lise, 208
Prophet
  of Islam, 1, 3, 8, 11–12, 15, 22, 30–32, 34, 41, 46, 50, 74–75, 84–85, 101, 114, 119, 122, 149, 166, 168, 171, 179, 194
Prophet Jonas, 105
Protestants, 3, 10, 26, 58, 127–28, 142, 152–53, 157
  Anglicans, 117, 234
  Evangelical, 159
  St Andrews Church, 127

Q

Qaddafi/Gaddafi, Mu'ammar, 3, 7, 74, 89
Qandahar, 139-40
Qaradawi, Sheikh Yussuf, 11, 49, 52, 116
Qatar, 11, 35, 52, 56, 116
  Doha, 52
  TV, 11
Qur'an, 11-12, 20, 32, 41, 46-47, 49, 53, 55, 59, 68, 80, 113, 115, 118-19, 128, 133, 139, 144, 154, 179, 180, 229
Qut'b, Sayyid, 41, 48

R

Radical Muslims, 35-36, 38, 40, 56, 81, 105, 107, 123, 153, 169, 211, 214, 221, 222, 231
  Ansar al-Islam, 12
  Ansar Beit al-Maqdas, 56
Jihadis, 3, 64, 70, 93, 102, 128, 137
Lashkar a-Tayiba, 150
Salafis, 3, 41, 43-44, 49, 65, 74, 77, 81, 83-84, 90, 123
Wahhabis/ Hanbalis, 3, 111, 113, 123, 132, 134, 172-73, 174
Ramallah, 35, 178, 181, 188, 189ff, 192ff
  Mayor of, 188
Raqqa -
  Orthodox Church of Annunciation at, 102
Regensburg Speech 24
  Benedict xvi, Pope, 148
Rome, 1, 11, 12, 58, 63, 65
Rushdie Affair, 17, 91, 148, 212
Russia, 5, 34, 199
  Moscow, 91

S

Sadat, President Anwar, 69-71, 73
Sahara, 28, 117
Saladin, 175, 194
Saliba, Bishop George, 60
Salah, Sheikh Ra'id, 52
Sarkozy, Nicolas, 210

Saudi Arabia, 10-11, 50, 52, 56, 110ff, 126, 132, 134, 138, 154, 172
  Riyadh, 111, 113
Scandinavia, 10, 30, 34, 211, 225ff
  Islamic Cultural Center, 225
September 11, (2001), 7, 24, 40, 49-50, 91, 112, 118, 120, 129, 140, 142, 179, 200-201, 204, 223
Shi'a, 14, 19, 57, 67, 127, 130
Shinouda, Patriarch, 11, 63, 71-72, 83
Sisi, President abd al-Fattah, 43, 51, 70, 73
Solana, Javier, 10
Somalia, ix, 28, 30, 56, 91, 119, 126, 129ff, 148, 216
  Ittihad Islami, 132
  Mogadishu, 130-31
  Shabab, ix, 28, 124, 126, 129ff
  Somaliland, 130-31
Sophronius, Patriarch, 179
Spain, (See also Iberia), 180, 200-201
  Cordova Mosque/ Church, 224
  Muslim Association of, 224
  Golden Age, 5, 18
  Madrid, 40, 201
  Valencia, 222
Sri Lanka, 135
Sudan, 19, 28, 56, 91ff, 118, 130, 140, 172
  Khartoum, 56, 91ff, 140
  South, 92ff
Suez, 37
Sufi, 17
  Qaderiyya, 131
Sunni, 57, 107, 109, 112, 116, 123
Sweden, 34, 211, 229
  Board of Agriculture, 225
  School Inspectorate, 226
Syria, ix, 3, 8, 19, 30, 37, 42, 74, 99ff, 108, 147, 229
  Damascus, x, 18, 230
  Damascus Plan, 64
  Free Syrian Army, 64
  Greater, 180
  Homs, 110
  Idlib, 109
Jabhat al-Nusra, ix, 99, 102, 199, 229
  Palmyra, x

Syriac Orthodox, 101-2, 108

T

Taliban 13, 45, 91, 119, 136, 138-39, 140ff
Tanzania, 91, 119, 129ff
    Dar al-Salam, 129
Tarsus
    St Paul Church at, 27
Tel Aviv, 20, 66, 130
Templars, 186
Thailand, 17, 29, 152
Timbuktu, 117
Tunisia, 37, 51, 91
    Al-Nahda Party, 51
Turabi, Hassan, 91ff, 117, 140
Turkey, 17-18, 21ff, 36, 102-3, 136, 191, 214
    Ankara, 22
    Izmir/ Smyrna, 26
    Malatya, 25
        Supreme Court, 22

U

UAE, 8, 52, 225
Umar/ Omar, Mullah, 138-39, 140, 142
Umar, Caliph, 139, 168
Umayyads, 18, 67, 166-67, 222
United Nations, 36, 50, 130, 169, 172
    Diplomacy, 141
    Headquarters, 121
    Human Rights Commission/ Council, 93, 169, 172
    Personnel, 56, 92, 148
    Secretary General, 73, 172
    UNESCO, 169ff, 175, 224
Unites States, 164, 169
    CAIR, 51, 216
    CIA, 138
    Commission on International Religious Freedom, 104
    Embassies of, 91, 118, 132, 140
    FBI, 215
    National Security Adviser, 216
    Open Door, 30, 56
    Pentagon, 112, 142
    State Department, 53
    Washington, 51, 64, 140
    White House, 37, 65, 114
Uzbekistan, 45, 136, 216

V

Vatican, 11, 234, 57, 78, 114, 178
    Council, 63
Vienna, 5, 201, 208, 223
Visigoths, 1, 18

W

Wars-
    World, I, ix, 5, 21, 25, 107, 165, 191, 201
    World, II, x, 5, 37, 51, 205, 209
    1967,, 177, 189
    1973,, 72
Cold, 137
    Gulf, 106, 111, 190
    Iran-Iraq, 106
    Lebanese, I, 94
    Lebanese, II, 94
West, ix, xi, 1, 5, 7, 12, 14, 22, 29, 31, 46, 49, 50, 65, 71, 112, 118, 156, 163, 170, 191, 202, 211, 228
    Dialogue with, 5ff
    Muslims in, 99ff
West Bank, ix, 8, 19, 68, 177-78, 181, 182-83, 187, 192, 210
World Watch, 21, 35, 56, 110, 119, 145, 165

Y

Yazidis, 62-63, 127
Yemen, 3, 8, 19, 56, 104, 129, 131, 147, 179, 215
Yusuf, Muhammed, 123ff

Z

Zanzibar, 133ff
    Anglican Church, 133
    Assembly of God Church, 133
    Roman Catholic Church, 134
    Seven Days Church, 133
    Wahhabis, 134

Zarqawi, Mus'ab, 101, 127, 130
Zawahiri, AYman, 14, 127
Zawiya al-Hamra, 69, 71, 73

Zionism, 37, 39, 62, 174
  Anti, 60, 62
Zoroastrians, 4, 205

www.ingramcontent.com/pod-product-compliance
Lightning Source LLC
Chambersburg PA
CBHW050436240426
43661CB00055B/2409